MEIN SPY

MEIN SPY

THE ULTIMATE GERMAN ESPIONAGE COLLECTION

SECRET ARMIES
THE NEW TECHNIQUE OF NAZI WARFARE

JOHN L. SPIVAK

THE GERMAN SPY
THE SECRET PLOTTING OF GERMAN SPIES IN
THE UNITED STATES AND THE INSIDE STORY
OF THE SINKING OF THE LUSITANIA

JOHN PRICE JONES

MAPLE SPRING PUBLISHING

Published 2025 by Maple Spring Publishing

Interior design by Jason Snyder
Cover design by Tom McKeveny

Library of Congress Cataloging-in-Publication Data is available upon request

ISBN: 979-8-3505-0218-3

10 9 8 7 6 5 4 3 2 1

SECRET
ARMIES

John L. Spivak

CONTENTS

PREFACE

THE MATERIAL IN THIS SMALL VOLUME just barely scratches the surface of a problem which is becoming increasingly grave: the activities of Nazi agents in the United States, Mexico, and Central America. During the past five years I have observed some of them, watching the original, crudely organized and directed propaganda machine develop, grow and leave an influence far wider than most people seem to realize. What at first appeared to be merely a distasteful attempt by Nazi Government officials at direct interference in the affairs of the American people and their Government, has now assumed the more sinister aspect of also seeking American naval and military secrets.

Further studies in Central America, Mexico and the Panama Canal Zone disclosed an espionage network directed by the Rome-Berlin-Tokyo axis and operating against the peace and security of the United States. A scrutiny of the Nazi Fifth Column[1] in a few European countries, especially in Czechoslovakia just before that Republic was turned over to Germany's mercy by the Munich "peace" and in France where Nazi and Italian agents built an amazing secret underground army, has made the fascist activities in the Western Hemisphere somewhat clearer to me.

I have included one chapter detailing events which cannot, so far as I have been able to discover, be traced directly to Nazi espionage; but it shows the influence of Nazi ideology upon England's now notorious "Cliveden set," which maneuvered the betrayal of Austria, sacrificed Czechoslovakia and is

1 When the Spanish Insurgents were investing Madrid early in November, 1936, newspaper correspondents asked Insurgent General Emilio Mola which of his four columns would take the city. Mola replied enigmatically: "The Fifth Column." He referred to the fascist sympathizers within Madrid—those attempting to abet the defeat of the Spanish Government by means of spying, sabotage and terrorism. The term "Fifth Column" is today widely used to describe the various fascist and Nazi organizations operating within the borders of non-fascist nations.

working in devious ways to strengthen Hitler in Europe. The "Cliveden set" has already had so profound an effect upon the growth and influence of fascism throughout the world, that I thought it advisable to include it.

The sources for most of the material, by its very nature, naturally cannot be revealed. Those conversations which I quote directly came from people who were present when they occurred or, as in the case of the Cagoulards in France, from official records. In the chapter on Czechoslovakia I quote a conversation between a Nazi spy and his chief. The details came to me from a source which in the past I had found accurate. Subsequently, the spy was arrested by Czech secret police, and his confession substantiated the conversation as I have given it.

Much of the material in this volume has been published in various periodicals from time to time, but so many Americans feel that concern over Nazi penetration in this country is exaggerated, that I hope even this brief and incomplete picture will serve to impress the reader, as it has impressed me, with the gravity of the situation.

J. L. S.

I

CZECHOSLOVAKIA— BEFORE THE CARVING

IT IS PRETTY GENERALLY ADMITTED now that the Munich "peace" gave Germany industrial and military areas essential to further aggressions. Instead of helping to put a troubled Europe on the road to lasting peace, Munich strengthened the totalitarian powers, especially Germany, and a strengthened Germany inevitably means increased activities of the Nazis' Fifth Column which is, in all quarters of the globe, actively preparing the ground for Hitler's greater plans.

If we can divine the future by the past, the Fifth Column, that shadowy group of secret agents now entrenched in every important country throughout the world, is an omen of what is to come. Before Germany marched into Austria, that unhappy country witnessed a large influx of Fifth Column members. In Czechoslovakia, especially in those months before the Republic's heart was handed to Hitler on a platter, there was a tremendous increase in the numbers and activities of agents sent into the Central European country.

During my stay there in the brief period immediately preceding the "peace," I learned a little about the operations of the Gestapo's secret agents in Czechoslovakia. Their numbers are vast and those few of whom I learned, are infinitesimal to the actual numbers at work then and now, not only in Czechoslovakia but in other countries. What I learned of those few, however, shows how the Gestapo, the Nazi secret service, operates in its ruthless drive.

For years Hitler had laid plans to fight, if he had to, for Czechoslovakia, whose natural mountain barriers and man-made defensive line of steel and concrete stood in the way of his announced drive to the Ukrainian wheat fields. In preparation for the day when he might have to fight for its control, he sent into the Republic a host of spies, provocateurs, propagandists and saboteurs to establish themselves, make contacts, carry on propaganda and build a machine which would be invaluable in time of war.

In a few instances I learned the details of the Nazis' inexorable determination and their inhuman indifference to the lives of even their own agents.

Arno Oertel, *alias* Harald Half, was a thin, white-faced spy trained in two Gestapo schools for Fifth Column work. Oertel was given a German passport by Richter, the Gestapo district chief at Bischofswerda on what was then the Czechoslovak-German frontier.

"You will proceed to Prague," Richter instructed him, "and lose yourself in the city. As soon as it is safe, go to Langenau near Boehmisch-Leipa and report to Frau Anna Suchy.[1] She will give you further instructions."

Oertel nodded. It was his first important espionage job—assigned to him after the twenty-five-year-old secret agent had finished his intensive course in the special Gestapo training school in Zossen (Brandenburg), one of the many schools established by the Nazi secret service to train agents for various activities.

After his graduation Oertel had been given minor practical training in politically disruptive work in anti-fascist organizations across the Czech border where he had posed as a German emigré. There he had shown such aptitude that his Gestapo chief at sector headquarters in Dresden, Herr Geissler, sent him to Czechoslovakia on a special mission.

Oertel hesitated. "Naturally I'll take all possible precautions but—accidents may happen."

Richter nodded. "If you are caught and arrested, demand to see the German Consul immediately," he said. "If you are in a bad predicament, we'll request your extradition on a criminal charge—burglarly with arms, attempted murder—some non-political crime. We've got a treaty with Czechoslovakia to extradite Germans accused of criminal acts but—" The Gestapo chief opened the top drawer of his desk and took a small capsule from a box. "If you find yourself in an utterly hopeless situation, swallow this."

He handed the pellet to the nervous young man.

---

1 Frau Suchy was one of the most active members of Konrad Henlein's *Deutscher Volksbund,* a propaganda and espionage organization masquerading as a "cultural" body in the Sudeten area. She is today a leading official in the new German Sudetenland.

"Cyanide," Richter said. "Tie it up in a knot in your handkerchief. It will not be taken from you if you are arrested. There is always an opportunity while being searched to take it."

Oertel tied the pellet in a corner of his handkerchief and placed it in his breast pocket.

"You are to make two reports," Richter continued. "One for Frau Suchy, the other for the contact in Prague. She'll get you in touch with him."

Anna Suchy, when Oertel reported to her, gave him specific orders: "On August 16 [1937], at five o'clock in the afternoon, you will sit on a bench near the fountain in Karlsplatz in Prague. A man dressed in a gray suit, gray hat, with a blue handkerchief showing from the breast pocket of his coat, will ask you for a light for his cigarette. Give him the light and accept a cigarette from the gentleman. He will give you detailed instructions on what to do and how to meet the Prague contact to whom in turn you will report."

At the appointed hour Oertel sat on a bench staring at the fountain, watching men and women strolling and chatting cheerfully on the way to meet friends for late afternoon coffee. Occasionally he looked at the afternoon papers lying on the bench beside him. He felt that he was being watched but he saw no one in a gray suit with a blue handkerchief. He wiped his forehead with his handkerchief, partly because of the heat, partly because of nervousness. As he held the handkerchief he could feel the tightly bound capsule.

Precisely at five he noticed a man in a gray suit with a gray hat and a blue handkerchief in the breast pocket of his coat, strolling toward him. As the man approached he took out a package of cigarettes, selected one and searched his pockets for a light. Stopping before Oertel, he doffed his hat and smilingly asked for a light. Oertel produced his lighter and the other in turn offered him a cigarette. He sat down on the bench.

"Report once a week," he said abruptly, puffing at his cigarette and staring at two children playing in the sunshine which flooded Karlsplatz. He stretched his feet like a man relaxing after a hard day's work. "Deliver reports to Frau Suchy personally. One week she will come to Prague, the next you go to her. Deliver a copy of your report to the English missionary, Vicar Robert Smith, who lives at 31 Karlsplatz."

Smith, to whom the unidentified man in the gray suit told Oertel to report, was a minister of the Church of Scotland in Prague, a British subject with influential connections not only with English-speaking people but with Czech government officials.[2] Besides his ministerial work, the Reverend Smith led an amateur orchestra group giving free concerts for German emigrés. On his clerical recommendation, he got German "emigré" women into England as house servants for British government officials and army officers.

The far-flung Gestapo network in Czechoslovakia concentrated much of its activities along the former German-Czech border. In Prague, even today when Germany has achieved what she said was all she wanted in Europe, the network reaches into all branches of the Government, the military forces and emigré anti-fascist groups. The country, before it was cut to pieces and even now, is honeycombed with Gestapo agents sent from Germany with false passports or smuggled across the border.

Often the Gestapo uses Czech citizens whose relatives are in Germany and upon whom pressure is put. The work of these agents consists not only of ferreting out military information regarding Czech defense measures and establishing contacts with Czech citizens for permanent espionage, but of the equally important assignment of disrupting anti-fascist groups—of creating opposition within organizations having large memberships in order to split and disintegrate them. Agents also make reports on public opinion and attitudes, and record carefully the names and addresses of those engaged in anti-fascist work. A similar procedure was followed in Austria before that country was invaded, and it enabled the Nazis to make wholesale arrests immediately upon entering the country.

Prague, with a German population of sixty thousand is still the headquarters for the astonishing espionage and propaganda machine which the Gestapo built throughout the country. Before Czechoslovakia was cut up, most of the espionage reports crossed the frontier into Germany through Tetschen-Bodenbach. The propaganda and espionage center of the Henlein group was in the headquarters of the *Sudeten Deutsche Partei* at 4 Hybernska St. A secondary headquarters, in the *Deutscher Hilfsverein* at 7 Nekazanka St., was directed by Emil Wallner, who was ostensibly representing the Leipzig Fair but was actually the chief of the Gestapo machine in Prague. His assistant, Hermann Dorn, living in Hanspaulka-Dejvice, masqueraded as the representative of the *Muenchner Illustrierte Zeitung.*

---

2 The Rev. Smith returned to England when he learned that the Czechoslovakian secret police were watching him. At the present writing he had not returned to his church in Prague.

Some aspects of the Nazi espionage and propaganda machine in Czecho-slovakia hold especial interest for American immigration authorities since into the United States, too, comes a steady flow of the shadowy members of the Nazis' Fifth Column. It is well to know that the letters and numbers at the top of passports inform German diplomatic representatives the world over that the bearer usually is a Gestapo agent. Whenever American immigration authorities find German passports with letters and numbers at the top, they may be reasonably sure that the bearer is an agent. These numbers are placed on passports by Gestapo headquarters in Berlin or Dresden. The agent's photograph and a sample of his (or her) handwriting is sent via the diplomatic pouch to the Nazi Embassy, Legation, Consulate or German Bund in the country or city to which the agent is assigned. When the agent reports in a foreign city, the resident Gestapo chief, in order to identify him, checks the passport's top number with the picture and the handwriting received by diplomatic pouch.

Rudolf Walter Voigt, *alias* Walter Clas, *alias* Heinz Leonhard, *alias* Herbert Frank—names which he used throughout Europe in his espionage work will serve as an illustration. Voigt was sent to Prague on a delicate mission. His job was to discover how Czechs got to Spain to fight in the International Brigade, a mystery in Berlin since such Czechs had to cross Italy, Germany or other fascist countries which cooperate with the Gestapo.

Voigt was given passport No. 1,128,236 made out in the name of Walter Clas, and bearing at the top of the passport the letters and numbers 1A1444. He was instructed, by Leader Wilhelm May of Dresden, to report to the Henlein Party headquarters upon his arrival in Prague. Clas, *alias* Voigt, arrived October 23, 1937, reported at the Sudeten Party headquarters and saw a man whom I was unable to identify. He was instructed to report again four days later, since information about the agent had not yet arrived.

Voigt was trained in the Gestapo espionage schools in Potsdam and Calmuth-Remagen. He operates directly under Wilhelm May whose headquarters are in Dresden. May is in charge of Gestapo work over Sector No. 2. Preceding the granting to Hitler of the Sudeten areas in Czechoslovakia, the entire Czech border espionage and terrorist activity was divided into sectors. At this writing the same sector divisions still exist, operating now across the new frontiers. Sector No. 1 embraces Silesia with headquarters at Breslau; No. 2, Saxony, with headquarters at Dresden; and No. 3, Bavaria, with headquarters at Munich. After the annexation of Austria, Sector No. 4 was added, commanded by Gestapo Chief Scheffler whose headquarters are in Berlin with a branch in Vienna. Sector No. 4 also directs *Standarte II* which stands ready to provide incidents to justify German invasion "because the situation has got out of control of the local authorities."

Another way in which immigration authorities, especially in countries surrounding Germany, can detect Gestapo agents is by the position of stamps on the German passport. Stamps are placed, in accordance with German law, directly under the spot provided for them on the passport on the front page, upper right hand corner. Whenever the stamps are on the cover facing the passport title page, it is a sign to Gestapo representatives and Consulates that the bearer is an agent who crossed the border hurriedly without time to get the regular numbers and letters from Gestapo headquarters. The agent is given this means of temporary identification by the border Gestapo chief.

Also, whenever immigration authorities find a German passport issued to the bearer for less than five years and then extended to the regulation five-year period, they may be certain that the bearer is a new Gestapo agent who is being tested by controlled movements in a foreign country. For his first Gestapo mission in Holland, for instance, Voigt was given a passport August 15, 1936, good for only fourteen days. His chief was not sure whether or not Voigt had agreed to become an agent just to get a passport and money to escape the country; so his passport period was limited.

When the fourteen-day period expired, Voigt would have to report to the Nazi Consulate for a renewal. In this particular instance, the passport was marked "Non-renewable Except by Special Permission of the Chief of Dresden Police." When Voigt performed his Holland mission successfully, he was given the usual five-year passport.

Any German whose passport shows a given limited time, which has been subsequently extended, gives proof that he has been tested and found satisfactory by the Gestapo.

II

ENGLAND'S CLIVEDEN SET

THE WORK OF FOREIGN AGENTS does not necessarily involve the securing of military and naval secrets. Information of all kinds is important to an aggressor planning an invasion or estimating a potential enemy's strength and morale; and often a diplomatic secret is worth far more than the choicest blueprint of a carefully guarded military device.

There are persons whom money, social position, political promises or glory cannot interest in following a policy of benefit to a foreign power. In such instances, however, protection of class interests sometimes drives them to acts which can scarcely be distinguished from those of paid foreign agents. This is especially true of those whose financial interests are on an international scale and who consequently think internationally.

Such class interests were involved in the betrayal of Austria to the Nazis only a few months before aggressor nations were invited to cut themselves a slice of Czechoslovakia; and it will probably never be known just how much the Nazis' Fifth Column, working in dinner jackets and evening gowns, influenced the powerful personages involved to chart a course which sacrificed a nation and a people and which foretold the Munich "peace" pact.

The story begins when Neville Chamberlain, Prime Minister of England, accepted an invitation to spend the weekend of March 26–27, 1938, at Cliveden, Lord and Lady Astor's country estate at Taplow, Buckinghamshire, in the beautiful Thames Valley. When the Prime Minister and his wife arrived at the huge Georgian house rising out of a fairyland of gardens and forests with the placid river for a background, the other guests who had already arrived and their hosts were under the horseshoe stone staircase to receive them.

The small but carefully selected group of guests had been invited "to play charades" over the weekend—a game in which the participants form opposing sides and act a certain part while the opponents try to guess what they are portraying. Every man invited held a strategic position in the British government, and it was during this "charades party" weekend that they secretly charted a course of British policy which will affect not only the fate of the British Empire but the course of world events and the lives of countless millions of people for years to come.

This course, which indirectly menaces the peace and security of the United States, deliberately launched England on a series of maneuvers which made Hitler stronger and will inevitably lead Great Britain on the road to fascism. The British Parliament and the British people do not know of these decisions, some of which the Chamberlain government has already carried out.

And without a knowledge of what happened during the talks in those historic two days and what preceded them, the world can only puzzle over an almost incomprehensible British foreign policy.

Present at this weekend gathering, besides the Astors and the Prime Minister and his wife, were the following:

Sir Thomas Inskip, Minister for Defense.

Sir Alexander Cadogan, who replaced Sir Robert Vansittart as adviser to the British Cabinet and who acts in a supervisory capacity over the extraordinarily powerful British Intelligence Service.

Geoffrey Dawson, editor of the London *Times*.

Lord Lothian, Governor of the National Bank of Scotland, a determined advocate of refusing arms to the Spanish democratic government while Hitler and Mussolini supplied Franco with them.

Tom Jones, adviser to former Premier Baldwin.

The Right Honorable E. A. Fitzroy, Speaker of the House of Commons.

The Baroness Mary Ravensdale, sister-in-law of Sir Oswald Mosley, leader of the British fascist movement.

To understand the amazing game played by the Cliveden house guests, in which nations and peoples have already been shuffled about as pawns, one must remember that powerful German industrialists and financiers like the Krupps and the Thyssens supported Hitler primarily in order to crush the

German trade-union and political movements which were in the late 1920s threatening their wealth and power.

The Astors are part of the same family in the United States. Lady Nancy Astor, born in Virginia, married into one of the richest families in England. Her interests and the interests of Viscount Astor, her husband, stretch into banking, railroads, life insurance and journalism. Half a dozen members of the family are in Parliament: Lady Astor, her husband, their son, in the House of Commons; and two relatives in the House of Lords. The Astor family controls two of the most powerful and influential newspapers in the world, the London *Times* and the London *Observer.* In the past these papers, whose influence cannot be exaggerated, have been strong enough to make and break Prime Ministers.

Cliveden House, ruled by the intensely energetic and ambitious American-born woman, had already left its mark upon current history following other weekend parties. Lady Astor and her coterie had been playing a more or less minor role in the affairs of the largest empire in the world, but decisions recently reached at her weekend parties have already changed the map of Europe, after almost incredible intrigues, betrayals and double-crossings, carried through with the ruthlessness of a conquering Caesar and the boundless ambitions of a Napoleon.

The weekends at Cliveden House which culminated in the historic one of March 26–27, began in the fall of 1937. Lady Astor had been having teas with Lady Ravensdale and had entertained von Ribbentrop, Nazi Ambassador to Great Britain, at her town house. Gradually the Astor-controlled London *Times* assumed a pro-Nazi bias on its very influential editorial page. When the *Times* wants to launch a campaign, its custom is to run a series of letters in its famous correspondence columns and then an editorial advocating the policy decided upon. During October, 1937, the *Times* sprouted letters regarding Hitler's claims for the return of the colonies taken from Germany after the war.

Rather than have Germany attack her, England preferred to see Hitler turn his eyes to the fertile Ukrainian wheat fields of the Soviet Union. It meant war, but that war seemed inevitable. If Russia won, England and her economic royalists would be faced with "the menace of communism." But if Germany won, she would expand eastward and, exhausted by the war, would be in no condition to make demands upon England. The part Great Britain's economic royalists had to play, then, was to strengthen Germany in her preparations for the coming war with Russia and at the same time prepare herself to fight if her calculations went wrong.

Cabinet ministers Lord Hailsham (sugar and insurance interests), Lord Swinton (railroads, power, with subsidiaries in Germany, Italy, etc.), Sir Samuel Hoare (real estate, insurance, etc.), were felt out and thought it was a good idea. Chamberlain himself had a hefty interest (around twelve thousand shares) in Imperial Chemical Industries, affiliated with *I. G. Farbenindustrie,* the German dye trust which is very actively supplying Hitler with war materials. The difficulty was Anthony Eden, British Foreign Minister, who was opposed to fascist aggressions because he feared they would eventually threaten the British Empire. Eden would certainly not approve of strengthening fascist countries and encouraging them to still greater aggressions.

At one of the carefully selected little parties the Astors invited Eden. In the small drawing room banked with flowers the idea was broached about sending an emissary to talk the matter over with Hitler—some genial, inoffensive person like Lord Halifax (huge land interests) for instance. Eden understood why the *Times* had suddenly raised the issue of the lost German colonies to an extent greater even than Hitler himself, and Eden emphatically expressed his disapproval. Such a step, he insisted, would encourage both Germany and Italy to further aggressions which would ultimately wreck the British Empire.

Nevertheless, the cabinet ministers who had been consulted brought pressure upon Chamberlain and while the Foreign Secretary was in Brussels on a state matter, the Prime Minister announced that Halifax would visit the Führer. Eden was furious and after a stormy session tendered his resignation. At that period, however, Eden's resignation might have thrown England into a turmoil—so Chamberlain mollified him. Public sympathy was with Eden and before he was eased out, the country had to be prepared for it.

In the quiet and subdued atmosphere of the diplomats' drawing rooms in London they tell, with many a chuckle, how Lord Halifax, his bowler firmly on his head, was sent to Berlin and Berchtesgaden in mid-November, 1937, with instructions not to get into any arguments. Lord Halifax, in the mellow judgment of his close friends, is one of the most amiable and charming of the British peers, earnest, well meaning and—not particularly bright.

In Berlin Halifax met Goering, attired for the occasion in a new and bewilderingly gaudy uniform. In the course of their conversation Goering, resting his hands on his enormous paunch, said:

"The world cannot stand still. World conditions cannot be frozen just as they are forever. The world is subject to change."

"Of course not," Lord Halifax agreed amiably. "It's absurd to think that anything can be frozen and no changes made."

"Germany cannot stand still," Goering continued. "Germany must expand. She must have Austria, Czechoslovakia and other countries—she must have oil—"

Now this was a point for argument but the Messenger Extraordinary had been instructed not to get into any arguments; so he nodded and in his best pacifying tone murmured, "Naturally. No one expects Germany to stand still if she must expand."

After Austria was invaded and Halifax was asked by his close friends what he had cooked up over there, he told the above story, expressing the fear that his conversation was probably misunderstood by Goering, the latter taking his amiability to mean that Great Britain approved Germany's plans to swallow Austria. The French Intelligence Service, however, has a different version, most of it collected during February, 1938, which, in the light of subsequent events, seems far more accurate.

Lord Halifax, these secret-service reports state, pledged England to a hands-off policy on Hitler's ambitions in Central Europe if Germany would not raise the question of the return of the colonies for six years. Within that period England estimated that Hitler would have expanded, strengthened his war machine and fought the Soviet Union to a victorious conclusion.

Late in January 1938, Lord and Lady Astor invited some guests for a weekend at Cliveden. The Prime Minister of England came and so did Lord Halifax, Lord Lothian, Tom Jones and J. L. Garvin, editor of the Astor-controlled London *Observer*. When Chamberlain returned to London, he asked Eden to open negotiations with Italy to secure a promise to stop killing British sailors and sinking British merchant vessels in the Mediterranean. During this time the British Foreign Office was issuing statements that Mussolini was "cooperating" in the hunt for the "unidentified" pirates.

British opinion, roused by the sinking of English ships, might hamper deals with the fascist leaders if such attacks were not ended. In return for the cessation of the piratical attacks, Chamberlain was ready to offer recognition of Abyssinia and even loans to Italy to develop her captured territory. It was paying tribute to a pirate chieftain, but Chamberlain was ready to do it to quiet opposition at home to the sinking of British vessels and to give him time in which to develop his policy.

Eden, who had fought for sanctions against the aggressor when Abyssinia was invaded, obeyed orders but insisted that Italy must first get her soldiers out of Spain. He did not want Mussolini to get a stranglehold upon Gibraltar, one of the strategic life lines of the British Empire. Mussolini refused and told the British Ambassador in Rome that he and Great Britain would never to able to get together because Eden insisted on the withdrawal of Italian troops from Spain, and that it might help if a different Foreign Secretary were appointed. Hitler, working closely with Mussolini in the Rome-Berlin axis, also began to press for a different Foreign Secretary but went Mussolini one better. Von Ribbentrop informed Chamberlain that Der Führer was displeased with the English press attacks upon him, Nazis and Nazi aggressions. Der Führer wanted that stopped.

The Foreign Office of the once proud and still biggest empire in the world promptly sent notes to the newspapers in Fleet Street requesting that stories about Nazis and Hitler be toned down "to aid the government," and most of the once proud and independent British newspapers established a "voluntary censorship" at what amounted to an order from Hitler relayed through England's Foreign Office. The explanation the newspapers gave to their staffs was that the world situation was too critical to refuse the government's request and, besides that refusal would probably mean losing routine Foreign Office and other government department news sources. The more than average British citizen doesn't know even today how his government and "independent" press took orders from Hitler.

In the latter part of January, 1938, the French Intelligence Service, still not knowing of the secret deal Halifax had made, learned that Hitler intended to invade Austria late in February and that simultaneously both Italy and Germany, instead of withdrawing troops as they had said they would, planned to intensify their offensive in Spain. When the French Intelligence learned of it, M. Delbos, then French Foreign Minister, and Eden were in Geneva attending a meeting of the Council of the League. Delbos excitedly informed Eden who, never dreaming that Great Britain had not only agreed to sacrifice Austria and betray France but was also double-crossing her own Foreign Minister, telephoned Chamberlain from Geneva.

The Prime Minister listened attentively, thanked him dryly, hung up, and promptly telephoned Sir Eric Phipps, British Ambassador to France. Sir Eric was instructed to get hold of M. Chautemps, the French Premier at the time, and ask that Chautemps instruct Delbos to stop frightening the British Foreign Secretary. But all during February the French Intelligence kept getting more information about the planned invasion of Austria and the proposed intensified offensive in Spain, and relayed it to England with insistent suggestions for joint precautions. Eden in turn relayed it to Chamberlain who always thanked him.

The date set for the invasion was approaching but Eden was still in office and Hitler began to fear that perhaps "perfidious Albion" with all her overtures of friendship might really be double-crossing Germany. If England could send a special emissary to offer to sell out Austria and double-cross her ally France, she might be quite capable of tricking Germany. Simultaneously the Gestapo stumbled upon information that the British Intelligence had reached into the top ranks of the German Army and was working with high officers. Hitler, not knowing how far the British Intelligence had penetrated, shook up his cabinet, made Ribbentrop Secretary for Foreign Affairs, and prepared for war in the event that England was leading him into a trap.

There are records in the British Foreign Office which show that Hitler, before invading Austria, tested England to be sure he wasn't being led into a trap. Von Ribbentrop informed Eden and Chamberlain that Hitler intended to summon Schuschnigg, the Austrian Chancellor, and demand that Austria rearrange her cabinet, take in Dr. Seyss-Inquart and release imprisoned Nazis. Hitler knew that Schuschnigg would immediately rush to England and France for aid. If they turned Austria down it was safe to proceed with the invasion.

The British Foreign Office records show that Schuschnigg did rush to England and France for support, that France was ready to give it, but that England refused, thereby forcing France to keep out of it.

While these frantic maneuvers were going on, the Astor-controlled *Times* and *Observer,* the Nazi and the Italian press simultaneously started a campaign against Eden. The date set for the sacrifice of Austria was approaching and Eden had to go or it might fail. The public, however, was with Eden; so another kind of attack was launched. Stories began to appear about the Foreign Secretary's health. There were sighs, long faces, sad regrets, but Eden stuck to his post in the hope that he could do something. On February 19, Hitler, tired of waiting, bluntly demanded that he be removed, and with the newspaper campaign in full swing, Chamberlain "in response to public opinion" removed him the very next day.

The amiable Lord Halifax was appointed Foreign Secretary. Pro-fascists like A. L. Lennon-Boyd, stanch supporter of Franco and admirer of Hitler and Mussolini, were given ministerial posts.

The Austrian invasion was delayed for three weeks because of the difficulty in getting Eden out. When the news flashed to a startled world that Nazi troops were thundering into a country whose independence Hitler had promised to respect, M. Corbin, the still unsuspecting French Ambassador, rushed to the Foreign Office to arrange for swift joint action. This was at four o'clock in the afternoon of March 11, 1938. Instead of receiving him immediately, Lord Halifax kept him waiting until nine o'clock in the evening. By that time Austria was Nazi territory. There was nothing to do but protest; so Lord Halifax, with a straight face, joined France in a "strong protest." It was not until a week after Austria had been absorbed that the French Intelligence Service learned the details of the Halifax deal and finally understood why England had side-stepped the pleas for joint action and why the French Ambassador had been kept cooling his heels until the occupation of Austria was completed.

From Austria Hitler got more men for his army, large deposits of magnesite, timber forests and enormous water-power resources for electricity. From Czechoslovakia, if he could get it, Hitler would have the Skoda armament works, one of the biggest in the world, factories in the Sudeten area, be next door to Hungarian wheat and Rumanian oil, dominate the Balkans, destroy potential Russian air and troop bases in Central Europe, and place Nazi troops within a few miles of the Soviet border and the Ukrainian wheat fields he has eyed so long.

Five days after Austria was invaded, on March 16, at 3:30 in the afternoon, Lord Halifax personally summoned the Czechoslovakian Minister. At four o'clock the Minister came out of the conference with a dazed and bewildered air. Lord Halifax had made some "suggestions." Revealing complete ignorance of what had happened and was happening in Czechoslovakian politics, Halifax was nevertheless laying down the law.

It was obvious that the British Foreign Secretary was getting orders from someone else, for Halifax suggested that the Central European Republic try to conciliate Germany (which it had been doing for months) and that a German be taken into the cabinet (there were already three in it). On March 22 there was another meeting at which the Minister learned that Halifax wanted the Czech Government to take a Nazi into the cabinet—as Austria took Dr. Seyss-Inquart at Hitler's orders.

This pressure from England for Czechoslovakian Nazis to be given more power in the government was virtually telling the beleaguered little democracy to fashion a strong rope and hang itself. Subsequent events showed that Chamberlain personally supplied the rope.

Then came the historic weekend of March 26–27, 1938.

The walls of the small drawing room at Cliveden House are lined with shelves filled with books. The laughing and chatting guests had gathered there after a delightful dinner. For the Prime Minister of England to go through all sorts of contortions in a game of charades might prove a trifle undignified; so the hostess suggested that they play "musical chairs."

Everyone thought it was a splendid idea and men servants in their impressive blue liveries arranged the chairs in the required order, carefully spacing the distances between them. One of the laughing and bejeweled women took her place at the piano. In "musical chairs" there is one person more than the number of chairs. When the music starts the players march around the chairs. The moment the music stops everyone dives for the nearest chair leaving the extra person standing and subject to the hilarious jibes of the other players and those rooting from the bleachers. It's one of the ways statesmen relax.

The music started and the dour Prime Minister of the greatest empire in the world, the Minister in charge of the Empire's defense measures, the editor of England's most powerful newspaper, the Right Honorable Speaker of the House of Commons, the sister-in-law of England's leading fascist and several others started marching while the piano tinkled its challenging tune. The Prime Minister, perhaps because he is essentially conservative, marched cautiously and stepped quickly between the spaces while Lady Astor eyed him shrewdly and the others suppressed giggles. The Prime Minister tried to maintain at least the dignity of his banking background but managed "to look only a little porky" as one expressed it afterward. Suddenly the music stopped. Everyone lunged for the nearest chair. The Prime Minister managed to get one and plopped into it heavily.

After half an hour or so some of the strategic rulers of Great Britain got a little winded and quit. A conversation started on foreign affairs and most of the wives retired to another room. When the discussion was ended the little

Cliveden house party had come to six major decisions which will change the face of the world if successfully carried through.

Those decisions (maneuvers to put some of them into effect have already begun) are:

1. To inform France that England will go to her aid if she is attacked, unless the attack results from a treaty obligation with another power.

2. To introduce peace time conscription in England.

3. To appoint three ministers to coordinate industrial defense (conscription in peace time); supervise military conscription; and, coordinate the "political education of the people" (propaganda).

4. To reach an agreement with Italy to preserve the legitimate interest of both countries in the Mediterranean.

5. To discuss mutual problems with Germany.

6. To express the hope to Germany that her methods of self-assertion be such as will not hinder mutual discussions by arousing British public opinion against her.

The two most important decisions in this plan are the one for the conscription of labor in peace time and the effort to force France to break the Franco-Soviet pact by choosing between England and Russia.

Consider conscription first and the motives behind it:

When any country whose workers are strongly organized starts veering towards fascism, it must either win over the trade-unions in one way or another or destroy them, for rebellious labor can prevent fascism by means of the general strike. British labor is known to hate fascism since it has learned that fascism destroys, among other things, the value of the trade-unions and all that they have gained after many years of struggle. Any veering by England toward fascism and fascist alliances spells trouble with the trade-unions; hence, the decision "to coordinate the political education of the people." This move is particularly necessary since some trade-union leaders, especially in the important armament industry, have already stated publicly that unless the workers were given assurances that the arms labor was manufacturing would be used in defense of democracy and not to destroy it, they would not cooperate.

Hence "the education of the people" and the conscription of labor in peace time which would ultimately lead to government control over the unions. With some variations it is the same procedure followed by Hitler in getting control of the once extremely powerful German trade-unions.

A few days after this historic weekend, the *Times* came out for "national organization" and the wisdom of "national registration." National registration, as the history of fascist countries has shown, is the first step in the conscription of labor. With this opening gun having been fired, it is a safe prophecy that if the Chamberlain government remains in office British labor will witness one of the most determined attacks ever made upon it in its history. All indications point to the ground being laid and it may result in splitting the trade-union movement, for some of the leaders are willing to go with the government while others have already indicated that they will refuse unless they know that it's for democracy and not for fascism.

The second important decision is to exert pressure upon France to break her pact with the Soviet Union—something Hitler has been unsuccessfully trying to accomplish for a long time. At the moment it appears that Great Britain will succeed just as she has already succeeded in breaking the Czechoslovakian-Soviet pact—another rupture Hitler was determined upon.

England has a reputation for shrewd diplomacy. In the past she has used nations and peoples, played one against the other, betrayed, sacrificed, double-crossed in the march of her empire. Since the Cliveden weekend, however, with its resultant intrigues, England has, to all appearances, finally double-crossed herself.

Those who guide her destiny and the destinies of her millions of subjects have apparently come to the conclusion that democracy, as England has known it, cannot survive and that it is a choice between fascism and communism. Under communism, the ruling class to which the Cliveden weekend guests belong, stand to lose their wealth and power. It is the fatuous hope of the economic royalists that under fascism they will still sit on top of the roost, and so the Cliveden weekenders move toward fascism.

Hitler's Fifth Column finds strange allies.

III

FRANCE'S SECRET FASCIST ARMY

NEITHER HITLER NOR MUSSOLINI COULD have foreseen the development of a Cliveden set or England's willingness to weaken her own position as the dominant European power by sacrificing Austria and a good portion of Czechoslovakia. The totalitarian powers proceeded on the assumption that when the struggle for control of central Europe, the Balkans and the Mediterranean came they would have to fight.

The Rome-Berlin axis reasoned logically that if, when the expected war broke out, France could be disrupted by a widespread internal rebellion, not only would she be weakened on the battlefield but fascism might even be victorious in the Republic. In preparation for this, the axis sent into France secret agents plentifully supplied with money and arms, and almost succeeded in one of the most amazing plots in history.

The opening scene of events which led directly to the discovery of how far the foreign secret agents had progressed took place in the Restaurant Drouant on the Place Gaillon which is frequented by leaders of Paris' financial, industrial and cultural life.

Precisely at noon, on September 10, 1937, Jacqueline Blondet, an eighteen-year-old stenographer with marcelled hair, sparkling eyes, and heavily rouged lips, passed through the rotating doors of the famous restaurant and turned right as she had been instructed. She had never been in so luxurious a place before—dining rooms done in gray or brown marble with furniture to match. Two steps lead from the gray to the brown room and Mlle. Blondet, not noticing them in her excitement, slipped and would have fallen had not the old wine steward who looks like Charles Dickens, caught and steadied her.

The two men with whom she was lunching were at a table at the far corner of the deserted room. The one who had invited her, François Metenier, a well-known French engineer and industrialist, powerfully built, with sharp eyes, dark hair, and a suave self-assured manner, rose at her approach, smiling at her embarrassment. The other man, considerably younger, was M. Locuty, a stocky, bushy haired man with square jaws and heavy tortoise-shell eyeglasses. He was an engineer at the huge Michelin Tire Works at Clermont-Ferrand where Metenier was an important official. The industrialist introduced the girl merely as "my friend" without mentioning her name.

With the exception of two couples having a late breakfast in the gray marble room, which they could see from their table, the three were alone.

"Shall we have a bottle of Bordeaux?" asked Metenier. "I ordered lunch by 'phone but I thought I would await your presence on the wine."

"Oh, anything you order," said Locuty with an effort at casualness.

"Yes, you order the wine," said the stenographer.

"*Garçon,* a bottle of St. Julien, Château Léoville-Poyferre 1870."

The ghost of Charles Dickens, who had been hovering nearby, bowed and smiled with appreciation of the guest's knowledge of a rare fine wine and personally rushed off to the cellars for the Bordeaux.

When the early lunch was over and the brandy had been set before them, Metenier studied his glass thoughtfully and glanced at the two portly men who had entered the brown dining room and sat some tables away. From the snatches of conversation the three gathered that one was a literary critic and the other a publisher. They were discussing a thrilling detective story just published which the critic insisted was too fantastic.

Metenier said to Locuty:

"You will have to make two bombs. I will take you to a very important man in our organization, a power in France. He will personally give you the material and show you how to make them. Then I will take you to the places where you will leave them. I do not want them to see me."

In low tones, they discussed the bombing of two places. Metenier, a pillar of the church, highly respected in his community and well-known throughout France, cautioned them as they left.

Why the vivacious blond stenographer was permitted to sit in on this conversation, Locuty did not know, unless it was to tempt him, for, as she bade him good-by, she squeezed his hand significantly and said she wanted to see him again.

Metenier drove Locuty to an office building where he introduced him to a man he called "Leon"—actually Alfred Macon, concierge of a building which Metenier and others used as headquarters for their activities. Within a few moments the door of an adjacent room opened and Jean Adolphe Moreau de la Meuse, aristocrat and leading French industrialist, came in. He had a monocle in his right eye which he kept adjusting nervously. His face was deeply marked and lined with heavy bluish pouches under the eyes. With a swift glance he sized up Locuty as Metenier rose.

"This is the gentleman whom I mentioned," he said.

"He understands his mission?" De la Meuse asked.

"Yes," said Locuty. "You will teach me how to make them?"

De la Meuse nodded. "It will be a time bomb which must be set for ten o'clock tomorrow night. There will be nobody in the building at that time, so no one will be hurt."

An hour later Locuty, who had made both bombs and set the timing devices, wrapped them into two neat packages. Metenier took him to the General Confederation of French Employers' Building in the Rue de Presbourg. In accordance with instructions he left one of the packages with the concierge, after which Metenier took him to the Ironmasters' Association headquarters on the Rue Boissiere, where Locuty left the second package.

On the evening of September 11, the General Confederation of French Employers was scheduled to hold a meeting in their building. This meeting was postponed; and, as De la Meuse had assured the Michelin engineer, the concierges and their wives, contrary to custom, were not in their buildings that evening.

At ten o'clock, both bombs exploded. The plans had gone off as arranged except for an accident, the investigation of which made public the whole amazing conspiracy. Two French gendarmes standing near one of the buildings were killed.

Immediately after the bombs exploded, the Employers' Confederation and the Ironmasters' Association issued statements charging the Communists and the Popular Front with being responsible for the outrages and accusing them of planning a reign of terror to seize control of France. The accusations left a profound effect upon the French people despite the Communists' assertions that they never countenance terrorism. The *Sûreté Nationale,* the French Scotland Yard, opened an intensive investigation which was spurred on by the deaths of the unfortunate gendarmes. It was not long before the

French people heard of the almost incredibly fantastic plot to destroy the Popular Front and establish fascism in France—a plot directed by leading French industrialists and high army officers cooperating with secret agents of the German and Italian Governments.

The ramifications of the plot are so packed with dynamite in the national and international arena that the French government, under pressure from England as well as from some of its own industrialists, government officials and army officers, has clamped the lid down on further disclosures lest continued publicity seriously affect the delicate balance of international relations.

It was obvious from what the police uncovered that it had taken several years to organize the gigantic conspiracy. Within the teeming city of Paris itself, steel and concrete fortresses had been secretly built. Other cities throughout France were similarly ringed in strategic places. Every one of these secret fortresses was stocked with arms and munitions, and throughout the country, once the confessions began, the police found thousands upon thousands of rifles and pistols, millions of cartridges, hundreds of machine guns and sub-machine guns. The fortresses themselves were fitted with secret radio and telephone stations for communication among themselves. Code books and evidence of arms-running from Germany and Italy were found. A vast espionage network and a series of murders were traced to this secret organization whose official name is the "Secret Committee for Revolutionary Action." At their meetings they wore hoods to conceal their identity from one another, like the Black Legion in the United States, and the press promptly named them the "Cagoulards" ("Hooded Ones").

Just how many members the Cagoulards actually have is unknown except to its Supreme Council and probably to the German and Italian Intelligence Divisions. Lists of names totaling eighteen thousand men were turned up by the *Sûreté Nationale,* and the hundreds of steel and concrete fortresses and the arms found in them point to a membership of at least 100,000. The way the fortresses were built and their strategic locations (blowing down the walls of the buildings where the fortresses were hidden would have given them command of streets, squares and government buildings) indicate supervision by high military officials.

When contractors buy enormous quantities of cement for dugouts, when butchers' and bakers' lorries rattle over ancient cobblestones with enormous loads of arms smuggled across German and Italian borders, when thousands of people are drilled and trained in pistol, rifle and machine-gun practice, it is impossible that the competent French Intelligence Service and the *Sûreté Nationale* should not get wind of it.

As far back as September, 1936, the *Sûreté Nationale* knew that some leading French industrialists with the cooperation of the German and Italian Governments were building a military fascist organization within France. Nevertheless it quietly permitted fortresses to be built and stocked with munitions. The General Staff of the French Army, from reports of Intelligence men in Germany and Italy, knew that those countries were smuggling arms into France, but they permitted it to go on. The General Staff knew that some eight hundred concrete fortresses were being built under the supervision of M. Anceaux, a building contractor of Dieppe, and that skilled members of the Secret Committee for Revolutionary Action had been recruited for the building and sworn to secrecy under penalty of death. They knew that these fortresses were equipped with sending and receiving radios, knew that some were within the shadow of military centers, knew that the Cagoulards had a far-flung espionage system. But the French General Staff made no effort to stop it.

The Popular Front Government was in power at the time, and heads of the Supreme War Council apparently preferred a fascist France to a democratic one. In fact, officers and reserve officers of the French Army cooperated with secret agents of their traditional enemy, Germany, to build up this formidable secret army.

The investigating authorities, stunned by their discoveries and the high officials and individuals to whom their investigations led, either did not dare go further with it, or, if they did, suppressed the information. Some of it, however, came out.

At the top of the Cagoulards is a Supreme War Council or General Staff whose members have not been disclosed. Working with them are several other organizations, all with innocent names, as for example the "Society of Studies for French Regeneration." The Cagoulards' activities are divided into broad general lines, each directed by an individual in complete command and embracing:

Buying war materials within France and smuggling war materials into the country from Germany, Italy and Insurgent Spain, along with the simultaneous weaving of an espionage network under Nazi and fascist direction and leadership.

Building concrete fortresses at strategic centers and storing smuggled arms in them.

Military training of secretly organized troops.

Getting the money to carry on these extensive activities.

Extreme care was, and still is, taken to conceal the identities of the ordinary members and especially the leaders. For instance, one of the leaders known to his subordinates as "Fontaine" is in reality Georges Cachier, director of a large company in Paris and chief of the Cagoulards' "Third Bureau," which is in charge of military movements. Cachier is an Officer of the French Legion of Honor and a reserve Lieutenant-Colonel in the French Army.

The Cagoulards are still very active. Members are being recruited with leaders pointing out to the fearful ones that there is nothing to worry about—almost all of those arrested in the early days of the investigation are free, out on bail or kept in a "gentleman's confinement" where they can do virtually as they please. "Our power is great," new members are told.

As is customary in secret terrorist societies, the members are sworn to silence with death as the penalty for indiscretion. The penalty when it is employed is usually administered in American gangster fashion. Each member is allotted to a "cell," the basic unit of the military organization, and assigned to a secretly fortified post for training. One of these posts discovered by the *Sûreté Nationale* was in an old boarding house run by two ancient spinsters with equally ancient guests who spent their time in rockers, knitting and reading and not dreaming that underneath the porch on which they sat so tranquilly was a fortress with enough explosives to blow the whole street to smithereens. Into this particular fortification, the cell members would steal one by one after the old maids had retired, entering by a concealed door three feet thick and electrically operated.

There are two different kinds of cells in the Cagoulards, "heavy" and "light" ones. They differ in the number of men and the quantity of armaments assigned to them. The "light" cell has eight men equipped with army rifles, automatics, hand grenades, and one sub-machine gun; the "heavy" one has twelve men similarly armed but with a machine gun instead of a sub-machine gun. Three cells form a unit, three units a battalion, three battalions a regiment, two regiments a brigade and two brigades a division of two thousand men. The battalions (one hundred and fifty men) are subdivided into squads of fifty to sixty men with ten to twelve cars at their disposal for quick movement throughout the city. These automobile squads are given intensive training.

Members are not required to pay dues, for enough money comes in from industrialists and the German and Italian Governments to eliminate the need of collecting money from members for operating expenses. Every effort is made to function without written communications. No membership cards are issued. Notices of meetings, drill and rifle practice are issued verbally, and so far as the mass membership is concerned, nothing in writing is placed in their hands.

A twenty-page handbook with instructions on street fighting was issued to group commanders and, lest a copy fall into wrong hands and betray the organization, it was boldly entitled: *Secret Rules of the Communist Party*. The instructions are specific and are based upon the insurrectionary tactics issued to the Nazi Storm Troopers. They fall into six sections: General Remarks; Group Fighting; Section Fighting; Choice of Terrain; Commissariat; and Policing Groups.

One or two excerpts from these instructions for street fighting follow:

> The particular force for street fighting is infantry, provided with automatic weapons and hand grenades. Members of the detachments should be instructed that automatic weapons must always be used in preference. Essential arms are: sub-machine guns, rifles including hunting rifles, hand grenades, revolvers, petards." (Petards are small bombs used for blowing in doors.)

With regard to "mopping up" in houses, the instructions state:

> If the door is barricaded, it must be opened with tools or explosives. If it is a heavy door, break it in by driving a lorry at it. Clean up basements and cellars by throwing bombs down through the air holes or other openings after your men have got into the house. Only after these have exploded should the cellar doors be forced. Then, when ascending the stairs, keep close to the walls while one of your men keeps firing straight

up the shaft. Mop up as you go down floor by floor. If necessary, pierce holes in the ceilings and mop up by throwing down hand grenades.

The chief of the Cagoulards' espionage system is Dr. Jean Marie Martin, a bushy-haired stocky man with dark, somber eyes. Dr. Martin usually travels with several false passports and with the utmost secrecy. At the moment he is in Genoa where he went to meet Commendatore Boccalaro, Mussolini's personal representative in charge of smuggling arms into foreign countries.

The preparations by the Rome-Berlin axis point to plans for a fight to a finish between fascist and non-fascist countries. A feeble or disrupted democracy will obviously strengthen the fascist powers in any coming struggle with anti-fascist powers. Germany and Italy, faced on their own borders with a democratic France allied with the Soviet Union in a military defense pact, would face a powerful enemy in the event of war. But if France were torn by a bloody civil war, she would be virtually unable even to defend her borders. Consequently, it is essential for Germany and Italy to weaken and if possible destroy France's democracy.

France and Germany have been traditional enemies in their struggle for land containing raw materials needed by their industries to compete in the world markets. But the growth of the French labor movement and the power of the Popular Front which threatened the control and the profits of French industrialists and financiers, made them find more in common with fascist and Nazi industrialists than with French workers who menaced their economic and political control. The result was that leading French industrialists were willing to cooperate with Nazi and fascist agents to destroy the Popular Front and establish fascism in France. About half of the 200,000,000 francs, which it is estimated the fortresses and arms cost, was contributed by French industrialists. The other half came from the German and Italian Governments.

Germany and Italy sent swarms of secret agents into France to supervise the building of the underground military machine and to carry on intensive espionage with the assistance of the French Army and Government officials who were members of the Hooded Ones. The espionage service was organized by Baron de Potters, an old international spy who travels with two or more passports under the names of Farmer and Meihert. De Potters gets his funds from the Nazis' strongly guarded "Bureau III B," established in Berne, Switzerland at 21 Gewerbestrasse. "Bureau III B" is the official name

SECRET ARMIES · **39**

of this branch of the Gestapo. At the head of it is Boris Toedli whose activities include not only espionage but underground diplomatic intrigue and propaganda. He works directly under Drs. Rosenberg and Goebbels. Toedli supplies not only the Baron but other espionage directors with money and there is plenty of it at his disposal for quick emergency uses. The money is deposited in the *Société des Banques Suisses,* account No. 60941.

The head of the Italian espionage system directing the work in France and cooperating closely with the Nazis is Commendatore Boccalaro, head of the Italian Government's Arsenal in Genoa. One of his specialties is the smuggling of arms into foreign countries.

Boccalaro's history shows that the not so fine Italian hand is interfering in the internal affairs of foreign governments. As far back as 1928, he secretly supplied carloads of arms from the Genoa Arsenal to Hungary, and in 1936 he supplied Yugoslavian terrorists with war materials in efforts to get those countries under Mussolini's sphere of influence. Boccalaro, too, seems to have had reasons to suppress information in at least one case where the death penalty was inflicted upon a member of the Cagoulards.

Among the Hooded Ones who have been found with bullets or knives in them was an arms runner named Adolphe-Augustin Juif, who tried to charge the secret organization a little more than he should for smuggling guns and munitions into France. When the organization threatened him, he advised it not to resort to threats because he knew a little too much.

On February 8, 1937, his bullet-riddled body was found in San Remo, Italy. When Juif's wife, not hearing from him, sought information about his whereabouts, she wrote to Boccalaro, since she knew he was working with the Genoa director. The Italian papers had announced the finding of his body; nevertheless, on March 3, Boccalaro wrote to the murdered man's widow:

"Your husband, my dear friend, is carrying on a special and delicate mission (perhaps in Spain or Germany) and has special reasons of a delicate nature not to inform even his own family where he is at the present moment."

Among the men whom Juif met before he was murdered was Eugène Deloncle, director of the Maritime and River Transport Mortgage Company and one of the most important industrialists in France. Deloncle, a high official in the Cagoulards, used the name of "Grosset" in his conspiratorial activities. The other man whom the murdered Juif met is General Edouard

Arthur Duseigneur, former Air Force chief and Military Adviser to the French Air Ministry. The General is one of the military heads of the Cagoulards and frequently met with Baron de Potters.

The *Sûreté Nationale,* the French Intelligence Service, and the examining magistrate have documentary evidence that Germany and Italy were and are deliberately conspiring to throw France, as they did Spain, into a civil war. Publication of these documents would have far-reaching effects, internally and externally. Great Britain, however, planning to establish a four-cornered pact between England, France, Germany and Italy, brought pressure to bear upon France to suppress further disclosures about the Cagoulards. To England's pressure was added that of leading French industrialists, financiers, government and army officials. Gradually, news about the Cagoulards is dying out. The real heads of the Hooded Ones either have not been named or, if arrested in the early days of the investigation, have been released on bail. And recruiting for the underground army is still going on.

IV

DYNAMITE UNDER MEXICO

MOST PEOPLE IN THE UNITED STATES feel secure from European or Asiatic aggression since wide oceans apparently separate us from the conquering ambitions of a Führer or a Son of the Sun. However, despite our desire to be left in peace, the Rome-Berlin axis, which Japan joined, has cast longing eyes upon the Western Hemisphere. The Monroe Doctrine is of value only so long as aggressor nations feel we are too strong for them to violate it; recent history has shown what pieces of paper are worth.

In the process of trying to get a foothold in the Americas, the Nazis have sent agents into all of the countries, but because most of the Central and South American republics are still resentful of past acts by the "Colossus of the North," they offer the most fertile fields.

The two spots on the Western Hemisphere most vital to the United States are the Panama Canal Zone and Mexico—the Zone because it is our trade and naval life line between the oceans and Mexico because potential enemies could find in it perfect military and naval bases.

Let us see what the totalitarian powers are doing in Mexico:

On June 30, 1937, the S.S. "Panuco" of the New York and Cuba Mail Steamship Co. steamed into Tampico, Mexico, from New York with a mysterious cargo consigned to one Armeria Estrada. As soon as she docked, the cargo was quickly transferred to the Atchison, Topeka and Santa Fe Railroad freight car No. 45169, which was awaiting it. A gentleman known around the freight yards as A. M. Cabezut, arranged for the car to leave immediately for the state of San Luis Potosí in the heart of Mexico.

There was no record on the bill of lading to show that the shipper was the Winchester Repeating Arms Company of New Haven, Conn., and that the cargo, ordered on January 23 and February 23, 1937, by an Italian named

Benito Estrada, was a large quantity of rifles, pistols and one hundred and forty cases of cartridges for various caliber guns.

When the car arrived in San Luis Potosí, it was met by an elderly, mustached German named Baron Ernst von Merck, who took the shipment to General Saturnino Cedillo, former governor of the state[3] and a well-known advocate of fascism. One week later the elderly German met a carload shipment of "farm implements." When it was unloaded in San Luis Potosi, the farm implements turned out to be dynamite.

Von Merck, who has been Cedillo's right-hand man, was during the World War a German spy stationed in Brussels. A member of Cedillo's staff[4] he traveled constantly between San Luis Potosí, where the arms were cached, and the Nazi Legation in Mexico City.

On December 21, 1937, Baron von Merck flew to Guatemala—the same day that a cargo of arms from Germany was to be landed off the wild jungle coast of Campeche in Southern Mexico.

Guatemala, just south of Mexico, is the most thoroughly organized fascist country in Central or South America. Its chief industries, coffee and bananas, are virtually controlled by Germans, whose enormous plantations overlap into the state of Chiapas, Mexico. But President Jorge Ubico, who is not much of an Aryan, prefers Mussolini's brand of fascism because the Nazi theory of Nordic supremacy does not strike a sympathetic chord in the President's heart. As a result, the Italian Minister to Guatemala is Ubico's adviser on almost all matters of state.

Guiseppe Sotanis, a mysterious Italian officer who sits in the Gran Hotel in San José, Costa Rica, collecting stamps and studying his immaculate fingernails, arranges for shipments of Italian arms into Guatemala. A few months ago Sotanis, the Italian minister to Guatemala, and Ubico met in Guatemala City. Shortly thereafter the Italian arms manufacturing company, Bredda, sent Ubico two hundred eighty portable machine guns, sixty anti-aircraft machine guns and seventy small caliber cannon.

But President Ubico is not hopelessly addicted to one brand of fascism. Nazi ships make no attempt to conceal their landing of arms and munitions at Puerto Barrios. From there they are transported by car, river and horse

---

3 In May, 1938, Cedillo launched an abortive rebellion and is now being hunted by the Mexican government.

4 After Cedillo's defeat von Merck fled to New York and went to Germany.

into the dense chicle forests in the mountain regions, then across the Guatemalan border into Chiapas and Campeche.

During March, 1938, mysterious activities took place in the heart of the chicle forests in Campeche. The region is a dense jungle inhabited by primitive Indian tribes. There is little reason for anyone to build an airport in this territory, much of which has not even been explored. But if the Mexican Government will instruct its air squadron to go to Campeche and fly forty miles north of the Rio Hondo and a little west of Quintana Roo border, they will find a completed airport in the heart of the chicle jungle; and if they will fly a little due west of the small villages of La Tuxpena and Esperanza in Campeche, they will find two more secret airports.

The Mexican Government knows that arms are being smuggled in through its own ports, across the Guatemalan border, and across the wide, sparsely inhabited two-thousand-mile stretch of American border. Both American and Mexican border patrols have been increased, but it is almost impossible to watch the entire region between Southern California and Brownsville. Few contraband runners are caught, apparently because neither the American nor Mexican Governments seem to know the routes followed or who the leading smugglers are.

On February 12, 1938, José Rebey and his brother Pablo, who live in the Altar district of Sonora and know every foot of the desert, drove to Tucson, Arizona, where they met two unidentified Americans. On February 16, 1938, José Rebey and Francisco Cuen, old and close friends of Gov. Roman Yocupicio, drove a Buick to the sandy, deserted wastes near Sonoyta, just south of the American border where one of the two unidentified Americans delivered a carload of cases securely covered with sheet metal. As soon as the cases were transferred into Rebey's car, he turned back on Sonora's flat, dusty roads, passing Caborca, La Cienega, and turning on the sun-dried rutted road to Ures, which lies parched and dry in the semi-tropical sun.

Ures is the central cache for arms smuggled into Sonora by Yocupicio, and the Rebey brothers and Cuen are among the chief contraband runners. The load they carried that day consisted of Thompson guns and cartridges, and the route followed is the one they generally use. A secondary route used by one of Cuen's chief aids, a police delegate from the El Tiro mine, lies over the roads to Ures by way of Altar.

If in time of war it becomes necessary for guard or patrol work to deflect any troops from the army, or ships from the navy, it is of advantage to the enemy. If a coming war found the United States lined up with the democratic as against the fascist powers and serious uprisings broke out in Mexico, it would require several U. S. regiments to patrol the border and a number of U. S. ships to watch the thousands of miles of coast line to prevent arms running to American countries sympathetic to the Berlin-Rome-Tokyo axis.

The three fascist powers that have cast longing eyes upon Central and South America have apparently divided their activities in the Americas, with Japan concentrating on the coast lines and the Panama Canal, Germany on the large Central and South American countries and Italy upon the small ones.

In Mexico, Nazi agents work directly with Mexican fascist groups, and have undertaken to carry the brunt of spreading anti-democratic propaganda to turn popular sentiment against the "Colossus of the North," and to develop a receptive attitude toward the totalitarian form of government.

Italy concentrates on espionage, with particular attention to Mexican aid to Loyalist Spain. It was the Italian espionage network in Mexico which learned the course of the ill-fated "Mar Cantabrico" which left New York and Vera Cruz with a cargo of arms for the Loyalists and was intercepted and sunk by an Insurgent cruiser.

Though Germany, even more than Italy, is utilizing her propaganda machine in the Americas' markets, the Japanese are not troubling about that just yet. Their commercial missions seem to be much less interested in establishing business connections than in taking photographs. The chief commercial activity all three countries are intensely interested in is getting concessions from Mexico for iron, manganese and oil—materials essential for war. President Lázaro Cárdenas, however, has stated his dislike of fascism on several occasions. Since Germany, Japan and Italy must obtain these products wherever they can get them, it would be to their advantage if a government more friendly to fascism were in power. But, should that prove impossible, the existence of a strong, fascist movement would have, in time of war, tremendous potentialities for sabotage.

Hence, Mexico is today being battered by pro-fascist propaganda broadcasts from Germany on special short-wave beams, and Nazi and fascist agents surreptitiously meet with discontented generals to weave a network throughout the country.

The radio propaganda is devoted chiefly to selling the wonders of totalitarian government, and to the dissemination of subtle, indirect comments calculated to turn popular feeling against the United States. In addition to regular broadcasts, material printed in Spanish and in German by the *Fichte Bund* with headquarters in Hamburg, Germany, is smuggled into Mexico in commercial shipments. A Nazi bund to direct this propaganda was organized secretly because of the government's unfriendly attitude toward fascism. The bund operates as the *Deutsche Volksgemeinschaft* and its propaganda center functions under the name of the "United German Charities." This organization, on the top floor of the building at 80 Uruguay Street, Mexico City, is actually the "Brown House," in direct contact with Nazi propaganda headquarters in Hamburg.

Some of the propaganda distributed in Mexico is smuggled off Nazi ships docking in Los Angeles, and is transported across the American border by agents working under Hermann Schwinn, director of Nazi activities for the West Coast of the United States. The propaganda sent by Schwinn across the American border is chiefly for distribution around Guaymas, where a special effort is being made to win the sympathy of the people. Meanwhile Yocupicio caches arms in Ures and the bland Japanese continue charting the harbors and coast lines.

The Nazis began to build fascism in Mexico right after Hitler got into power. In 1933 Schwinn called a meeting in Mexicali of several Nazi agents operating out of Los Angeles, including General Rodriguez, and several members of a veterans organization. It was at this meeting that the Mexican Gold shirts were organized. Under the direction of Rodriguez and his right-hand men (Antonio F. Escobar was one of them), the fascist organization drilled and paraded, but little official attention was paid to them. Five years ago few people realized the intensity and possibilities of Nazi propaganda and organization. The only ones in Mexico who watched the growth of the fascist military body were the trade-unionists and the Communists. They remembered what happened in Italy and Germany when the Black Shirts and the Brown Shirts were permitted to grow strong.

On November 20, 1935, Rodriguez and his organization staged a military demonstration in Mexico City, and marched upon the President's palace. Trade-unionists, liberals and Communists barred their way. When the pitched battle was over, five Gold Shirts were dead, some sixty persons wounded, and Rodriguez himself had been stabbed by a woman worker, on her lips the furious cry, "Down with fascism!"

When the Gold Shirt leader was discharged from the hospital, he found that his organization had been made illegal, and he himself exiled. Rodriguez went to El Paso, Texas, and immediately, working through Escobar, set about establishing the "Confederation of the Middle Class" to take over now the illegal Gold Shirt work and consolidate the various Mexican fascist groups. Its headquarters was established at 40 Passo de la Reforma.

Rodriguez kept in touch with Schwinn through Henry Allen, a native American of San Diego, who acts as liaison man. It was Allen, on orders from Schwinn, who last year secretly met in Guaymas Ramon F. Iturbe, a member of the Mexican Chamber of Deputies. Iturbe is in constant touch with the fascist groups in Mexico City.

The Gold Shirts smuggled arms into Mexico along the border between Laredo and Brownsville, and cached them in Monterrey. On January 31, 1938, Gold Shirts attempted to attack Matamoros, near Brownsville. A Mexican policeman was killed and another wounded in the fighting. Two days later Gold Shirts surrounded Reynosa, some distance west of Matamoros, but met peasants armed with rifles, pistols and knives. The fascists withdrew and Rodriguez vanished, only to appear in San Diego, California, on February 19, 1938 for a secret meeting with Plutarco Elias Calles, the former President of Mexico. After a three-hour conference Rodriguez went to Los Angeles, met Schwinn, and proceeded to Mission, Texas, where he established new headquarters.

A few days after these conferences, he sent two men into Mexico under forged passports to discuss closer cooperation among the fascist leaders. The men sent into Mexico were an American named Mario Baldwin, one of Rodriguez's chief assistants, and a Mexican named Sanchez Yanez. They established headquarters at 31 José Joaquin Herrera, apartment 1-T, and met for their secret conferences in Jesus de Avila's tailor shop at 22 Isabel la Catolico.

In the latter part of June, 1935, an amiable bar fly arrived in Mexico City from Berlin as civilian attaché to the German Legation. A civilian attaché is the lowest grade in the diplomatic ranks and the salary is just about enough to keep him going. Nevertheless, Dr. Heinrich Northe, at that time not quite thirty, and not especially well-to-do, established a somewhat luxurious place at 64 Tokyo St. and bought a private airplane for "pleasure jaunts" about Mexico. Northe is seldom at the Nazi Legation. He is more apt to be found in Sonora, where Yocupicio is storing arms and where the Japanese fishing fleet is active, or in Acapulco, whose harbor fascinates the Japanese. He used to make frequent visits to Cedillo just before the General started his rebellion. On March 4, 1938, Northe took off "for a vacation" in the Panama Canal Zone. He stopped off in Guatemala on the way down.

The persistently vacationing commercial attaché, before coming to Mexico, was part of the Gestapo network in Moscow and Bulgaria. Immediately after the Nazis got control of Germany, Northe went into the German "diplomatic service," and was one of the first secret agents sent to the German Embassy in Moscow. The Russian secret service apparently watched him a little too closely, for he was shifted to Sofia, Bulgaria, where he bought a private plane and flew wherever he wished. In 1935, when the signers of the "anti-Communist pact" decided to concentrate upon Mexico, Northe was transferred to Mexico City.

One of Northe's chief aids is a German adventurer who was a spy during the World War. When the War ended, Hans Heinrich von Holleuffer, of 36 Danubio St., Mexico City, worked hard at earning a dishonest penny in Republican Germany. When the law got after him, he skipped to Mexico, where, without even pausing for breath, he went to work on his fellow countrymen in the New World. Berlin asked for his arrest and extradition and von Holleuffer fled to Guatemala. That was in 1926. He came back to Mexico in 1931 under the name of Hans Helbing.

When Hitler got into power von Holleuffer's brother-in-law became a high official in the Gestapo. Since there was no danger of the Nazis extraditing him on charges of fraud and forgery, Hans Helbing became Hans Heinrich von Holleuffer again and, without any visible means of support, established a swanky residence at the above address, got an expensive automobile, a chauffeur, and some very good-looking maids. Since he has not defrauded anyone lately, the German colony in Mexico still wonders how he does it.

He does it by being in charge of arms smuggling from Germany to Mexican fascists. During the latter part of December, 1937, he directed the unloading of one of the heaviest cargoes of arms yet shipped into Mexico. Northe had informed von Holleuffer that a German vessel whose name even Northe had not yet been given, would be ready to land a cargo of guns, munitions and mountain artillery somewhere along the wild and deserted coast of Campeche where there are miles of shore with not even an Indian around. Von Holleuffer was instructed to arrange for unloading the cargo and having it removed into the interior.

On December 19, 1937, von Holleuffer arranged a meeting in Mexico City with Julio Rosenberg of 13 San Juan de Letran and Curt Kaiser at 34 Bolivar, the latter's home. He offered them fifty thousand pesos to take the contraband off the boat and transport it through the chicle jungles to the destination he would give them.

Shortly after the Japanese-Nazi pact was signed, the Japanese Government arranged with the somewhat naive Mexican Government for Japanese fishing experts to conduct "scientific explorations" along Mexico's Pacific Coast in return for teaching Mexicans how to catch fish scientifically. The agreement provided that two Japanese, J. Yamashito and Y. Matsui, be employed by the Mexican Government for the exploratory work.

Matsui arrived in Mexico in 1936 and immediately became interested in the fish situation at Acapulco, which from a naval standpoint has the best harbor on the entire long stretch of Mexico's Pacific coast line. In February, 1938, he decided that it was important to the west-coast shrimp-fishing studies for him to do some exploratory work along the northeast part of the Mexican coast, near the American border, and there he went.

Immediately after the agreement was signed, three magnificent fishing boats, the "Minatu Maru," the "Minowa Maru" and the "Saro Maru," which had been hovering out on the Pacific while the negotiations were going on, appeared in Guaymas. Their captains reported to the Nippon Suisan Kaisha, a fishing company with headquarters in Guaymas. Eighty per cent of this company's stock is owned by the Japanese Government.

Each ship is equipped with large fish bins which can easily be turned into munition carriers, each has powerful short-wave sending and receiving sets; and each has extraordinarily long cruising powers ranging from three to six thousand miles. These boats do not do much fishing. They confine themselves to "exploring," which includes the taking of soundings of harbors, especially Magdalena Bay. Apparently the explorers want to know how deep the fish can swim and whether there are any rocks or ledges in their way.

That Germany, Japan and Italy are not working toward peaceful ends in Mexico is slowly dawning upon the Mexican Government. Influential government and trade-union leaders have repeatedly shown their dislike of Nazism and fascism and have urged propaganda against them.

On the morning of October 5, 1937, Freiherr Riedt von Collenberg, Nazi minister to Mexico, telephoned the Japanese and Italian ministers to suggest a joint meeting to discuss steps to counteract the attacks on fascism and their countries. The Japanese minister, Sacchiro Koshda, suave and skilled in such matters, thought it would not be wise to meet in any of the legations. The Italian minister suggested the offices of the Italian Union on San Cosne Avenue.

At half past one in the afternoon of October 7, the ministers arrived, each in a taxi instead of the legation car which carries a conspicuous diplomatic license plate. At this secret meeting which lasted until after four, they concluded that it would be unwise for them personally to take any steps to counteract the anti-fascist activities—that it would be wiser to work indirectly through fascist organizations like the Confederation of the Middle Class and its associated bodies. A few days earlier each minister had received a letter from several organizations allied with the Confederation of the Middle Class. It was an offer to help the Berlin-Tokyo-Rome combination. A free translation of the passage which the ministers discussed (from the letter received by the Japanese minister which I now have) follows:

"We, exactly like the representatives of the three powers, love our Fatherland and are disposed to any sacrifice to prevent the intervention of these elements [Jews and Communists] in our politics, in which, unfortunately, they have begun to have great influence. And we will employ, and are employing, all legal methods of struggle to make an end of them."

The phrase "legal methods" is frequently employed by those who suggest illegal activity. The German Minister knew that the *Union Nacionalista Mexicana,* one of the signers of the letter, was run by Escobar, and that Carmen Calero, 12 Place de la Concepcion, Mexico City, an elderly woman physician active in many fascist organizations, was a member of the *Partido Anti-reelectionista Accion,* another of the signers.

One month later the various fascist groups got enough money to launch an intensive pro-fascist drive under the usual guise of fighting Communism. José Luis Noriega, Secretary of the Nationalist Youth of Mexico, which also signed the letters to the ministers, left for the United States to organize an anti-Cárdenas drive. At the same time, Carmen Calero left on a mysterious mission to Puebla on November 12, 1937, with a letter from Escobar to J. Trinidad Mata, publisher of the local paper *Avance*. She carried still another letter addressed to their "distinguished comrades," without mentioning names, and signed by both Escobar and Ovidio Pedrero Valenzuela, President of the *Accion Civica Nacionalista*. The "distinguished comrades" to whom she presented the letter were the Nazi honorary consul in Puebla, Carl Petersen, Avenida 2, Oriente 15, and a Japanese agent named L. Yuzinratsa with whom the consul has been in repeated conferences.

Six weeks after the secret meeting of the Japanese, German and Italian ministers, and one week after she went to Puebla, Dr. Carmen Calero got twenty-two kilos of dynamite and stored it in a house at 39 Juan de la Mateos, in Mexico City. She, her sister, Colonel Valenzuela, and four others, met at her home and laid plans to assassinate President Cárdenas by blowing up his train when he left on a proposed trip to Sonora.

On November 18, 1937, the secret police made a series of simultaneous raids upon Dr. Calero's and Valenzuela's homes and the house where the dynamite was cached. They arrested everyone in the houses. But once the arrests had been made, the Mexican Government found itself in a quandary. To bring the prisoners to trial would involve foreign governments and create an international scandal; so Cárdenas personally ordered the secret police to release them.

The arrests, however, scared the wits out of the ministers, and their horror was not lessened when they discovered that the letters from the fascist organizations had vanished from their files. They wouldn't even answer the telephone when one of the released fascist leaders called. It was then that the Mexican fascists decided to send a special messenger to Francisco Franco in Spain (November 30, 1937) with the request that Franco intercede to get money from Hitler to help overthrow Cárdenas, since the Nazi minister was too scared to cooperate. The special messenger was Fernando Ostos Mora. He never got there.

V

SURROUNDING
THE PANAMA CANAL

THERE IS A LITTLE SHIRT SHOP in Colon, Panama, on Calle 10a between Avenida Herrera and Avenida Amador Guerrero, whose red and black painted shingle announces that Lola Osawa is the proprietor.

Across the street from her shirt shop, where the red light district begins, is a bar frequented by natives, soldiers and sailors. Tourists seldom go there, for it is a bit off the beaten track. In front of the bar is a West Indian boy with a tripod and camera with a telescopic lens. He never photographs natives, and wandering tourists pass him by, but he is there every day from eight in the morning until dark. His job is to photograph everyone who shows an undue interest in the little shirt shop and particularly anyone who enters or leaves it. Usually he snaps your picture from across the street, but if he misses you he darts across and waits to take another shot when you come out.

I saw him take my picture when I entered the store. It was almost high noon and Lola was not yet up. The business upon which she and her husband are supposed to depend for a living was in the hands of two giggling young Panamanian girls who sat idly at two ancient Singer sewing machines.

"You got shirts?" I asked.

Without troubling to rise and wait on me, they pointed to a glass case stretched across the room and barring quick entrance to the shop proper. I examined the assortment in the case, counting a total of twenty-eight shirts.

"I don't especially like these," I said. "Got any others?"

"No more," one of them giggled.

"Where's Lola?"

"Upstairs," the other said, motioning with her thumb to the ceiling.

"Looks like you're doing a rushing business, eh?" They looked puzzled and I explained: "Busy, eh?"

"Busy? No. No busy."

There is little work for them and neither Lola nor they care a whoop whether or not you buy any of the shop's stock of twenty-eight shirts. Lola herself pays little attention to the business from which she obviously cannot earn enough to pay the rent, let alone keep herself and her husband, pay two girls and a lookout.

The little shirt shop is a cubbyhole about nine feet square, its wooden walls painted a pale, washed-out blue. A deck which cuts the store's height in half, forms a little balcony which is covered by a green and yellow print curtain stretched across it. To the right, casually covered by another print curtain, is a red painted ladder by which the deck is reached. On the deck, at the extreme left, where it is not perceptible from the street or the shop, is another tiny ladder which reaches to the ceiling.

If you stand on the ladder and press against the ceiling directly over it, a well-oiled trap door will open soundlessly and lead you into Lola's bedroom above the shop. In front of the window with the blue curtain is a worn bed, the hard mattress neatly covered with a counterpane. At the head of the mattress is a mended tear. It is in this mattress that Lola hides photographs of extraordinary military and naval importance. I saw four of them.

The charming little seamstress is one of the most capable of the Japanese espionage agents operating in the Canal Zone area. Lola Osawa is not her right name. She is Chiyo Morasawa, who arrived at Balboa from Yokahama on the Japanese steamship "Anyo Maru" on May 24, 1929, and promptly disappeared for almost a year. When she appeared again, she was Lola Osawa, seamstress. She has been an active Japanese agent for almost ten years, specializing in getting photographs of military importance. Her husband, who entered Panama without a Panamanian visa on his passport, is a reserve officer in the Japanese Navy. He lives with Lola in the room above the shop, never does any work though he passes as a merchant, and is always wandering around with a camera. Occasionally he vanishes to Japan. His last trip was in 1935. At that time he stayed there over a year.

To defend the ten-mile-wide and forty-six-mile-long strip of land, lakes and canal which the Republic of Panama leased to the United States "in perpetuity," the army, navy and air corps have woven a network of secret fortifications, laid mines and placed anti-aircraft guns. Foreign spies and international adventurers play a sleepless game to learn these military and naval secrets. The Isthmus is a center of intrigue, plotting, conniving, conspiracy and espionage, with the intelligence departments of foreign governments bidding high for information. For the capture or disablement of the Canal by an enemy would mean that American ships would have to go around the Horn to get from one coast to another—a delay which in time of war might prove to be the difference between victory and defeat.

Because of the efficiency and speed of modern communication and transportation, any region within five hundred to a thousand miles of a military objective is considered in the "sensitive zone," especially if it is of great strategic importance. Hence, espionage activities embrace Central and South American Republics which may have to be used by an enemy as a base of operations. Costa Rica, north of the Canal, and Colombia, south of it, are beehives of secret Japanese, Nazi and Italian activities. Special efforts are made to buy or lease land "for colonization," but the land chosen is such that it can be turned into an air base almost overnight.

For decades Japanese in the Canal Zone area have been photographing everything in sight, not only around the Canal, but for hundreds of miles north and south of it; and the Japanese fishing fleet has taken soundings of the waters and harbors along the coast. Since the conclusion of the Japanese-Nazi "anti-Communist pact," Nazi agents have been sent to German colonies in Central and South America to organize them, carry on propaganda and cooperate secretly with Japanese agents. Italy, which had been only mildly interested in Central America, has become extremely active in cultivating the friendship of Central American Republics since she joined the Tokyo-Berlin tie-up. Let me illustrate:

The recognized vulnerability of the Canal has caused the United States to plan another through Nicaragua. The friendship of the Nicaraguan Government and people, therefore, is of great importance to us from both a commercial and a military standpoint. It is likewise of importance to others.

Italy undertook to gain Nicaragua's friendship when she joined the Japanese-Nazi line-up. First, she offered scholarships, with all expenses paid, for Nicaraguan students to study fascism in Italy. Then, on December 14, 1937, about one month after a secret Nazi agent arrived in Central America with orders to step on the propaganda and organizational activity, the Italian S.S. "Leme" sailed out of Naples with a cargo of guns, armored cars, mountain artillery, machine guns and a considerable amount of munitions.

On January 11, 1938, the Secretary of the Italian Legation in San José, Costa Rica, flew to Managua, Nicaragua, to witness the delivery of arms which arrived in Managua on January 12, 1938. Diplomatic representatives do not usually witness purely business transactions, but this was a shipment worth $300,000 which the Italian Government knew Nicaragua could not pay. But, as one of the results, Italy today has a firm foothold in the country through which the United States hopes to build another Canal. The international espionage underground world, which knew that the shipment of arms was coming, has it that Japan, Germany and Italy split the cost of the arms among themselves to gain the friendship of the Nicaraguan Government.

A flood of Nazi propaganda sent on short-wave beams is directed at Central and South America from Germany. In Spanish, German, Portuguese and English, regular programs are sent across at government expense. Government subsidized news agencies flood the newspapers with "news dispatches" which they sell at a nominal price or give away. The programs and the "news dispatches" explain and glorify the totalitarian form of government, and since many of the sister "republics" are dictatorships, they are ideologically sympathetic and receptive.

The Nazis are strong in Colombia, south of the Canal, with a Bund training regularly in military maneuvers at Cali. Since the Japanese-Nazi pact, the Japanese have established a colony of several hundred at Corinto in the Cauca Valley, thirty miles from Cali.

The Japanese colony was settled on land carefully chosen—long, level, flat acres which overnight can be turned into an air base for a fleet landed from an airplane carrier or assembled on the spot. And it is near Cali that Alejandro Tujun, a Japanese in constant touch with the Japanese Foreign Office, is at this writing dickering for the purchase of 400,000 acres of level land for "colonization." On such an acreage enough military men could be colonized to give the United States a first-class headache in time of war. It is two hours flying time from Cali to the Canal.

The entrances on either side of the Panama Canal are secretly mined. The location of these mines is one of the most carefully guarded secrets of the American navy and one of the most sought after by international spies.

The Japanese, who have been fishing along the West Coast and Panamanian waters for years, are the only fishermen who find it necessary to use sounding lines to catch fish. Sounding lines are used to measure the depths of the waters and to locate submerged ledges and covered rocks in this once mountainous area. Any fleet which plans to approach the Canal or use har-bors even within several hundred miles north or south of the Canal must have this information to know just where to go and how near to shore they can approach before sending out landing parties.

The use of sounding lines by Japanese fishermen and the mysterious going and comings of their boats became so pronounced that the Panama-nian Government could not ignore them. It issued a decree prohibiting all aliens from fishing in Panamanian waters.

In April, 1937, the "Taiyo Maru," flying the American flag but manned by Japanese, hauled up her anchor in the dead of night and with all lights out chugged from the unrestricted waters into the area where the mines are generally believed to be laid. The "Taiyo" operated out of San Diego, Califor-nia, and once established a world's record of being one hundred and eleven days at sea without catching a single fish. The captain, piloting the boat from previous general knowledge of the waters rather than by chart, unfor-tunately ran aground. The fishing vessel was stranded on a submerged ledge and couldn't get off.

In the morning the authorities found her, took off her captain and crew—all of whom had cameras—and asked why the boat was in restricted waters.

"I didn't know where I was," said the captain. "We were fishing for bait."

"But bait is caught in the daytime by all other fishermen," the officials pointed out.

"We thought we might catch some at night," the captain explained.

Since 1934, when rumors of the Japanese-Nazi pact began to circulate throughout the world, the Japanese have made several attempts to get a foothold right at the entrance to the Canal on the Pacific side. They have moved heaven and earth for permission to establish a refrigeration plant on Taboga Island, some twelve miles out on the Pacific Ocean and facing the Canal. Taboga Island would make a perfect base from which to study the waters and fortifications along the coast and the islands between the Canal and Taboga.

When this and other efforts failed and there was talk of banning alien fishing in Panamanian waters, Yoshitaro Amano, who runs a store in Pan-ama and has far flung interests all along the Pacific coasts of Central and South America, organized the Amano Fisheries, Ltd. In July, 1937, he built in

Japan the "Amano Maru," as luxurious a fishing boat as ever sailed the seas. With a purring diesel engine, it has the longest cruising range of any fishing vessel afloat, a powerful sending and receiving radio with a permanent operator on board, and an extremely secret Japanese invention enabling it to detect and locate mines.

Like all other Japanese in the Canal Zone area, Amano, rated a millionaire in Chile, goes in for a little photography. In September, 1937, word spread along the international espionage grapevine that Nicaragua, through which the United States was planning another Canal, had some sort of peculiar fortifications in the military zone at Managua.

Shortly thereafter the Japanese millionaire appeared at Managua with his expensive camera and headed straight for the military zone. Thirty minutes after he arrived (8:00 a.m. of October 7, 1937), he was in a Nicaraguan jail charged with suspected espionage and with taking pictures in prohibited areas.

I mention this incident because the luxurious boat was registered under the Panamanian flag and immediately began a series of actions so peculiar that the Republic of Panama canceled the Panamanian registry. The "Amano" promptly left for Puntarenas, Costa Rica, north of the Canal, which has a harbor big enough to take care of almost all the fleets in the world. Many of the Japanese ships went there, sounding lines and all, when alien fishing was prohibited in Panamanian waters. Today the "Amano Maru" is a mystery ship haunting Puntarenas and the waters between Costa Rica and Panama and occasionally vanishing out to sea with her wireless crackling constantly.

Some seventy fishing vessels operating out of San Diego, California, fly the American flag. San Diego is of great importance to a potential enemy because it is a naval as well as an air base. Of these seventy vessels flying the American flag, ten are either partially or entirely manned by Japanese.

Let me illustrate how boats fly the American flag:

On March 9, 1937, the S.S. "Columbus" was registered as an American fishing vessel under certificate of registry No. 235,912, issued at Los Angeles. The vessel is owned by the Columbus Fishing Company of Los Angeles. The captain, R. I. Suenaga, is a twenty-six-year-old Japanese, born in Hawaii and a full-fledged American citizen. The navigator and one sailor are also

Japanese, born in Hawaii but American citizens. The crew of ten consists entirely of Japanese born in Japan.

The ten boats which fly the American flag but are manned by Japanese crews are: "Alert," "Asama," "Columbus," "Flying Cloud," "Magellan," "Oipango," "San Lucas," "Santa Margarita," "Taiyo," "Wesgate."

Each boat carries a short-wave radio and has a cruising range of from three to five thousand miles, which is extraordinary for just little fishing boats. They operate on the high seas and where they go, only the master and crew and those who send them know. The only time anyone gets a record of them is when they come in to refuel or repair.

In the event of war half a dozen of these fishing vessels, stretched across the Pacific at intervals of five hundred or a thousand miles, would make an excellent system of communication for messages which could be relayed from one to another and in a few moments reach their destination.

In Colón on the Atlantic side and in Panama on the Pacific, East and West literally meet at the crossroads of the world. The winding streets are crowded with the brown and black people who comprise three-fourths of Panama's population. On these teeming, hot, tropical streets are some three hundred Japanese storekeepers, fishermen, commission merchants and barbers—few of whom do much business, but all of whom sit patiently in their doorways, reading the newspapers or staring at the passer-by.

I counted forty-seven Japanese barbers in Panama and eight in Colón. In Panama they cluster on Avenida Central and Calle Carlos A. Mendoza. On both these streets rents are high and, with the exception of Saturdays when the natives come for haircuts, the amount of business the barbers do does not warrant the three to five men in each shop. Yet, though they earn scarcely enough to meet their rent, there is not a lowly barber among them who does not have a Leica or Contax camera with which, until the sinking of the "Panay," they wandered around, photographing the Canal, the islands around the Canal, the coast line, and the topography of the region.

They live in Panama with a sort of permanence, but nine out of ten do not have families—even those advanced in years. Periodically some of them take trips to Japan, though, if you watch their business carefully, you know they could not possibly have earned enough to pay for their passage. And those in the outlying districts don't even pretend to have a business. They just sit and wait, without any visible means of support. It is not until you study their locations, as in the Province of Chorrera, that you find they are in spots of strategic military or naval importance.

Since there were so many barbers in Panama, the need for an occasional gathering without attracting too much attention became apparent. And so the little barber, A. Sonada, who shaves and cuts hair at 45 Carlos A. Mendoza Street, organized a "labor union," the Barbers' Association. The Association will not accept barbers of other nationalities but will allow Japanese fishermen to attend meetings. They meet on the second floor of the building at 58 Carlos A. Mendoza Street, where many of the fishermen live. At their meetings one guard stands outside the room and another downstairs at the entrance to the building.

On hot Sunday afternoons when the Barbers' Association gathers, the diplomatic representatives of other nations are usually taking a siesta or are down at the beach, but Tetsuo Umimoto, the Japanese Consul, climbs the stairs in the stuffy atmosphere and sits in on the deliberations of the barbers and visiting fishermen. It is the only barbers' union I ever heard of whose deliberations were considered important enough for a diplomatic representative to attend. This labor union has another extraordinary custom. It has a special fund to put competitors up in business. Whenever a Japanese arrives in Panama, the Barbers' Association opens a shop for him, buys the chairs—provides him with everything necessary to compete with them for the scarce trade in the shaving and shearing industry!

At these meetings the barber Sonada, who is only a hired hand, sits beside the Japanese Consul at the head of the room. Umimoto remains standing until Sonada is seated. When another barber, T. Takano, who runs a little hole-in-the-wall shop and lives at 10 Avenida B, shows up, both Sonada and the Consul rise, bow very low and remain standing until he motions them to be seated. Maybe it's just an old Japanese custom, but the Consul does not extend the same courtesy to the other barbers.

In attendance at these guarded meetings of the barbers' union and visiting fishermen, is Katarino Kubayama, a gentle-faced, soft-spoken, middle-aged businessman with no visible business. He is fifty-five years old now and lives at Calle Colón, Casa No. 11.

Way back in 1917 Kubayama was a barefoot Japanese fisherman like the others now on the west coast. One morning two Japanese battleships appeared and anchored in the harbor. From the reed- and vegetation covered jungle shore, a sun-dried, brown *panga* was rowed out by the barefooted fisherman using the short quick strokes of the native. His brown, soiled dungarees were rolled up to his calves; his shirt, open at the throat, was torn and his head was covered by a ragged straw hat.

The silvery notes of a bugle sounded. The crew of the flagship lined up at attention. The officers, including the Commander, also waited stiffly at attention while the fisherman tied his *panga* to the ship's ladder. As Kubayama clambered on board, the officers saluted. With a great show of formality they escorted him to the Commander's quarters, the junior officer following behind at a respectful distance. Two hours later Kubayama was escorted to the ladder again, the trumpet sounded its salute, and the ragged fisherman rowed away—all conducted with a courtesy extended only to a high ranking officer of the Japanese navy.

Today Kubayama works closely with the Japanese Consul. Together they call upon the captains of Japanese ships whenever they come to Panama, and are closeted with them for hours at a time. Kubayama says he is trying to sell supplies to the captains.

Japanese in the Canal Zone area change their names periodically or come with several passports all prepared. There is, for instance, Shoichi Yokoi, who commutes between Japan and Panama without any commercial reasons. On June 7, 1934, the Japanese Foreign Office in Tokyo issued passport No. 255,875 to him under the name of Masakazu Yokoy with permission to visit all Central and South American countries. Though he had permission for all, he applied only for a Panamanian visa (September 28, 1934), after which he settled down for a while among the fishermen and barbers. On July 11, 1936, the Foreign Office in Tokyo handed Yokoy another passport under the name of Shoichi Yokoi, together with visas which filled the whole passport and overflowed onto several extra pages. Shoichi or Masakazu is now traveling with both passports and a suitcase full of film for his camera.

Several years ago a Japanese named T. Tahara came to Panama as the traveling representative of a newly organized company, the Official Japanese Association of Importers and Exporters for Latin America, and established headquarters in the offices of the Boyd Bros, shipping agency in Panama.

Nelson Rounsevell, publisher of the *Panama American,* who has fought Japanese colonization in Canal areas, printed a story that this big businessman got very little mail, made no efforts to establish business contacts and, in talking with the few businessmen he met socially, showed a complete lack of knowledge about business. Tahara was talked about and orders promptly came through for him to return to Japan.

This was in 1936. Half a year later, a suave Japanese named Takahiro Wakabayashi appeared in Panama as the representative of the Federation of Japanese Importers and Exporters, the same organization under a slightly changed name. Wakabayashi checked into the cool and spacious Hotel Tivoli, run by the United States Government on Canal Zone territory and, protected by the guardian wings of the somewhat sleepy American Eagle, washed up and made a beeline for the Boyd Bros. office, where he was closeted with the general manager for over an hour.

Wakabayashi's business interests ranged from taking pictures of the Canal in specially chartered planes, to negotiating for manganese deposits and attempting to establish an "experimental station to grow cotton in Costa Rica."

The big manganese-and-cotton-photographer man fluttered all over Central and South America, always with his camera. One week he was in San José, Costa Rica; the next he made a hurried special flight to Bogotá, Colombia (November 12, 1937); then back to Panama and Costa Rica. He finally got permission from Costa Rica to establish his experimental station.

In obtaining that concession he was aided by Giuseppe Sotanis, an Italian gentleman wearing the fascist insignia in the lapel of his coat, whom he met at the Gran Hotel in San José. Sotanis, a former Italian artillery officer, is a nattily dressed, slender man in his early forties who apparently does nothing in San José except study his immaculate finger nails, drink Scotch-and-sodas, collect stamps and vanish every few months only to reappear again, still studying his immaculate finger nails. It was Sotanis who arranged for Nicaragua to get the shipment of arms and munitions which I mentioned earlier.

This uncommunicative Italian stamp collector paved the way for Wakabayashi to meet Raul Gurdian, the Costa Rican Minister of Finance, and Ramon Madrigal, Vice-president of the government-owned National Bank and a prominent Costa Rican merchant. Shortly after Costa Rica gave Wakabayashi permission to experiment with his cotton growing, both the Minister of Finance and the Vice-president of the government bank took trips to Japan.

The ink was scarcely dry on the agreement to permit the Japanese to experiment in cotton growing before a Japanese steamer appeared in Puntarenas with twenty-one young and alert Japanese and a bag of cotton seed. They were "laborers," Wakabayashi explained. The "laborers" were put up in first-class hotels and took life easy while Wakabayashi and one of the laborers started hunting a suitable spot on which to plant their bag of seed. All sorts of land was offered to them, but Wakabayashi wanted no land anywhere near a hill or a mountain. He finally found what he wanted half-way between Puntarenas and San José—long, level, flat acres. He wanted this land at any price, finally paying for it an annual rental equal to the value of the acres.

The twenty-one "laborers" who had been brought from Chimbota, Peru, where there is a colony of twenty thousand Japanese, planted an acre with cotton seed and sat them down to rest, imperturbable, silent, waiting. The plowed land is now as smooth and level as the acres at Corinto in Colombia, south of the Canal.

The harbor at Puntarenas, as I mentioned earlier, would make a splendid base of operations for an enemy fleet. Not far from shore are the flat, level acres of the "experimental station" and the twenty-one Japanese who could quickly turn these smooth acres into an air base. It is north of the Panama Canal and within two hours flying time of it, as Corinto is south of the Canal and within two hours flying time.

The Boyd Bros, steamship agency, to which Tahara and Wakabayashi went immediately upon arrival, is an American concern. The manager, with whom each was closeted, is Hans Hermann Heildelk of Avenida Peru, No. 64, Panama City, and, though efforts have been made to keep it secret, part owner of the agency. Heildelk is also the son-in-law of Ernst F. Neumann, the Nazi Consul to Panama.

On November 15, 1937, Heildelk returned from Japan by way of Germany. Five days later, on November 20, 1937, his father-in-law, who, besides being Nazi Consul, owns in partnership with Fritz Kohpcke, one of the largest hardware stores in Panama, told his clerks that he and his partner would work a little late that night. Neither partner went out to eat and the corrugated sliding door of the store, at Norte No. 54 in the heart of the Panamanian commercial district, was left open about three feet from the ground so that passers-by could not see inside unless they stooped deliberately.

At eight o'clock a car drew up at the corner of the darkened street in front of Neumann & Kohpcke, Ltd. Two unidentified men, Heildelk and Walter Scharpp, former Nazi Consul at Colón who had also just returned from Germany, stepped out, and stooping under the partly open door, entered the store. Once inside Scharpp quietly assumed command. To all practical purposes they were on German territory, for the Nazi consulate office was in the store.

Scharpp announced that the group had been very carefully chosen because of their known loyalty to Nazi Germany and because of their desire to promote friendship for Germany in Latin American countries and to cooperate with the Japanese, who had their own organization functioning efficiently in Central and South America.

"Some of these countries are already friendly," said Scharpp, "and we can work undisturbed provided we do not interfere in the Panama Canal Zone. It is North American territory, and you will have trouble from their officials and intelligence officers as well as political pressure from the States. You understand?"

"Panama is friendly to North America," said Kohpcke.

"Precisely. At the present time it is not wise to do much more than broadcast, but at a propitious time we shall be able to explain National Socialism to the Panamanians."

He looked at Kohpcke, whose left eyelid droops more than his right, giving him the appearance of being perpetually sleepy. Kohpcke looked at Neumann.

"Tonight we want to organize a Bund in Panama. In a few days I am going to Costa Rica to organize another and then leave for Valparaiso."

The others nodded. They had been informed that Scharpp was to have complete charge of Nazi activities from Valparaiso to Panama. That night they established *Der Deutsch-Ausländische Nazi Genossenschafts Bund,* with the understanding that it function secretly. The list of members was to be controlled by Neumann.

Scharpp explained that secrecy was advisable to avoid antagonizing the Panamanian Government, "which is friendly to Italy and we can cooperate with the Italian Legation here."

"The Japanese are more important that the Italians," Kohpcke pointed out.

"The Japanese will work with us," Heildelk assured him.

"But we can't be seen with them—"

"Fritz [Kohpcke] will call a meeting in Jacobs' house," said Scharpp.

"Jacobs!" exclaimed one of the unidentified men. "You don't mean the Austrian Consul!"

Scharpp nodded slowly. "He is generally believed to be anti-Nazi. His partner spent twelve years in Japan and speaks Japanese perfectly. The Japanese Consul knows and trusts both. We cannot find a better place."

On the night of December 13, 1937, forty carefully selected Germans who, during the intervening month had become members of the Bund in Panama, arrived singly and in small groups at the home of August Jacobs-Kantstein, Panamanian merchant and Austrian Honorary Consul.

Five Japanese, headed by Tetsuo Umimoto, also came. One, K. Ishibashi, formerly captain of the "Hokkai Maru" and a reserve officer in the Japanese Navy; K. Ohihara, a Japanese agent staying with the Japanese Consul but having no visible reason to be in Panama; two captains of Japanese fishing boats and A. Sonada, the barber who organized the labor union and in whose presence the Consul does not sit until the barber is seated.

Throughout the meeting, presided over by the elderly but tall and soldierly Austrian Consul, the Japanese said little. It was primarily the first get-together for Nazi-Japanese cooperation in the Canal Zone area.

"Mr. Umimoto has not said much," remarked Jacobs.

"There is so little to say when there are so many present," said the little Consul apologetically.

The others understood. The Japanese were too shrewd to discuss detailed plans with so many present.

A few days later Umimoto called upon Heildelk and was closeted with him for three hours. Shortly after that Sonada made a hurried trip to Japan.

VI

SECRET AGENTS ARRIVE IN AMERICA

GERMANY'S INTEREST IN THE Panama Canal became acute only after Japan joined the Rome-Berlin axis "to exchange information about Communism"—an exchange which appears to be more concerned with military secrets than with Communism.

The activities of Japanese and Nazi agents in Latin American countries and especially around the Canal, the organizing of a fascist rebellion in Mexico to the south of us and intensive propaganda carried on in Canada to the north, are but part of the broad invasion of the Western Hemisphere by the Fifth Column—an invasion which began almost immediately after Hitler got into power. Since the United States is the most important country in the Americas, it was and is subject to special concentration by secret Nazi agents.

The first threads spun spread out in many directions, with propaganda as the base from which to broaden espionage activities. One of the earliest of the secret agents sent to this country was an American, Colonel Edwin Emerson, soldier of fortune, mediocre author and fairly competent war correspondent. Emerson lived at 215 East 15th Street, New York City and had an office in Room 1923 at 17 Battery Place, the address of the German Consulate General. Room 1923 was rented by a representative of the German Consul General. The rent paid was nominal and in at least one instance, to avoid its being traced, it was paid in cash by Hitler's diplomatic representative. Prior to the renting of this room, Emerson had desk space with the German Consulate General for six weeks.

The May 15, 1933, issue of the *Amerika Deutsche Post,* a Nazi propaganda organ published in New York, carried an advertisement stating that the editor of this paper made his headquarters in Emerson's room. This was the first indication that Emerson had arrived in this country to handle Nazi propaganda.

For many years Emerson had wandered about the globe covering assignments for newspapers and magazines and always bragging about his Americanism and his "patriotism." One of his great boasts was that he was with Roosevelt's Rough Riders during the Spanish-American war; what he never told was that Roosevelt brought him back from Cuba in irons.

From his room paid for by the German Consul General, Emerson launched the "Friends of Germany."[5] This organization was the chief disseminator of pro-Hitler and anti-democratic propaganda in the United States, but the Colonel directed the propaganda somewhat stupidly. The "Friends of Germany" held meetings with "storm troops" in full uniform; bitter attacks were made against Jews and Catholics at large mass meetings. Visiting officers and sailors, from German ships docked in New York, appeared at these meetings to preach fascism and Nazism, until a wave of resentment swept the country. One of the keynotes of these talks was sounded by Edward F. Sullivan of Boston at a meeting held at Turnhalle, Lexington Avenue and 85th Street, on June 5th, 1934, when he repeatedly referred to Jews as "dirty, stinking kikes" and announced that he proposed to organize a strong Nazi group in Boston.

Propaganda Minister Goebbels in Berlin became annoyed at the public reaction, and the entire Nazi foreign propaganda service was reorganized. Emerson was ordered back to Germany for explicit instructions on how to carry on propaganda without antagonizing the entire country.

In October, 1933, Royal Scott Gulden (who has no connection with the mustard business, but is a distant relative of the head of it), who had been cooperating with Emerson, tried to organize an espionage system to watch Communists. In this effort Gulden enlisted the aid of Fred R. Marvin, a professional patriot. At three o'clock on the afternoon of March 10, 1934, a very secret meeting was called by Gulden at 139 East 57th Street. Present were Gulden, J. Schmidt and William Dudley Pelley, head of the Silver Shirts.

The meeting decided to adopt anti-semitic propaganda—to play on latent anti-semitism—as part of the first campaign to attract followers. The country was in a serious economic crisis with considerable unrest throughout the land. Both Hitler and Mussolini got into power in periods of great unrest by

5 Subsequently changed to "Friends of the New Germany" and then to the current "German-American Bund."

promising peace and security to the bewildered people. Men of means were terrified by fears of "revolution" and this group, directed by Emerson, began to preach that the revolution might come any minute and that the Jews were responsible for Moscow, the Third International, the Mississippi flood and anything else that troubled the people. When the meeting ended the "Order of '76"[6] had been born and Royal Scott Gulden appointed Secretary to direct espionage and propaganda.

From the very beginning Emerson tried to get people into places which would provide access to important information. On February 22, 1934, a merger of the Republican Senatorial and Congressional Campaign Committees to conduct the Party's Congressional campaign independent of the Republican National Committee was announced in a joint statement by Senator Daniel O. Hastings of Delaware and Representative Chester C. Bolton of Ohio, chairmen, respectively, of the two committees.

Several weeks before this announcement, the two committees had employed Sidney Brooks, for years head of the research bureau of the International Telephone and Telegraph Company. Brooks, because of his position, was close in the confidences of Republican Senators and Congressmen. He heard state secrets and had his fingers on the political pulse of the country.

Shortly after he took charge of the joint committee for the Senators and Congressmen, Brooks made a hurried visit to New York. On March 4, 1934, he drove to the Hotel Edison and went directly to Room 830 where a man registered as "William D. Goodales—Los Angeles," was awaiting him. Mr. "Goodales" was William Dudley Pelley, head of the Silver Shirts, who had come to New York to confer with Brooks and Gulden. After this conference the two went to Gulden's office where they had a confidential talk that lasted over an hour during which an agreement was made to merge the Order of '76 with the Silver Shirts so as to carry on their propaganda more effectively.

Brooks himself, on his mysterious visits to New York, went to 17 Battery Place, which houses the German Consulate General. At that address he visited one John E. Kelly. In a letter to Kelly dated as far back as December 27, 1933, he wrote: "I will be in New York Friday to Monday and can be reached in the usual manner—Gramercy 5-9193 (care Emerson)."

---

6 Still functioning on a minor scale. The Fifth Column has since these early beginnings established much more efficient groups.

Sidney Brooks also was a member of the secret Order of '76. Before anyone could join he had to give, in his own handwriting and sealed with his own fingerprints, certain details of his life. Brooks' application for membership in this espionage group organized with the help of a Nazi sent to this country, revealed that he was the son of the Nazi agent, Colonel Edwin Emerson, and that he was using his mother's maiden name so that connection could not be traced too easily.

One of the other early propagandists who is still active as a "patriot" was Edward H. Hunter, Executive Secretary of the Industrial Defense Association, Inc., 7 Water Street, Boston. Early in 1934, while the negotiations for the merging of the espionage order and the Silver Shirts were going on, this rooter for American liberty heard Germany was spending money in this country and on March 3, he wrote to the "Friends of Germany":

> Under separate cover we are sending you twenty-five copies of our *Swan Song of Hate* as requested and you may have as many as you wish.
>
> Several times I have conferred with Dr. Tippelskirch and at one time suggested that if he could secure the financial backing from Germany, I could start a real campaign along lines that would be very effective.
>
> All that is necessary to return America to Americans is to organize the many thousands of persons who are victims of Judaism and I am ready to do that at any time.

Dr. Tippelskirch, with whom Hunter discussed getting money from Germany for anti-semitic work, was the German Consul in Boston.

The activities of the early agents ranged from propaganda to smuggling and espionage, though at the beginning the espionage was on a minor scale. It took several years of organizing pro-German groups in this country before they could pick the most reliable for the more dangerous spy work. Much of the propaganda was sent in openly through the mails, but some of it was of so vicious and anti-democratic character that the Propaganda Ministry in Germany decided it was wiser to smuggle it in from Nazi ships.

One of the chief smugglers was Guenther Orgell,[7] at that time head of the "Friends of Germany," through whom the propaganda was distributed to

---

7 Following passage of the new 1938 law requiring all foreign agents to register, Orgell registered with the State Department as a German agent.

*Application by Sidney Brooks for membership in the secret Order of '76,
showing him to be a son of the Nazi agent, Colonel Edwin Emerson.*

various branches of the organization throughout the country. In those days
Orgell lived at 606 West 115th Street, New York City,[8] and was ostensibly
employed as an electrical engineer by the Raymond Roth Co., 25 West 45th
Street. Let me illustrate how he worked:

At twenty minutes to ten on the evening of March 16, 1934, the North
German Lloyd "Europa" was preparing to sail at midnight. The gaily illumi-
nated boat was filled with men and women, many in evening dress, seeing
friends off to Europe. German stewards, all of them members of the ship's
Nazi *Gruppe,* stood about smiling, bowing, but watching every passenger
and visitor carefully.

People wandered all over the boat. Many visited the library on the main
promenade deck, which has a German post office. There was a great deal of
laughter and chatter. Orgell, dressed in an ordinary business suit and carrying a folded newspaper in his hands, wandered in. Catching the post office
steward's eye, he casually took four letters from his coat pocket and handed
them to the steward who as casually slipped them into his pocket. There were
no stamps on the letters, which, incidentally, constituted a federal offense.

Still so casual in manner that the average observer would not even have
noticed the transfer of the letters, Orgell wandered over to a desk in the

8 He now lives at Great Kills, Staten Island, N. Y.

library and rapidly wrote another letter—so important, apparently, that he dared not carry it with him for fear of a mishap. The letter was sealed and handed to the steward.

The library had a great many visitors. No one seemed to be paying any attention to this visitor or passenger talking to the steward. With a quick glance around him, Orgell took in everyone in the library and seemed satisfied. He caught the steward's eye again and nodded. The steward opened a closet in the library, the second one left of the main aisle on the port side toward the stern of the boat. A thin package was taken from its hiding place and quickly slipped to Orgell who covered it with his newspaper and promptly left the ship.

This was the manner in which Nazi secret instructions and spy reports were sent and received—a procedure that kept up until the arrest of the Nazi spies who were tried late in 1938.

When Orgell needed trusted men to deliver messages to and from the boats as well as to smuggle off material, he usually called upon the American branch of the *Stahlhelm,* or Steel Helmets, which used to drill secretly in anticipation of *Der Tag* in this country. Only when he felt that he was not being watched, or only in the event of the most important messages, did he go aboard the ships personally. Orgell's liaison man in the smuggling activities was Frank Mutschinski, a painting contractor who used to live at 116 Garland Court, Garritsen Beach, N.Y.

Mutschinski came to the United States from Germany on the S.S. "George Washington," June 16, 1920. He was commander of one of the American branches of the *Stahlhelm* which had offices at 174 East 85th Street, New York. While he was in command, he received his orders direct from Franz Seldte, subsequently Minister of Labor under Hitler. Seldte at that time was in Magdeburg, Germany. Branches of the *Stahlhelm* were established by him and Orgell in Rochester, Chicago, Philadelphia, Newark, Detroit, Los Angeles and Toronto (the first step in the Fifth Column's invasion of Canada).

To help Orgell in his smuggling activities, Mutschinski supplied him with a chief assistant, Carl Brunkhorst. It was Brunkhorst's job to deliver the secret letters. Nazi uniforms for American Storm Troopers were smuggled into this country off German ships by Paul Bante who lived at 186 East 93rd Street, New York City. Bante, at the time he was engaged in the smuggling activities, was a member of the 244th Coast Guard as well as the New York National Guard.

In the early days of organizing the Nazi web over the United States, the German agents received cooperation from racketeering "patriots" who saw possibilities of scaring the wits out of the American people by announcing that the "revolution" was just around the corner. The country was in an economic crisis, the American people were bewildered and didn't know which way to turn, there was considerable unrest in the land, and the Nazi agents and their American counterparts visualized in Hitler's cry that "Communism and the Jews" were responsible, grand pickings from the scared suckers.

Since Communism, especially in those restless days in the depths of the depression, was the bugaboo of the rich, it was inevitable that some unscrupulous but shrewd observers of the American scene would take advantage of this fear and capitalize on it. One of the chief racketeers, a man who subsequently worked very closely with secret Nazi agents in this country, was Harry A. Jung, Honorary General Manager of the American Vigilant Intelligence Federation, Post Office Box 144, Chicago. This organization was originally founded to spy on Communists and Socialists. For a while Jung collected from terrified employers by promising to inform them about the threat of revolution—what time it would occur and who would lead it. In return he collected plenty.

In time employers got fed up when the rowboat loaded with bomb-throwing Bolsheviks failed to arrive from Moscow. Pickings became slim. Jung was badly in need of a new terror-inspiring "issue" with which to collect from the suckers. He found it at the time Emerson was sent here from Germany. Gulden, Pelley and their associates were launching an anti-semitic campaign as the first step to attract people to the "Friends of Germany." Jung likewise discovered the "menace of the Jew" and peddled it for all it was worth.

There was an air of secrecy about the whole outfit. Even the location of the office in the Chicago Tribune Tower was kept from the membership; all they were given was the post office box number. As soon as he collected enough material from the *Daily Worker* and other Communist publications, he sent agents to call on the gullible businessmen with horrendous stories of the Muscovites now on the high seas on their way to capture the American Government. The salesmen collected and in turn got forty per cent of the pickings.

When Jung heard that William Dudley Pelley was making money on the Jew-and-Catholic scare and that others like Edward H. Hunter of the Industrial

American Vigilant Intelligence Federation

INCORPORATED—NOT FOR PROFIT

NATIONAL HEADQUARTERS

P. O. BOX 144

CHICAGO, ILL.   December
One
1 9 3 3

TELEPHONE
SUPERIOR
4646

C—10247
H-7-S

Mr. Harry F. Sieber, Treasurer,
Silver Legion of America,
Asheville, N. C.

DEC 7 1933

Dear Mr. Sieber:

            In response to yours
addressed to R. L. Peterson on November 26, we can give you a price of
sixty cents per copy in quantity lots
of the "Protocols".

            As for "Halt, Gentile!
and Salute the Jew", same can be had
at ten cents per copy, in quantity
lots or fifteen cents apiece.

                              Very truly yours,

                              Harry A. Jung
                              Harry A. Jung,
                              Honorary General Manager

HAJ/RP

435 No. Michigan Ave., R.2212

Showing the type of literature peddled by patrioteer Harry A. Jung.

Defense Association were talking with the German Consul General about getting money from Germany for propaganda, he got busy peddling "The Protocols of the Elders of Zion," long discredited as forgeries. Armed with these, Jung's high pressure salesmen scoured the country, collecting shekels from Christian businessmen and getting their forty per cent commissions.

It was not long before Jung, Pelley and others were working in full swing with secret Nazi agents sent into this country for propaganda and espionage purposes.

VII

NAZI SPIES and AMERICAN "PATRIOTS"

ONCE THE SPADEWORK WAS done by the early Nazi agents sent into the United States, the web rapidly embraced native fascists, racketeering "patriots" and deluded Americans who swallowed their propaganda. When Japan joined the Rome-Berlin axis, espionage directed against American naval and military forces became one of the major interests of the foreign agents, especially on the West Coast.

Some five years ago, after the McCormick Congressional Committee investigation into Nazi activities turned up a number of propagandists, there was a lull in their activity until the nationwide denunciations died out. In the meantime Goebbels again ordered the reorganization of the entire propaganda machine in this country.

It was during this period that the approaching Presidential elections presented an immediate task for the Nazis to work on. The Roosevelt Administration was considered by the Nazis both here and in Germany as none too friendly to Hitler, and before the election got well under way the Nazis here, upon instructions from their local leaders who act only upon instructions from the German Propaganda Bureau, became active in the anti-Roosevelt campaign. Both Nazi agents and "patriotic" American groups working with Nazi agents (without much money after the Congressional Committee's exposés) suddenly found themselves possessed of more than enough capital with which to operate. Some of the money came from the Nazis and some from anti-Roosevelt forces.

One of the most vicious of the anti-Roosevelt propaganda mediums was established by Nazi agents in a carefully hidden printing plant.

No one who got off on the sixth floor at 325 W. Ohio St., Chicago, and entered the John Baumgarth's Specialty Company, would have suspected anything out of the ordinary about the place. It looked just like hundreds of other business firms where pale girls and anemic-looking men made calendars.

People came up on the ancient elevator, attended to their affairs at the desks in front of the door, and left. Very few of them ever went behind the enormous piles of cardboard and paper which almost obstructed the passage to the right of the desks. But if you turned into this passage and then turned to the left, you came upon a wooden partition. Unless you were watching for it you would think it a wall.

There was no indication of what was behind the partition. There was only a shiny Yale lock in a door carefully hidden from the eyes of casual visitors. If you knew nothing about it and tried to open the the door, you would find it locked. If you knocked or banged on it, there would be no answering sign from the other side, and the young man operating the cutting machine alongside the partition would merely stare at you blankly.

But if you knocked three times quickly, paused for a split second and then knocked once more, the door would be opened immediately. Without the proper signal all the knocking in the world would not help, for this was the entrance to the carefully guarded publication rooms of the *American Gentile* and the headquarters for Nazi anti-democratic activities in the Middle West. But even more guarded than the location of the printing plant were the goings and comings of the paper's editor, Captain Victor DeKayville and his financial backer, Charles O'Brien.

This brings me to two of the leading Nazi agents in the United States, one of whom originally started the newspaper. Certainly none of the American suckers who gave them money to spread pro-Nazi propaganda knew that both were masquerading under false names and that one of them is an ex-convict.

Those social leaders in Chicago and San Francisco, whose doors were always open to the handsome, dashing Prince Peter Kushubue with his sad eyes and his talk of how the Bolsheviki had confiscated his vast estates and family jewels in Old Russia, may be interested to learn that his Highness, the Prince, is really—well, let me give a brief sketch of his activities before he became a Nazi agent:

In 1922, a Russian emigré, born in Petrograd and christened Peter Afanassieff or Aphanassieff, came to the United States seeking his fortune, preferably in the form of a wealthy heiress. As an ordinary run-of-the-mill Afanassieff, he was just an unemployed White Russian looking for a job and it didn't take

Anti-Semitic anti-Roosevelt handbill issued by
the American White Guard in California.

him long to discover that in this democratic country heiresses and their doting papas go nuts over titles. So overnight Peter Afanassieff blossomed out into Prince Peter Kushubue; and as a Prince whose wealth had been confiscated by the Bolsheviki, the doors of San Francisco society opened to him.

Afanassieff just barely missed marrying a wealthy heiress on the West Coast, and in his despondence he tried his hand at a little forgery. But he picked the wrong outfit to practice penmanship on. He forged a United States Treasury check and when the federal men got after him he fled to Chicago. He was picked up and on November 29, 1929, he found himself before a U.S. Commissioner who ordered his return to San Francisco. On December 19 of the same year he pleaded guilty before Federal Judge F. J. Kerrigan and was given a year and a half. At the trial he admitted to being just an ordinary Afanassieff and served his sentence under that name.

When he came out he alternated between being Prince Kushubue and an ordinary Afanassieff and then, because the 1930 crash had kicked the bottom out of the market for foreign titles, he picked himself a good solid American name: Armstrong. He said it was his mother's maiden name. For convenience we'll call him Armstrong from now on.

When he arrived in Chicago in 1933, he met some White Russians who were working with Harry A. Jung on an altogether new translation of the

Grand Rapids Michigan.

Dear # I.

Yours of Twelvth instant received and Mr.Shera delivered your package to me last Saturday.

Refering to my of II/inst.I was able to accomplish only part of a job.Mr.Thompson and Mr.Tolliefiere were out of townes I'll try to get in tuch with both on Monday. Saturday a.m.I had one hour and 20m.talk with editor of G.R.Herald Mr.Frank Sparks. He read my credentials and after coversing a while we agreed upon that something should be done and done in a hurry.I left with that chap our 3 documents(legal sise), memo on Foster ,A.V/I.F. programme/blue/C.P.U.S.A.chart,Facing the facts and Vigilant. I think it will be good idea if you send him a few lines mentioning how glad you are e.t.c.Same evening I received invitation to attend diner at Dr.Ferris N.Smith (639 Plymouth blwd.Grand Rapide,Mich.)He is a very prominent ,rich and internationaly known Plastic Surgery specialist.In my honour we had 2 bottles of champaign and other things beside.Diner party ended at 4.30 a.m.Sunday.Most interesting part of it that Mrs.Smith' just few weeks ago came back from U.S.S.R.where she spend 10 days in Moscow.She is very wellversed in Bolshevik end of our problems But also very much like to find outother "ENI-S!".So last nite she pledged herself to A.V.I.F.and wills sighn card on my return back to Grand Rapids.Mr.Gerry D.Pettibone of 206 Lafayette Ave.N.E.-signed card last Tuesday but did not paid money-will Collect later.

Speaking of #679 according to opinion of Dr.S.G.he lakes backbone as an organizer, please remember that I am Quoting some one else opinion.I can not have of my own in this case 'cose I saw him so little.

Tomorrow I'll try to see Tolliefiere and also Thompson.Then in an Evening to see again Dr. F.N.Smith.

Yours Art

Enclos.

P.S. Tuesday leaving for Detroit, ill stay with Dr. at Tuller Hotel.

Letter written by secret agent No. 31 (Peter Afanassieff, alias Prince Kushubue, alias Peter V. Armstrong) to No. 1 (Harry A. Jung).

"Protocols." Jung planned to publish and distribute the forgeries in order to scare the wits out of his Christian suckers, but changed his mind when he discovered he could buy them cheaper and resell at a higher price. Jung, in turn, introduced Armstrong to Nazi agents.

Jung and the ex-convict hit it up. Before long Armstrong became Jung's secret agent No. 31 (Jung is No. 1 and always signs his letters to agents with

Nibelungen-Verlag G.m.b.H.

Berlin NW 40, In den Zelten 9a

Auslieferungsstelle nur Leipzig C 1, Täubchenweg 17
Fernruf: Berlin A 1 Jäger-5644, Leipzig 71246
Postscheckkonto: Berlin 78302
Bankkonto: Deutsche Bank und Disconto-Gesellschaft, Depositenkasse B 2,
Berlin NW 40, Alt-Moabit 109

Herrn
Peter V. Armstrong
i.Fa. Patriotic Publishing Co.
C h i c a g o .

Dear Sir,
By Mr. Lilienfeld we were informed that you are interested in
the english edition of our book: Herman Fehst, Bolschewism and
Jewry. We beg to inform you that the right of edition of this
~~k and all

a   ...t in a~ ance
later on we will deduct the sale every half a year.

We await with interest your answer.

Yours faithfully
Nibelungen-Verlag
G. m. b. H.

*Letter showing contact between Peter V. Armstrong (the White Russian
ex-convict Peter Afanassieff) and German publishers of anti-Semitic literature.*

that number. His agents, too, sign only their numbers. They are not supposed even to write the number but every once in a while an agent slips up and scribbles a postscript in his own handwriting. A reproduction of one of No. 31's reports to the No. 1 Guy appears on the opposite page.)

It was not long after Jung introduced Armstrong to Nazi agents that the White Russian decided that he could work the racket himself. He began to meet secretly with Nazi agents without telling Jung about it. Their favorite meeting place was at Von Thenen's Tavern, 2357 Roscoe St., Chicago. Present at these meetings, usually called by Fritz Gissibl, head of the "Friends of the New Germany,"[9] were Armstrong, Captain Victor DeKayville, J. K. Leibl (who organized an underground Nazi clique in South Bend, Ind.), Oscar Pfaus, Nick Mueller, Toni Mueller, Jose Martini, Franz Schaeffer and Gregor Buss. When Gissibl couldn't attend, his right-hand man Leibl acted for him.

9 Gissibl left for Stuttgart, Germany, and leadership was taken over by his brother, Peter.

In March, 1936, Armstrong and the others decided to establish a "National Alliance" to aid in Nazi work. They decided to use the utmost secrecy lest what they were doing and who were behind it, leak out. They met only in private homes and so careful were they that the host of one meeting would not be told where the next meeting was to be held. Only a picked handful of the most trusted Nazi agents were invited.

The first meeting was held at Bockhold's home, 1235 Waveland Ave., Chicago; the second at the home of Mrs. Emma Schmid, 4710 Winthrop Ave., Chicago. To the second meeting they invited C. O. Anderson of 601 Diversey Parkway, Chicago. He was listed by the Nazis and the White Russians as a good sucker because he had contributed money to Jung.

The White Russians and the Nazi agents then decided to start a publishing business as the first step to attract followers. They issued a paper called the *Gentile Front.* They were extremely careful to keep the editorial and publication addresses secret. All mail was sent only to Post Office Box No. 526 in the old Chicago Post Office. The company was named the Patriotic Publishing Co. and with the utmost secrecy editorial offices were established at 5 S. Wabash in Chicago and the paper printed in the basement at 4233 N. Kildare where the Merrimac Press functioned.

Subsequently, to throw anyone who might be watching them off the trail, they changed the name of the publishing company to the Right Cause Publishing Co. and issued an avalanche of Nazi propaganda. It was through this secretly organized and secretly functioning propaganda center that Harry A. Jung, ultra-"patriot," distributed printed attacks on Roosevelt just before the Presidential election.

The *American Gentile,* backed by Nazi money, published the most insane rantings imaginable. But when one is inclined to dismiss them as insanity, one remembers that it was the same sort of stuff Hitler used in winning millions of bewildered Germans to his banner. The pre-election issue (October, 1936) of the *Gentile* will serve as an illustration of what they published and distributed through the United States mails:

Former Congressman Louis T. McFadden[10] died on October 1 from a stroke. He was sixty years old. The *American Gentile,* however, implied that

10 Before McFadden died, I published evidence that while he was a member of Congress he worked with Nazi agents in this country.

he had been murdered by Jews; Senator Bronson Cutting (killed in an airplane crash) also was murdered by Jews. Huey Long was murdered by Jews. Walter A. Liggett, the newspaper editor, was murdered by Jews, and it was an international ring of Jewish bankers who hired Booth to murder Abraham Lincoln.

Of course it was crazy, but the coal digger in Kentucky or the bedeviled farmer in the Middle West who couldn't pay his taxes or the unemployed worker in an industrial center who couldn't find a job did not know history any too well nor understand the workings of the economic system; and when they were told by newspapers brought to them by the United States Government mails that their economic difficulties were due to a Jewish-Communist plot, that Roosevelt was a Jew and was controlled by Jews and Communists, some of them were prone to believe it. With this irresponsible propaganda anti-semitism grew. Men and women were attracted to the Nazi web without dreaming of the forces disseminating the propaganda of the motives behind them.

The most capable of those drawn into the Nazi propaganda machine were chosen for more serious work. Some were used for propaganda; others were given definite espionage assignments. The espionage and propaganda divisions of the Nazi machine in this country are separate bodies. They overlap only in serving as a recruiting ground.

The smuggling of anti-democratic propaganda off Nazi ships entering American ports was exposed by the McCormick Congressional Committee, but it stopped only for a brief period. The Nazi ships which bring in propaganda also bring secret instructions to agents here and take back their reports. To eliminate tell-tale evidence, Dr. George Gyssling, Nazi Consul in Los Angeles, has paid out cash to leaders of the German propaganda machine on the West Coast. Affidavits to this effect are in my possession.

The headquarters for the West Coast propaganda machine which dabbles a little in espionage, is the *Deutsches Haus,* 634 W. 15th Street, Los Angeles. The building is supposed to be merely a meeting place for German-Americans and sympathizers of the Hitler regime. Actually its functions are far more sinister.

The *Deutsches Haus,* before it was turned into a center of Nazi activity, had been a typical Los Angeles home. When the Nazis took it over, they ripped out several of the front rooms and turned it into a barn-like affair with a skylight overhead and a raised platform from which speakers sing the praises of Hitler and fascism. In the rear part of the hall is a combined bar and restaurant where the German-Americans drink their beer and whiskies and plot the smuggling of propaganda from Nazi ships and the carrying on of espionage against American military and naval forces.

I use the word "plot" for precisely what it means. From this house, naturalized American citizens and native Americans direct espionage and propaganda activities paid for by a foreign government and designed against the peace and security of the United States.

The leader of this group, Hermann Schwinn, was appointed by Minister of Propaganda Goebbels in Germany and is the recipient of personal letters of praise from Adolf Hitler for his work. Schwinn is a naturalized citizen,[11] a comparatively young man in his early thirties, ruddy-faced and with a thin, quivering mustache on his upper lip. This little Führer's office is just off the meeting hall and adjoins the small bookstore where the purchaser can get pamphlets, books, and newspapers attacking democracy.

When I called upon Schwinn at the Nazi headquarters and introduced myself, he smiled amiably and granted my request for an interview. The German-American Bund, he explained immediately (the reorganized Friends of the New Germany), is now a patriotic organization, consisting only of American citizens.

The German-American Bund, Schwinn continued as we seated ourselves in his office, was now a "patriotic organization striving to create among Americans a better understanding of Nazi Germany, to combat anti-Nazi propaganda and the boycott against Germany, and to fight Communism." He took about ten minutes to explain their peaceful objectives and their great love for the United States.

"Everything is America for the Americans and to fight all alien theories and interests?" I asked, summing up his explanation.

"That's right," he beamed.

"Does any propaganda come from Germany to help save America for the Americans?"

---

11 As this book went to press, the U. S. Government had just begun action to revoke Schwinn's citizenship, claiming that he had obtained it by making false statements.

"No, sir!" he said. "We have nothing to do with Germany; we are Americans first. Mr. Dickstein[12] says that there is propaganda coming, but he was never able to prove any of his statements."

"Then how does propaganda like *World Service* from Erfurt, Germany, get into this country?"

"Oh, I get it," he said casually. "Anyone can subscribe to it for a dollar and a half a year. We get two or three copies around here—by subscription, of course."

"There must be a lot of subscribers in the United States for I've seen a great many copies. I thought that perhaps it comes in batches from Germany for distribution here so members of the Nazi groups in the United States could use it to help save America for the Americans."

"No," he smiled. "It's all a subscription matter."

"I see. Do you know Captain George Trauernicht?"

Schwinn shot a startled glance at me and nodded slowly. "Yes," he said, "he's Captain of the Hapag Line ship 'Oakland.'"

"Do you ever visit him?"

"Yes; he was here last week."

"Doesn't he bring batches of *World Service* and other propaganda for you every time he comes into port?"

"No," Schwinn said sharply. "The visits I pay him are purely social. Just to drink a glass of good German beer."

"Do you usually pay social visits carrying a brief case?"

"Now, wait a minute," he protested. "Don't write down the answer until I think."

I stopped typing on his office machine which he had permitted me to use to take verbatim notes of the interview and waited while he thought. After a lengthy silence I added:

"You had a brief case on Thursday when you visited him."

He continued thinking for a little longer and then said that he thought he had had a brief case on that trip.

"But why do you ask me that?" he demanded. "There was nothing in that brief case."

---

12 Congressman Samuel Dickstein. The McCormick Congressional Committee was frequently referred to as the "Dickstein Committee" because Dickstein had introduced the resolution for the investigation.

"Sure there was. The brief case always contains reports you send back to Germany and instructions from Germany are brought to you by Captain Trauernicht as well as other captains of German ships docking here and in San Diego."

"I have never taken off propaganda nor given nor received reports," Schwinn insisted. "Somebody told you something and you've got it all wrong."

"Suppose I mention a few instances. At four o'clock on Monday afternoon, March 9, 1936, your beer-drinking friend, Captain Trauernicht, waited for you at the gangplank of his boat—for your 'social' visit. What he wanted was the package of sealed reports from Nazi agents throughout the United States which you were bringing in your brief case. In due time you arrived and gave him the reports. Then you started on a drinking spree—"

"I don't know what you're talking about," Schwinn interrupted.

"Maybe I can refresh your memory. That was the evening the Captain took a lady from Beverly Hills, to the first mate's cabin—remember? You know, the lady who lives on North Crescent Drive—shall I mention her name?"

Schwinn's face turned an apoplectic red and he became quiet.

"On Monday, February 10, 1936," I continued. "Reinhold Kusche, leader of the O. D. unit in your organization and a 'patriotic' naturalized American citizen, was on board the steamer 'Elbe' docked in Los Angeles harbor. He telephoned to one of your Nazi agents, Albert Voigt, that the Captain was sailing at five o'clock for Antwerp and was furious because the agents' reports had not yet been delivered to him. Kusche told Voigt to bring the reports in a hurry—which Voigt promptly did.

"On Tuesday evening, May 12, 1936, the Captain of the Nazi ship 'Schwaben', which had just arrived from Antwerp, Belgium, came to your office and handed you a sealed package of orders and propaganda. He laid it on your desk in this room. The package contained copies of *World Service*—which is obtainable, you remember, only by subscription at a dollar and a half a year."

"It is not true—" Schwinn interrupted excitedly.

"I have a copy from the batch he brought to you. But let's continue. On Monday, June 8, 1936, you yourself went to the Nazi ship 'Weser' and gave the captain secret reports to take back to Germany and left with secret orders he had brought over—orders sealed in brown, manila paper[13]—and a large package of *Fichte-Bund* propaganda. I have a copy from that batch, too."

---

13 During the trial of the four Nazi spies in New York the Federal prosecutor brought out that they also carried orders sealed in brown, manila paper.

Schwinn stared at me and then smiled. "You can't prove anything," he said with assurance.

"I have affidavits about all these items and more—affidavits from men on board the Nazi ships."

"It's impossible!" he exclaimed. "No German on the ship would dare to sign an affidavit!"

"But I have them," I repeated.

"You intend to publish them?" he asked, a cunning look appearing in his eyes.

His eagerness to discover who had given me affidavits was funny and I laughed. "I'll publish the information contained in them," I explained. "The names of the signers will be given only to an American governmental or judicial body which may look into your 'patriotic' activities. But let's get on. Do you know the Nazi Consul in Los Angeles—Dr. George Gyssling?"

He sat silently for a moment as if hesitating whether to speak.

"Don't be afraid to talk," I said. "The Consul isn't. You know, of course, that he does not like you?"

A deep red flush suffused his face. "It's mutual!" he said. "I know he talks—"

Throughout the interview Schwinn tried almost pathetically, despite his obvious dislike of Gyssling, to cover up the Consul's interference in American affairs. When I told Schwinn I had affidavits showing that Rafael Demmler, President of the Steuben Society of Los Angeles, got two hundred dollars in April, 1936, from the Nazi Consul to help maintain the *Deutsches Haus* as a center of Nazi propaganda, he shook his head bewilderedly; and when I pointed out that he himself got one hundred and forty-five dollars in cash from the Nazi Consul on Tuesday, April 28, 1936, to cover expenses incurred by Schwinn in the effort to bring the German-American groups together for the better dissemination of Nazi propaganda, his face turned alternately white and red and finally he exploded:

"Did Gyssling tell you that?"

"I'm not saying who told it to me. But let's get on with some of your other 'patriotic' activities. On Thursday, June 18, 1936, you visited Captain Trauernicht in company with Count von Bülow—"

For the first time since the interview began Schwinn sat upright in his chair as if I had struck him. All the other subjects had left him slightly disturbed but still with an obvious sense that he was not on particularly dangerous ground. But at the mention of Von Bülow's name a look of actual fear spread over his face.

"On that day," I continued, "you and the Count went directly to the Captain's cabin where you handed over your reports—"

"What are you getting at?" Schwinn demanded sharply.

"I'm getting at the Count. What do you know about him?"

"Nothing. I know nothing about him. I've met him, that's all."

"Have you ever visited his home at Point Loma,[14] San Diego?"

Schwinn stared at me without answering.

"Have you ever been there?" I repeated.

"Yes," he said slowly.

"Did you ever observe how, through his study windows, you could see almost everything going on at the American naval base—"

"I have nothing to say," Schwinn interrupted excitedly.

Among the men sent here directly by Rudolf Hess, Hitler's right-hand man, is a former German-American businessman named Meyerhofer. This Nazi came here with special instructions from Hess, a personal friend of his, to reorganize the Nazi machine in the United States. He arrived early in 1935 posing as a businessman. After consultations with Nazi leaders in New York, including the Nazi Consul General, he went to Detroit to confer with Fritz Kuhn,[15] national head of the German-American Bund. From Detroit he went to Chicago where he held more conferences with Nazi agents and then went directly to Los Angeles for conferences with Schwinn, Von Bülow and other secret agents operating in the United States. Meyerhofer's mission was not only to reorganize the propaganda machine but to try to place it on a self-supporting basis so that in the event of war when funds from Germany would be cut off, an efficient Nazi machine could continue functioning.

It was with this knowledge in mind that I asked Schwinn what he knew about Meyerhofer. At the mention of his name the Nazi leader for the West Coast again showed a flash of fear. He hesitated a little longer than usual and then said in a low voice, "He is a member of our organization. He came from Germany about thirty or forty years ago." Suddenly he added, "He's an American citizen."

"I know he's an American citizen. But are you sure he didn't come from Germany—on his latest trip—in January of last year?"

14 Von Bülow has since sold his home and moved into the El Cortez Hotel in San Diego.

15 At that time working for Henry Ford.

Schwinn smiled a little wryly. "He might have," he said in the same low tone.

"He's a personal friend of Rudolf Hess—"

"Listen!" Schwinn exclaimed. "You're on the wrong track!"

"Maybe; but what's his business here?"

"He's a businessman!"

"What's his business?"

Schwinn shrugged his shoulders. "I don't know," he said and then with growing excitement, "I tell you you're on the wrong track!"

"Then what are you so excited about?"

"Because you're on the wrong track—"

"Okay. I'm on the wrong track and you know nothing about Nazi spies. Do you know of the visits paid by the Japanese Consul in Los Angeles to Nazi ships when they come into port and of his conferences with Nazi captains—"

"The Japanese! We have nothing to do with the Japanese. We are a patriotic group—"

"Yes, I know. What do you know about Schneeberger?"

Schwinn answered with an "M-m-m-m." His jaw bones showed against the ruddy flesh of his cheeks. He stared up at the ceiling. "He was a Tyrolian peasant boy," he said without looking at me. "A boy traveling around the world; you know, just chiseling his way around—"

"Just a bum, eh?"

"That's it," he agreed quickly. "Just a bum."

"What would your connections be with bums? Do you usually associate with Tyrolian bums who are chiseling their way around the world?"

"Oh, he just came here like so many other people. He wanted money; so I gave him a little help and he went to San Francisco and Oakland. He vanished. I haven't any idea where he might be now. Maybe he's in Chicago now."

"He couldn't possibly be in Japan now, could he?"

"He spoke of going to Japan," Schwinn admitted.

"You saw him off on a Japanese training ship which the Japanese Government sent here from the Canal Zone, didn't you?"

"I don't know," he said defiantly. "I know nothing about him."

"The treaty between Japan and Germany providing for exchange of information about Communists was signed November 25, 1936. But in September, 1936, Schneeberger told you he was leaving on a Japanese training ship for

Japan. No training ship was expected on the West Coast at that time by the United States port authorities, and yet a Japanese training ship appeared—ordered here from the Canal Zone. It was on this ship that Schneeberger left. Apparently, then, the Nazis and the Japanese had already been working together—and you were cooperating because you took Schneeberger around. You took him to Count von Bülow's home at Point Loma, overlooking the American naval base. You know that Schneeberger was not broke because he was spending money freely—"

"He was broke," Schwinn interrupted weakly.

"If he was so broke, how do you account for his carrying around an expensive camera and always having plenty of film with which to photograph American naval and military spots?"

"I don't know. Maybe he carried the camera around to hock in case he went broke."

The absurdity of the excuse was so patent that I laughed. Schwinn smiled a little.

"All right. What do you know about a man named Maeder?"

Again that long, drawn-out "M-m-m-m." A long pause and Schwinn said, "Maeder is an American citizen, I believe."

"Yes; you are, too. But what's his business in this country?"

"I don't know," Schwinn said helplessly. "I really don't know."

"You know nothing about his activities or observations of American naval and military bases? Do you usually take in members without knowing anything about them?"

"Sometimes we do and sometimes we do not—"

"But orders were sent from Germany to make this an American organization—"

Schwinn nodded without admitting it verbally.

"And since you throw out all Germans who are not American citizens, you check with the Consul General in New York as to whether they are fit—"

"We have nothing to do with the Consul General—"

"What happened to Willi Sachse who used to be a member here?"

"He is supposed to have gone back to Germany."

"Have you heard from him from Germany?"

"No; I haven't heard since he left."

"You received a letter recently from him from San Francisco where he is watching foreign vessels—"

"Oh," said Schwinn, raising his hands in a helpless gesture, "I know you have spies in my organization."

We talked a little longer—of visits he made to Nazi agents in the Middle West and in New York, of secret conferences with propagandists and spies. But he refused to do any more than shrug his shoulders at all new questions.

"I have said too much already," he said.

VIII

HENRY FORD and
SECRET NAZI ACTIVITIES

ONE OF THE CHIEF NAZI propagandists in the United States recently ran in the United States Senate primaries in Kansas and was almost nominated. He is Gerald B. Winrod, who poses as a Protestant minister but has no affiliations with any reputable church.

Winrod, even before he tried to get into the Senate, was one of the most brazen of the Nazis' Fifth Column operating in this country. He has held secret consultations with officials in the German Embassy in Washington and carries on his propaganda under Fritz Kuhn's direction.

Shortly after Winrod returned from a mysterious trip to Germany and held an equally mysterious long consultation at the Nazi Embassy in this country (1935), he organized the *Capitol News and Feature Service,* with offices at 209 Kellogg Building, Washington. The "news service" supplied smaller papers throughout the land with "impartial comments" on the national scene. The *Service* was edited by Dan Gilbert, a San Diego newspaperman, and the material was sent free of charge (as is the material sent to the Latin American countries from Germany and Italy). It was of course, deliberately calculated to spread pro-Hitler sentiment and propaganda.

Few who read Winrod's publications realize the extent of his activities. On March 1, 1937, Senator Joseph T. Robinson addressed the United States Senate on what appeared to him to be "unfair propaganda" carried on by Winrod against President Roosevelt's proposed reorganization of the judiciary system. The Senator stated that he could not understand why the issues should be deliberately falsified by a gentleman of the cloth—that it reminded him of the old Ku Klux Klan tactics.

The Senator did not know that Winrod's propaganda against Roosevelt was only part of a propaganda campaign cunningly and brazenly organized by Nazis in this country in an effort to defeat a man who, they felt, was not friendly to them. In this campaign, Nazi agents worked openly and secretly with a few unscrupulous members of the Republican Party in an effort to defeat Roosevelt.

Several years ago Winrod was a poverty-stricken man living at 145 N. Green Street, Wichita, Kansas. He called himself a minister but all church bodies have repudiated him. Without a church, he did a little evangelistic preaching and lived off collections made from his audience. It was a precarious livelihood and often the "Reverend" did not have enough money to buy even ordinary necessities.

Records in several Wichita department stores tell the story of the evangelist's poverty before an angel came to visit him. All the storekeepers with whom Winrod dealt requested that their names be withheld, but signified their willingness to present their records to any governmental body which might be interested in the sudden wealth he acquired after he became an intense Hitler propagandist. In the days of his poverty Winrod, the records show, could afford to buy only the cheapest furniture, the cheapest clothes, and pay for them on the installment plan in weekly payments ranging from fifty cents to two or three dollars a week.

I am reproducing with this chapter several of the installment cards. The reader will notice that as late as 1934 Winrod was paying at the rate of one dollar a week. It was in this period that Nazi agents in the United States were carrying on their intensive campaign, and it was also in this period that Winrod began to harangue his audiences about the "menace of the Jews and the Catholics."

Then one day, the Reverend Gerald B. Winrod suddenly found himself possessed of enough money to go to Germany. When he came back in February, 1935, he had new suit cases, new clothes and a fat check book. The records in the Wichita department stores where he had been getting credit for clothes and furniture show that after his return from Germany he paid all his debts in lump sums—by check. Then he became a publisher.

In his newspaper, *The Revealer,* he published a report on his trip to Europe, but did not mention where he got the money for the jaunt. The report (February 15, 1935) told of his discovery that the German people loved Hitler and that only "Jewish influence in high circles of certain governments is making it impossible for Germany to carry on normal trade and financial relations with other countries."

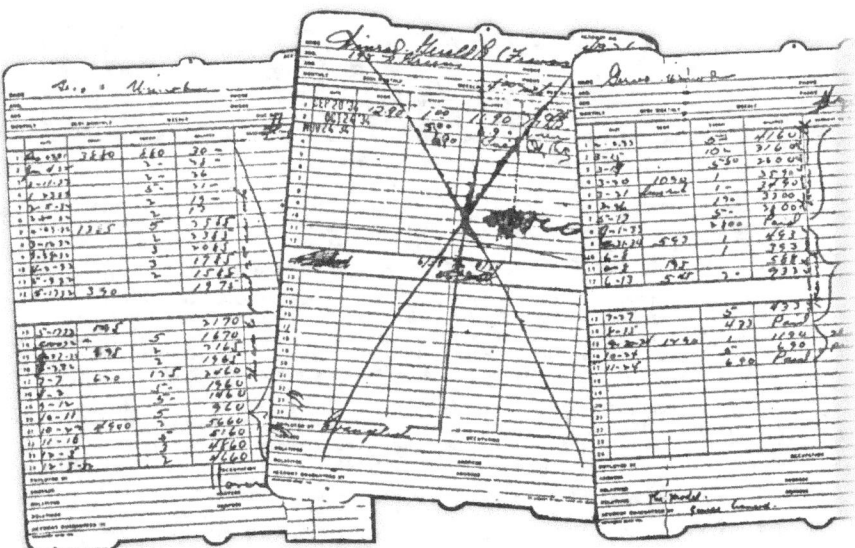

Account cards for the Reverend Gerald B. Winrod in a Wichita department store, showing his straitened financial circumstances during the early thirties.

In this period of his new-found prosperity he established contacts with Nazi agents and pro-fascists like Harry A. Jung of the American Vigilant Intelligence Federation, Colonel Edwin Emerson, James True and a host of other patrioteers.

Before the Presidential election he made another trip to Germany. When he returned, he enlarged his distribution apparatus and was apparently important enough for high Nazi officials visiting the United States to meet with him. One of these was Hans von Reitenkranz, who came quietly to the United States as Hitler's personal representative to arrange for oil purchases—oil which Germany needed badly for her factories and especially for her growing war machine.

Von Reitenkranz is a friend of Professor Kurt Sepmeier of the University of Wichita. He introduced Winrod to the Professor. They became friendly. When I was in Wichita making inquiries about the Reverend Winrod, I constantly came across the Professor's trail. Both he and Winrod had been meeting regularly but with an effort at secrecy.

In January, 1937, after several meetings with Professor Sepmeier, Winrod went to Washington. I also went to Washington and found that the Reverend

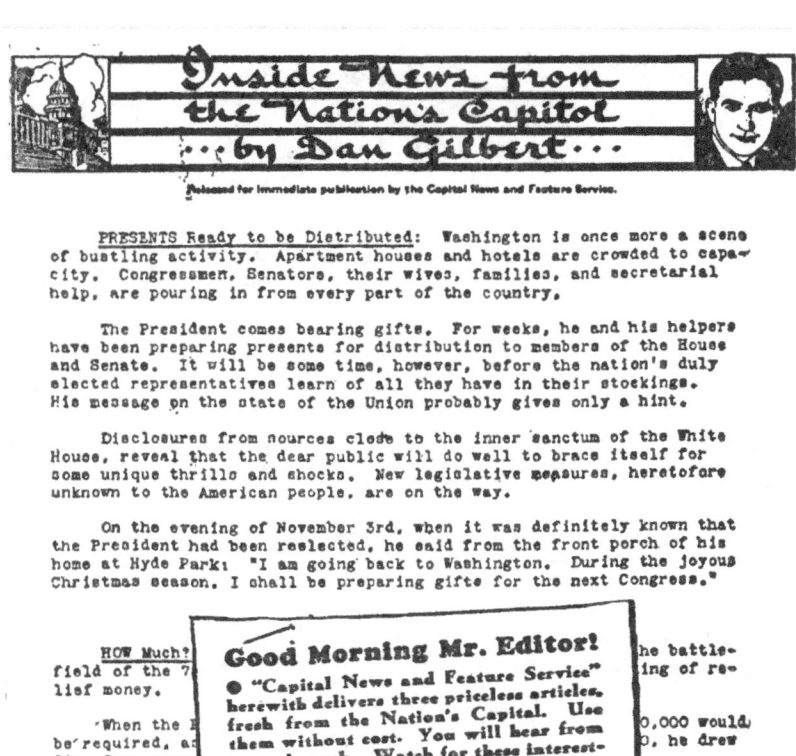

Sample of the "Capital News and Feature Service," in the establishment and distribution of which the Reverend Gerald B. Winrod had a hand.

was calling at the German Embassy. On one of his visits he remained inside for an hour and eighteen minutes. Whom he saw or what he discussed I do not know; but immediately after this long visit, the *News and Feature Service* was organized with money enough to send its items out free of charge to the papers that would accept them.

Gilbert, who headed the *Service,* was for many years the personal representative of William Dudley Pelley, leader of the Silver Shirts. The Nazis had been trying to get the Silver Shirts to cooperate with them in a fascist "united front" and the appointment of Gilbert was the first indication that a friendly cooperation had been established.

The Wessington Springs Independent

C. J. WEBB, PUBLISHER

Wessington Springs, South Dakota

January 19, 1937

Capital News & Feature Service
Ben Franklin Station
Box 771
Washington, D.C.

Gentlemen:-

    We are in receipt of a service from you
entitled "Inside News from the Nations Capital,"
by Dan Gilbert, which we do not recollect
ordering. We wish to know the source of this
service, if it is free, and why? We are running
a Washington Service and of course would have to
have some definite reason for changing, and if we
started to use yours we would want the assurance
that it would come regularly, until advance notice
was received to stop it.

                Respectfully,

CJW:GB

*Letter from a small-town newspaper showing the kind of confusion
caused by the "Capitol News and Feature Service."*

Winrod had been in constant communication with Pelley, and Pelley had conferred several times with Schwinn. The Nazis were eager to get a native American body into the organization so they would have an American "front."

Gilbert opened offices in Washington and, fearful lest their location become known, rented Post Office Box No. 771, Ben Franklin Station, for use as a mailing address. After the first issue had been sent out, Winrod and his agents canvassed prominent industrialists for donations to support the "news service" on the grounds that it was furthering religious activities and fighting Communism. The money collected was actually used to carry on anti-democratic propaganda. A number of industrialists contributed. I have a list of them, but since there is no conclusive evidence that they knew the money was being spent by Nazi agents, I shall not publish the names. I mention it merely as an illustration of how wealthy men are victimized by racketeers with pleas of "patriotism" and "public service." Harry A. Jung did the same thing by getting money from rich Jews "to fight Communism" and from rich gentiles "to fight the menace of the Jew."

With the first issue of the *Capitol News and Feature Service,* the following announcement was mailed to the editors of rural weeklies:

"Good Morning, Mr. Editor! *Capitol News and Feature Service* herewith delivers three priceless articles, fresh from the Nation's capitol. Use them without cost. You will hear from us each week. Watch for these interesting articles."

An examination of the "priceless articles" showed that they were designed primarily to attack American democracy.

Since his return from Germany and his conferences at the Nazi Embassy, Winrod has made frequent trips into Mexico where he has met with Mexican fascists—especially with leaders of the Mexican Gold Shirts which were organized by Hermann Schwinn. Again we discover the tie-up between fascist organizations in the United States and those to the south of us.

When the Nazis reorganized their propaganda machine several years ago and established smuggling headquarters on the West Coast, propaganda taken off Nazi ships docking in San Diego and Los Angeles included material printed in Spanish for the special use of General Nicholas Rodriguez, head of the Gold Shirts.

The Spanish as well as the English material was taken to the *Deutsches Haus* in Los Angeles and turned over to Schwinn, who forwarded the batches to Rodriguez. The contact man between Schwinn and the head of the fascist movement in Mexico is a native American named Henry Douglas Allen of San Diego. Allen, under the pretext of being a mining engineer and interested in prospecting in Mexico, went repeatedly into the neighboring country with the smuggled propaganda and delivered it to Rodriguez' agents.

Since native Americans, especially if they say they wish to prospect, can travel across the international boundary into Mexico as often as they please without arousing suspicion, Allen was chosen as the liaison man between Nazi agents in the United States and Rodriguez. As I said earlier, the Nazis tried from the beginning to get an American "front" and to draw as many Americans into it as possible—obviously strategic preparation for future work more serious than mere propaganda. Hence Allen was instructed to become active in the Silver Shirt movement. He organized Down Town Post

No. 47-10 and established Silver Shirt recruiting headquarters in Room 693 at 730 South Grand Ave., Los Angeles.

In August, 1936, when a lot of Nazi and anti-Roosevelt money was being shelled out in efforts to defeat Roosevelt, Allen became extremely active. While Pelley was out of town, he was instructed to work with Kenneth Alexander, Pelley's right-hand man. Alexander was formerly a still-photographer at United Artists Studios. The two opened offices in the Broadway Arcade Building and on October 1, 1935, moved to the Lankersheim Building at Third Street near Spring, Los Angeles.

Rodriguez, after he was given assurances of Nazi aid, worked not only with Nazi agents in this country but also with Julio Brunet, manager of the Ford factory in Mexico City.

The earliest documentary record I have of their tie-up is a letter Rodriguez wrote to Ford's manager on September 27, 1934, on Gold Shirt stationery. The letter merely asks Brunet to give jobs to two "worthy young men" and is written in a manner that shows Rodriguez and Brunet are rather close.

By February 7, 1935, Rodriguez and the Ford executive in Mexico had become sufficiently intimate for the fascist leader to express his appreciation of Brunet's placing Gold Shirts in the plant. His letter addressed to the manager of the Ford Company follows:

We have been informed by our delegate, Senora N. M. Colunga, that she was very well treated by you and that in addition you informed her that our request for work for some of our comrades who needed it has also been heard. Not doubting but that this will be fulfilled, A.R.M. [the Gold Shirts] sends you the most expressive thanks for having seen in you the recognition of one of the greatest obligations of humanity to Mexicanism.

On November 19, 1935, shortly before the Gold Shirts felt they were powerful enough to attempt the overthrow of the Mexican Government and the establishment of a fascist dictatorship, Rodriguez wrote to the manager of the Ford plant, asking for the two ambulances which had been promised the fascists by the Ford manager. Rodriguez had organized his attempted Putsch carefully, with a women's ambulance corps to care for the wounded in the expected fighting. The letter, again translated almost literally, follows:

Sr. Manager of the Ford Company   Nov. 19, 1935.
Mexico City
Highly Esteemed Señor:

This will be delivered to you personally by Sr. General Juan Alvarez C., who comes with the object of ascertaining if that company would be able to supply two ambulances which they had already offered, for the transportation of the Women's Sanitary Brigade on the 20th day of this month at 8 a.m.

Thanking you in advance for the references, I am happy to repeat that I am at your command. Affectionately and attentively, S. S.

NICHOLAS RODRIGUEZ C.
Supreme Commander.

In the street fighting that followed the attempted fascist Putsch a number were killed and wounded. It was after this fight that Rodriguez was exiled.

I am reproducing some of these letters from carbon copies, initialed by Rodriguez, which were in his files. Why he initials carbon copies I don't know, but I have a stack of his correspondence with Nazi agents and almost all of his carbons are initialed.

On October 4, 1936, Allen wrote to the exiled fascist leader. Ostensibly the letter invited him to address the Silver Shirts. Actually it was for a special conference about "matters of vital importance to us both." This letter was written when Schwinn was holding conferences with Pelley to merge forces in a fascist united front, and when Schneeberger was preparing to leave for Japan on a training ship ordered up from the Canal Zone by the Japanese to take him on board. The letter follows:

Dear General Rodriguez:

Upon receipt of this letter will you kindly communicate with me and advise me whether it would be possible for you to come to Los Angeles in the near future to make an address to our organization here. We shall be glad to defray all expenses which will include airplane both ways if you desire it. We shall also offer you bodyguard for your protection if you deem it necessary. Your fight is our fight and it is our desire to have you come to Los Angeles especially to confer with us relative to matters of vital importance to us both. I would suggest that if you can arrange to come, you telegraph me (charges collect) upon receipt of this letter so that I may make arrangements without delay.

Fraternally yours,
HENRY ALLEN.

When I went to Mexico to look into Nazi activities, I gave a copy of this letter to the Minister of the Interior. At that time Allen was again in Mexico under the pretense of looking into his mining interests, but a check showed that he had actually gone there to confer secretly with a Mexican army man, General Iturbe. At my request the Mexican Government looked into Allen's movements and learned that he had entered Guaymas, center of Japanese activities, with Kenneth Alexander, Pelley's chief aid.

noviembre 19 de 1935.

Sr. Gerente de la Cia. FORD.
C i u d a d.

Senor de mi respeto:

La presente le sera entregada personalmente por el Sr. General JUAN ALVAREZ C., quien va con el objeto de saber si esa Compania podra facilitar dos ambulancias que ya con anticipacion habian ofrecido, con objeto del transporte de la Brigada Sanitaria Femenil el dia 20 del actual a las 8 a.m.
Anticipandole las gracias por el favor de referencia, me es grato repetirme a sus ordenes como su afmo. atto., y S.S.

NICOLAS RODRIGUEZ C.
Jefe Supremo.

Letter from General Rodriguez to the Ford manager in Mexico City. The translation is given on page 112.

The connection between Ford's Mexican manager and General Rodriguez might be considered an unfortunate incident for which Ford could not be held responsible. This would be a reasonable assumption if the Nazi-Rodriguez-Ford tie-up in Mexico were an isolated case. The facts, however, show it is not.

Letter from Henry Allen to General Rodriguez, showing the tie-up between American and Mexican fascist organizations.

The national leader of the Nazi propaganda machine in this country has been on the Ford pay roll. Kuhn was supposed to work for Ford as a chemist, but while on Ford's pay roll he traveled around the United States conferring with other secret Nazi agents and actively directing Nazi work in this country.

Ford has a highly developed and exceedingly efficient espionage system of his own which, among other things, watches what his employees do—even to their home life. Kuhn's activities were known to Harry Bennett, head of the

LEFT: *American-made anti-Semitic sticker of a type appearing with increasing frequency in recent times.* RIGHT: *Title-page of the German edition of "The International Jew," by Henry Ford, of which 100,000 copies have been distributed.*

Ford secret service or "Personnel Department," as it is called, and Bennett reports to Ford. Furthermore, Kuhn's Nazi connections had been publicized in both the American and the Nazi press and were no secret. Jews and Christians alike protested to Ford about his employee's anti-democratic work while on the motor magnate's pay roll, but Kuhn was left undisturbed to travel around organizing Nazi groups. In 1938 Ford was given the highest medal of honor which Hitler can give to a foreigner. No statement was ever made as to just what Henry Ford had done for the Nazi Führer to merit the honor.

Simultaneously with Kuhn's intensified work, Ford's confidential secretary, William J. Cameron, became active again. Cameron was editor of Ford's *Dearborn Independent* when that newspaper published the "Protocols of the Elders of Zion" after they had been proved to be forgeries. When a nation-wide protest arose from Jews and Christians who were shocked at seeing one of the richest and most powerful men in the country use his wealth to disseminate race hatred, and when the protest grew into a boycott of his cars, Ford apologized and discontinued the newspaper. But instead of easing his editor out or giving him some other job, he made him his confidential secretary.

When Kuhn went to work for Ford, the national headquarters of the Nazi propaganda machine was moved to Detroit, and the anti-democratic activities increased in intensity. Employing Nazi anti-semitism as the bait to attract dissatisfied and bewildered elements in the population, a new organization made its appearance: The Anglo-Saxon Federation, headed by Ford's private secretary. Headquarters were established in the McCormick Building in Chicago, Room 834, at 332 S. Michigan Ave. and in the Fox Building in Detroit.

In July, 1936, Cameron, obviously because Ford was violently anti-Roosevelt, stepped out as head of the organization and became its Director of Publications. When Winrod was raising money from American industrialists to support the *Capitol News and Feature Service,* Cameron was among the contributors.

The Anglo-Saxon Federation began to distribute the "Protocols" again. I bought a copy in the Detroit offices of the organization, stamped with the name of the organization. The introduction quotes Ford as approving of them. It states:

Mr. Henry Ford, in an interview published in the *New York World,* February 17, 1921, put the case for Nilus[16] tersely and convincingly thus:

"The only statement I care to make about the 'Protocols' is that they fit in with what is going on. They are sixteen years old, and they have fitted the world situation up to this time. They fit it now."

When Ford was on the witness stand in a libel suit some fifteen years ago and admitted his ignorance of matters with which even grammar school children are familiar, the country laughed. His ignorance, however, is his own affair, but when he takes no step to curb his personal representative from working with secret foreign agents to undermine a friendly government, it becomes a matter, it appears to me, of importance to the people of this country and the Government of the United States.

16 The man who forged the "Protocols" originally and who subsequently confessed to having done so.

IX

NAZI AGENTS in AMERICAN UNIVERSITIES

THE UNIVERSITIES ARE TOO IMPORTANT A TRAINING GROUND for Nazi agents to ignore. A few professors in some of our universities have joined the growing list of anti-democratic propagandists. Some of them are German subjects and do not disguise their pro-Nazi bias; others carry on their propaganda as a "scholarly analysis" of the Hitler regime—with a fervor, however, that smacks of the paid propagandist.

German exchange students, too, studying at some of our universities, are active in various efforts to draw native Americans within the sphere of Nazi influence. Some of these students came here ostensibly to study for degrees, but devote most of their time to spreading Nazi ideology and meeting with secret Nazi agents and military spies. Such was Prince von Lippe of the University of Southern California.

Von Lippe is not an American citizen as so many of the agents are. With no visible means of support, he received expenses from a total stranger—oddly enough, Count von Bülow whose home overlooked the naval base in San Diego and who was constantly in conferences with Nazi agents. It was to Count von Bülow, you recall, that Hermann Schwinn brought Schneeberger as soon as he arrived on his way to Japan, and von Bülow took him around while Schneeberger photographed areas in the military and naval zone. A number of very secret conferences were held while Schneeberger was on the West Coast, in the home of Dr. K. Burchardi, a Los Angeles physician who visits Nazi ships with Schwinn and von Bülow (on one occasion Schneeberger summoned Burchardi to come with him to a Nazi ship which had just docked in Los Angeles—and the physician dropped his work and went).

German exchange students, when they enter this country, are under instructions to report to the German-American Bund. On July 4, 1936, three exchange students—a young lady and two young men—entered Los Angeles while on a motor tour of the country. They were students at Georgia Tech. In Los Angeles they went directly to the *Deutsches Haus* and presented a letter of introduction to Hermann Schwinn who assigned them quarters at the home of Max Edgan, one of Schwinn's lieutenants. The students then made a detailed report to Schwinn on the political work they were carrying out at Georgia Tech.

But the professors are the chief hope of Nazi agents attempting to spread the idea of totalitarian government and a bit of race hatred as the bait to attract some elements in the population. Some of the professors and some of their activities follow briefly:

Professor Frederick E. Auhagen, formerly of the German Department, Seth Low Junior College, Columbia University.

Dr. Auhagen came to this country in 1923 and worked as a mining engineer in Pennsylvania. From 1925 to 1927 he was with the Foreign Department of the Equitable Trust Co.; then became connected with Columbia University in 1927. He is not an American citizen and constantly refers to Germany as "my native country."

This professor is one of the leading academic apologists for Herr Hitler in the United States. Besides carrying on his pro-Nazi propaganda in the classroom, he does a great deal of lecturing, sometimes appearing before the Foreign Policy Association. On one occasion, in an address before the Men's Club of the Baptist Church at Rockville, Long Island, he stated that Seth Low Junior College was opened "in order to keep Hebrew faces off the campus at Columbia University."

Auhagen never tried to hide his sympathies with Nazism. Preceding a debate on February 1, 1936, before the City Club of Cleveland, he gave press interviews as a Nazi, and in the debate upheld Hitler as the savior of Germany and world civilization. With a fervor far removed from professorial calm, he explained that American newspaper dispatches about the treatment of Jews and Catholics in Germany were exaggerated.

"As to criticism of Germany's treatment of Catholics," he said again in Denver, Colorado on July 26, 1935, "that is not true!"

Professor Frederick K. Krueger, of Wittenberg college, with whom Auhagen is rather closely identified in arranging and giving talks about Nazis and totalitarian government, at every opportunity issues press interviews along the same line. In them he explains that the anti-Nazi sentiment in the United States press does not represent the editors, but is dictated by Jews who "control the press, the motion pictures and other organs of public opinion."

Because of the high scientific standing of Professor Vladimir Karapetoff of the Cornell engineering faculty, he is listened to with more attention and respect than are the more blatant propagandists for the adoption of fascist tactics and principles. Shortly after Hitler took power, the Professor started to do his share on the campus. At first he did it subtly, but when this made little headway he began to talk of the "growing domination of Jews in American life, politically as well as economically" and emphasized that the large number of Jews in the Law School and on the campus generally was becoming a problem.

"It's the smooth-faced Jew whom we must fear," he kept repeating, "and not the long-bearded Jewish rabbi."

Not content with expressing personal opinions, he took to organizing groups, addressing them on the subject of the Jew; and on one occasion he called a special meeting of the Officer's Club with the proviso that Jews be excluded.

Paul F. Douglas,[17] teacher of German, Economics and Political Science at Green Mountain College, wrote a book, *God Among the Germans,* which purports to be an introduction to the mind and method of Nazism.

I have information coming from a reputable source that Dr. Douglas was paid by the Nazi Government to write the book. This source is unwilling to let his name be used, but is ready to testify and lay his information before any governmental body which will investigate the devious methods of Nazi agents in this country.

There are at various universities throughout the country other professors and instructors quite active in spreading pro-Hitler propaganda. Some of them meet with Nazi agents closely allied to the espionage machine. I offer only these few as illustrations of Nazi efforts to get footholds in the American universities.

---

17 Not to be confused with Prof. Paul H. Douglas of the University of Chicago, a highly reputable scholar and a stanch defender of democracy.

Along with efforts to carry on their work in the universities, Nazi agents tried to get a foothold in the political life of the country by finding a few Republicans who were willing to use anti-democratic propaganda in their efforts to defeat Roosevelt during the Presidential campaign. At no time in American history did secret agents of a foreign power so brazenly attempt to interfere in the internal affairs of the American people. Nor at any time in American history did agents of a foreign government find such willing cooperation from unscrupulous American politicians.

Among those who worked with Hitler agents was Newton Jenkins, director of the Coughlin-Lemke Third Party.[18] The Detroit Priest and the Congressman were fully aware, preceding and during the campaign, that Jenkins supported Hitler and was a Jew-baiter of the first order. They were aware of this while they were appealing for Jewish votes. The Radio Priest and the Congressman kept in constant touch with their campaign manager and knew what sort of government Jenkins wanted.

Jenkins' association with Nazis dates to the days preceding the launching of the Presidential campaign. At that time he participated in a secret conference held in Chicago with the object of uniting the scattered fascist forces in the United States to form a powerful fascist united front. Among those who attended where Walter Kappe, Fritz Gissibl and Zahn—three active Hitler agents assigned to the Mid-West area; William Dudley Pelley, leader of the Silver Shirts; Harry A. Jung, the ultra-"patriot"; George W. Christians of Chattanooga, Tenn., head of the American fascists; and several others. The conference ended with an agreement to support a Third-Party movement directed by Jenkins.

Throughout the campaign Jenkins stressed an exaggerated nationalism, advocated "party patrols" similar to Hitler's storm troops and adopted the Nazi Jew-baiting tactics. His first public appearance with the Nazis was on October 30, 1935, at a meeting held in Lincoln Turner Hall, 1005 Diversey Building, Chicago. Uniformed storm troopers with the swastika on their arm bands patrolled the room. In the course of his talk he said:

The trouble with this country now is due to the money powers and Jewish politicians who control our Government. The Federal Treasury is being

18 Father Coughlin was finally reprimanded by the Vatican for his unpriestly attacks upon the President.

controlled by a Jew, Morgenthau, and a Jew, Eugene Meyer. The State, County and our own Municipal Government is being controlled by Jewish politicians. Our own Mayor signs what the Jews want him to sign. Nearly in every department of our country and local government you will find a Jew at the head of it. Not only under a Democratic administration but also under a Republican administration we will find the same conditions. . . . The American people must free itself from the money plunderers who have thrown this country into the World War and also a possibility of dragging them into the present war for private gain and shake off their shoulders the Jewish politicians. The Third Party promises to do both.

This is precisely the sort of stuff paid Nazi agents in the propaganda division are ordered to disseminate, and this is the man Father Coughlin and Congressman Lemke picked to direct their campaign.

It was a Nazi agent, Ernst Goerner of Milwaukee, who spread the story, aided by anti-Roosevelt forces, that Frances Perkins, Secretary of Labor, was a Jewess. The story received such wide publicity that she had to issue a public statement giving her birth and marriage records.

Goerner is one of the important Nazi agents in the Mid-West. He's a bit eccentric and the Nazis sometimes have difficulty keeping him in line, but when Schwinn made a trip East shortly before the election campaign, he stopped off specially to see Goerner who thereupon sent a flood of propaganda throughout the country about Secretary Perkins' ancestry as well as charges that Roosevelt and almost all Government officials were Jews.

It was after Schwinn's trip to the East that other disseminators of anti-democratic propaganda, like Robert Edward Edmondson and James True, came to life in a big way. One of the penniless men who suddenly blossomed into the money after Schwinn's trip East was Olov E. Tietzow, who used Post Office Box No. 491 in Chicago lest the fact that he lived at 715 Aldine Ave. be discovered.

Up until a few months before the campaign Tietzow was an unemployed electrical engineer who had difficulty paying the three-dollar weekly rent for his hall bed-room at the Aldine Ave. address. After Schwinn's visit and meeting with him, Tietzow began to commute by air between Chicago and Buffalo where he opened a branch office.

Tietzow was tested out a little at first. He was put to work in the offices of the Friends of the New Germany on Western Ave. and Roscoe St., Chicago. In his spare time he worked out of 1454 Foster Ave., Chicago. A quotation or two from some of his letters will give an indication of his activities. On February 21, 1936, he wrote to William Stern, Fargo, N. D., a member of the Republican National Committee. He said in part:

Information about the so-called fascist movement here in the U.S. A. will be furnished by me if you so desire, together with other data you might be interested in. An opportunity to discuss our national problems and to lay before patriotic persons of means and influence and before national organizations my plans for a nationwide movement would be welcome. . . .

This letter to a high Republican Party official was written after Tietzow had outlined the contents to Toni Mueller, Nazi agent in Chicago reporting directly to Fritz Kuhn.

Since most of the patrioteers were opposed to the New Deal and since some of them were already working with Nazi agents in this country, it was not long before they were going full blast in their "Save America" racket. The people of the United States, though they don't talk much about it, are thoroughly patriotic in the fullest sense of the word. To accuse anyone of not being a patriot is almost worse than telling a man that he is a son of not quite a lady. The racketeers in patriotism long ago discovered that people would contribute to a "patriotic cause" if only to escape the reputation of being unpatriotic; and the racketeers have made a nice living out of it. For some of the patrioteers it has become a thriving business, with everybody involved—except the suckers—getting his cut. Some of the big "patriotic" organizations are really influential, and the small ones are hopefully struggling along in the expectation of bigger and better and more patriotic days when the pickings will be more than attractive.

Every time I start looking into organizations with high-sounding and impressive names, I am profoundly impressed with the accuracy of Barnum's noted observation. Raise the cry of "patriotism" and perfectly good Americans forget to try to find out just what the "patriotic" activities are, and shell out without a murmur. Industrialists particularly like the "Americanism" of the patriotic groups because almost all of them incorporate an anti-labor policy. The propaganda, of

©1936 – O.E.T.

THE AMERICAN GUARD

8-15-1936

Mr. Warner M. Pearson, Architect,
8 North Michigan Ave.,
Chicago, Illinois.

Dear Mr. Pearson:

Received your request for literature. From time to time, pamphlets dealing with the Jewish-Communistic problems will be sent to you. Extra copies of especially interesting ones will be sent to you with request that you distribute them among your friends; there is no charge for any of those leaflets.

The American Guard is now being organized by me in the states of Illinois and Minnesota, and later on the activities will be extended to other states as well. The purpose is to help counteract the undermining influence of Jews and other communists, and to restore White rule here in America. Members of the organization do not, for the time being, pay any fees or dues; reliance is made entirely upon voluntary contributions. – The main activities now center upon distribution of educational propaganda; active participation in politics will start in a couple of months when, I hope, the organization of this party has been completed.

Trusting that you will actively support the organization, I am

Sincerely yours,

Olov E. Tietzow
P.O.Box 491, Chicago, Illinois

Letter by Olov E. Tietzow, showing typical methods of American fascists.

course, is rarely conducted as an open fight against labor, but is put across as a fight to save America from the Communists.

Some of the racketeering patriotic organizations with a more or less devout following include the National Republican Publishing Company, Washington, D. C., the American Vigilant Intelligence Federation, Chicago, Ill., the Paul

Reveres, Chicago, Ill., the Industrial Defense Association, Boston, Mass., the American Nationalists, Inc., New York, N.Y. and the American Nationalist Party, Los Angeles, Calif. There are a number of others, but these are some of the most blatant.

The National Republican Company, 511 11th Street, N.W., Washington, D.C., is one of the most influential. It publishes the *National Republic,* a journal accepted by men high in public office and by leading industrialists as earnestly trying to inculcate "Americanism" into Americans.

The *National Republic* has an amazing list of endorsers—governors, mayors, senators, congressmen and nationally-known industrialists. The magazine is virtually the entire organization and is dedicated "to defending American ideals and institutions." It is headed by Walter S. Steele, who was tied up with Harry A. Jung of the American Vigilant Intelligence Federation before he went into business for himself. While Steele was working with the ace of racketeers in patriotism, the president-editor of the *National Republic* also eked out a few pennies by distributing the "Protocols of the Elders of Zion." Today, however, he confines himself chiefly to fighting Communism, spreading race hatred only when it is paid for in advertisements. Books distributed by Nazi propagandists in furthering their anti-democratic campaign—such books as *T.N.T.* by Colonel Edwin Hadley and *The Conflict of the Ages* find space in the *National Republic's* pages. Colonel Hadley headed the Paul Reveres which tried to organize fascist groups on American university campuses, and *The Conflict of the Ages* devotes a full chapter to the Nazi "proofs" of the authenticity of the "Protocols."

I mention these to show the type of stuff Steele is willing to disseminate—if he is paid for it. And by permitting the use of their names, the sponsors, consciously or unconsciously, aid him in his anti-American activities.

The detailed aims of the *National Republic* are to provide a "weekly service to twenty-three hundred editors, to defend American institutions against subversive radicalism; a national information service on subversive organizations and activities; an Americanization bureau serving schools, colleges and patriotic groups; conducted for the public good from Washington, D.C., by nationally known leaders."

The procedure of conducting the organization "for the public good" includes high-pressuring the shekels from the suckers. Steele, a former newspaperman, learned from his association with that other arch-patriot, Jung. So when Steele established his own racket, he found one of his early aids in former Senator Robinson of Indiana. Robinson was closely tied up with the Ku Klux Klan. Through Robinson and through other politicians reached with the cry "Save America," he got a long list of prominent sponsors and gradually increased it until now it reads like a *Who's Who* of reactionary industrialists and innocent politicians. With letters of introduction from Senator Robinson, Steele's high pressure gang set out to collect in the name of patriotism.

The procedure was simple. Salesmen presented their letters of introduction to the mayor of a city. The mayor was impressed with the high "patriotic" motives and especially with the imposing list of names sponsoring the efforts. The mayor introduced the high-pressure fellows to other people—and the milking began.

Let me illustrate a little more specifically:

On March 4, 1936, Steele sent two of his ablest dollar-pullers, Messrs. Fahr and Hamilton, into the Oklahoma oil fields where the industrialists would like to see a minimum of 200 per cent Americanism instilled in the public mind. Messrs. Fahr and Hamilton had letters of introduction to Mayor T. A. Penny of Tulsa, Okla. When the salesmen approached the Mayor, they had not only the long and imposing list of names on the letterhead but additional letters of introduction from ex-Governor Curley of Mass., ex-Senator Robinson of Indiana and Congressman Martin Dies of Texas. The drummers wanted the Mayor to introduce them to the Chairman of the Tulsa Board of Education who could help them get funds in Tulsa and elsewhere. The funds were to be used to place the "patriotic" magazine in the public school system in order "to preserve this country against subversive activities, particularly Communism."

It was a neat circulation-getting stunt, performed without Fahr and Hamilton telling what percentage of the take they got.

The Mayor gave the letters of introduction. With these letters and the excellent contacts thus established, they started down the sucker list from W. G. Skelly, head of the Skelly Oil Co., Tulsa to Waite Phillips of the Phillips Petroleum Co.

Like his former colleague Harry A. Jung, Steele works on the big industrialists by whispering confidentially that he has sources of information about which he can't talk much but which make it possible for him to keep the industrialists informed about "subversive radicals." For a reasonable price and perhaps a contribution to a worthy cause, Steele would supply the industrialist with "confidential information for members only" which would keep him up to date about the radicals threatening America. The "confidential information" must not be shown to anybody else. Extreme caution is necessary lest the radicals find out about the "information service." With all this hocum, secrecy and whispering, the industrialist becomes a member at so much per not realizing that the information thus peddled can be got for three cents a day—five cents on Sundays—by buying the *Daily Worker*. It's just one of the little patriotic rackets the boys have cooked up.

Working closely with Steele is James A. True of the James True Associates, another precious racketeer who stepped from patrioteering into efforts to organize in conjunction with Nazi agents a secret armed force in the United States. With True in this effort to establish a Cagoulard organization in this country, were some of the most active Nazi agents and patrioteers.

X

UNDERGROUND ARMIES in AMERICA

EARLY IN 1938 NATIVE AMERICANS, working with Nazi agents, completed plans to organize a secret army along the general lines of the Cagoulards in France. The decision was made after the liaison man between Nazi agents here and plotters for the secret army met with Fritz Kuhn and Signor Giuseppe Cosmelli, Counselor to the Italian Embassy in Washington.

The liaison man is Henry D. Allen, who moved from San Diego to 2860 Nina St., Pasadena, Calif. Allen, the reader may recollect, helped Schwinn organize the Mexican Gold Shirts which unsuccessfully attempted to seize the Mexican Government. Allen is still active in a plot to overthrow the Cárdenas Government, working at the moment with Gen. Ramon F. Iturbe, a member of the Mexican Chamber of Deputies, with Gen. Yocupicio who is smuggling arms as part of a plan to rebel, and with Pablo L. Delgado who took over the fascist Gold Shirt work under a different name after Rodriguez was exiled when his attempt to march on the Government failed.

To understand the feverish activities of foreign agents and native Americans working with foreign agents, one must remember that when the World War broke out in 1914, Germany was caught with only small espionage and sabotage organizations in the United States. It cost the German War Office large sums of money to build them under difficult and dangerous conditions. The Nazis do not intend to be caught the same way in the event a war finds the United States on the enemy side or, if neutral, supplying arms and materials to the enemy.

The first step to prevent such a development is to build an enormous propaganda machine and to draw into it as many native Americans as possible. Because of the future potentialities of natives as spies and *saboteurs,* the Nazi leaders take extraordinary precautions to safeguard their identities.

Should the United States become involved in a war with fascist powers, especially Germany, the German members of the Bund can be watched and, if necessary, interned; but native Americans not known as Bund members can move about freely, hence the care to prevent their identities from becoming known. Schwinn, for instance, keeps a regular list of the German-American Bund members at the *Deutsches Haus* in Los Angeles. The native American members, however, are not listed. The names are kept in code and only Schwinn knows the code numbers.

Military considerations thus lead the Nazi General Staff to maintain this propaganda in the United States, despite the knowledge Nazi leaders in Germany have that its activities and distasteful propaganda here are seriously hampering German-American commercial relations.

The propaganda machine is already functioning as the German-American *Volksbund*. The second step, as was demonstrated in France with the Cagoulards and in Spain with Franco's Fifth Column, is to organize secret armies capable of starting sporadic outbreaks tantamount to civil war—a procedure which would naturally deflect the country's energies in war time.

This second step was taken after careful study, and Henry D. Allen was chosen as the liaison man between those maneuvering the plot.

The private letters exchanged between Allen and his fellow conspirators are now in my possession. Some of the letters exchanged were signed with the writers' real names and some with code names. Allen's code name, for instance, is "Rosenthal."

On April 13, 1938, he wrote to a "G.D." (of whom more shortly) as follows:

> Have just sent Delgado into Sonora incognito. This move has resulted from a four-party conference held in Yuma a few days ago. This party was composed of Urbalejo, chief of the Yaqui nation, Joe Mattus, his trusted lieutenant, Delgado and myself. Yocupicio has completely come over to our side, which you can perceive from the outcome of the little tryout in Aqua Prieta a few weeks ago. Delgado has arrived safely at Bocatete, and will get the boys in that part of the country pretty active. . . . Inasmuch as I am his legal and properly accredited representative in the United States, you may rest assured that there will be no doubt as to the objectives of this movement south of the Rio Grande.

I have received three letters from General Iturbe in which he tells me that they are taking the Spanish copies of the Protocols which K. sent me, and making 5,000 copies of same. In each letter he begs me to set a time and date for meeting him at Guadalajara for the purpose of effecting the necessary plans for active campaigning with Delgado. I will arrange all of this as soon as you consider it expedient. . . .

Rosenthal.

Two days later (April 15, 1938) he wrote from Fresno, Calif. under his own name to F. W. Clark, 919½ S. Yakima Ave., Tacoma, Wash. The letter reads in part:

Relative to the Gold Shirts of Mexico, please be advised that we found it necessary to reorganize this group in August, 1937. The activist elements have proceeded and are now carrying on under the name of the Mexican Nationalist Movement of which Pablo L. Delgado is the nominal head. I am the legal and personal representative of Delgado in the movement in the United States.

So much for his current activities to establish fascism to the south of us.

Most Americans who fall for Nazi propaganda do not suspect that they are being played for suckers by shrewd manipulators pulling the strings in Berlin, and probably not one of the many reputable and sincerely patriotic Americans who fell for Allen's "patriotic" appeals suspects his activities against the country he so zealously wants to "save."

Some shrewd observer once remarked that "patriotism is the last refuge of a scoundrel." Whenever I come across an "ultra-patriot" with foam dripping from his mouth while he beats his chest with loud cries about his own honesty and the crookedness of those running the country, I suspect a phony. As a rule, I look for the criminal record of a man who's yelling "Chase out the crooks" and "Let's have honest government," and all too often I find one. Henry D. Allen, *alias* H. O. Moffet, *alias* Howard Leighton Allen, *alias* Rosenthal, etc., ex-inmate of San Quentin and Folsom prisons, is no exception; his criminal record extends over a period of twenty-nine years.

Let me give the record before I start quoting from his letters, chiefly for the benefit of those sincere and loyal Americans who thought his Swastika-inspired activities represented honest convictions.

May 17, 1910: Arrested in Los Angeles charged with uttering fictitious checks. In simple language this means just a little bit of forgery. Los Angeles Police Department file, No. 7613.

June 10, 1910: Sentenced to three years imprisonment; sentence suspended upon tearful assurances of good behavior.

May 12, 1912: Picked up in Philadelphia charged with being a fugitive; brought back to Los Angeles.

July 1, 1912: Committed to San Quentin. Guest No. 25835.

April 21, 1915: Committed to Folsom from Santa Barbara on a forgery charge. Guest No. 9542.

Feb. 1, 1919: Arrested in Los Angeles County charged with suspicion of a felony. Los Angeles County No. 14554.

June 31, 1924: Arrested in San Francisco, charged with uttering fictitious checks. No. 35570.

Oct. 5, 1925: Los Angeles Police Department issued notice that Allen was wanted for uttering fictitious checks. Bulletin No. 233.

Allen is apparently a prolific writer—of bad checks and of long reports about his activities to his superiors.

Two of Allen's close friends are also native Americans: C. F. Ingalls of 2702 Bush St., San Francisco and George Deatherage (the G. D. mentioned earlier). Deatherage now lives and operates out of St. Albans, W. Va. He organized the American Nationalist Confederation which used to have its headquarters in Palo Alto, Calif. Both these gentlemen also work with Schwinn.

On January 7, 1938, Deatherage received from San Francisco a letter signed "C.F.I."—in a plain envelope without a return address. The letter is very long and detailed. I quote in part:

> We must get busy organizing grid-lattice-work or skeleton for a military staff throughout the nation, and in this we need representatives of fascist groups, and we need Americans with whom these others may be incorporated. . . . All must believe in being ruthless in an emergency. . . .
>
> The political and the military organizations must not be unified. They have different aims. With one hand we offer the public a potential

program. Whether they accept it or not and whether they wish to return to the ideals embodied in a representative form of a constitutional federal republic or not, is of secondary importance. Of first importance is the need of the emergency military organization to function simultaneously should our enemies revolt if we should win politically or should we revolt if our enemies win politically.

On January 19, 1938, Deatherage received a letter signed with the code name "Laura and Clayton." "Laura" is Hermann Schwinn. This letter, too, is long and goes into details on how best to organize the secret military group and have it ready for instant action. The letter states at one point:

> After we do all this, now then we shall have the national military frame-work all steamed up and oiled and coupled to the multiplicity of working parts ready to appear on all fronts. . . .

After "C.F.I." and "Laura and Clayton" had decided on the details of the secret military body in which they needed the aid of "Nazi and fascist" forces, they needed money and arms.

Early in January, Allen received from "Mrs. Fry and C. Chapman" four hundred and fifty dollars for a trip to Washington, D. C. "Mrs. Fry and C. Chapman" live in Santa Monica, but use Glendale, Calif. for a post office address. This money was spent between January 13 and February 10, 1938, according to the expense account Allen turned in to the Fry-Chapman combination.

Three days after Allen got the money (January 16, 1938), he received from Schwinn a letter of introduction to Fritz Kuhn, addressed to the *Amerikadeutscher Volksbund*, 178 E. 85th Street, New York City. The letter was written in German. Following is the translation:

My Bund Leader:

> The bearer of this letter is my old friend and comrade-in-arms, Henry Allen, who is coming East on an important matter.

> Mr. Allen knows the situation in Los Angeles and California very well and can give you important information. We can give Allen absolute confidence.

Hail and Victory,

HERMANN SCHWINN.

The "important matter" on which Allen was going East and which he wanted to discuss with the national Nazi leader in this country, was to contact the Italian Embassy, the Hungarian Legation, James True of the James True Associates (distributors of "Industrial Control Reports" from its headquarters in Washington, D.C.), George Deatherage in St. Albans, W. Va., and several others.

Allen reported regularly to Chapman, signing his letters with the code name "Rosenthal." I quote in part from one letter written from Washington on January 24, 1938:

> Upon calling at the Rumanian Embassy I found the Ambassador with all his attachés are of the Carol-Tartarescu regime, and they are sailing on Wednesday, January 26. The new Ambassador will arrive with his staff on Saturday, I am told. The letter which you gave me I mailed to Budapest myself, not daring to entrust it to the present staff at the Embassy. At the Italian Embassy I found the Ambassador away, but I had a very delightful and satisfactory conference with Signor G. Cosmelli, who is the Italian counselor. . . .

Shortly after the conference at the Italian Embassy, True and Allen conferred. Subsequently, True wrote to Allen and added a postscript in long hand: "But be very careful about controlling the information and destroy this letter."

Allen did not destroy it immediately. The letter, dated February 23, 1938, reads in part:

> The bunch of money promised off and on for three years may come through within the next week or two. We have had so many disappointments that I hardly dare hope but there seems a fair chance of results. If it comes through we will have you back here in a hurry. You, George, and I will get together and prepare for real action.
>
> If your friends want some pea shooters, I have connections now for any quantity and at the right price. They are United States standard surplus. Let me know as soon as you can.

To these events must be added the peculiar and unexplained actions of the Dies Congressional Committee appointed to "investigate subversive activities." The Committee employed a Nazi propagandist as one of its chief investigators and refused to question three suspected Nazi spies working in the Brooklyn Navy Yard. Congressman Martin Dies of Texas, chairman of the Committee, gave two of the *National Republic's* high-pressure men letters of introduction when they started out on a little milking party in the name of patriotism. He received the cooperation of Harry A. Jung, and he refused to examine the files of James A. True when the above letter was brought to his Committee's attention.

But these actions merit more detailed consideration.

XI

THE DIES COMMITTEE SUPPRESSES EVIDENCE

THREE SUSPECTED NAZI SPIES WERE quietly taken out of the Brooklyn Navy Yard to the Dies Congressional Committee headquarters in New York in Room 1604, United States Court House Building. The three men were each questioned for about five minutes by Congressman J. Parnell Thomas[19] of New Jersey and Joe Starnes of Alabama. The men were asked if they had heard of any un-American goings-on in the Navy Yard. Each of the three subpoenaed men said he had not, and the Congressmen sent them back to work in the Navy Yard after warning them not to say a word to anyone about having been called before the Committee.

When I learned of the Congressional Committee's refusal to question men they had subpoenaed, I wondered at the unusual procedure—especially since it promptly put Nazi propagandists (such as Edwin P. Banta, a speaker for the German-American Bund) on the stand as authorities on "un-American" activities in the United States. A little inquiry turned up some interesting facts.

One of the Committee's chief investigators, Edward Francis Sullivan of Boston, had worked closely with Nazi agents as far back as 1934. Sullivan's whole record was extremely unsavory. He had been a labor spy, had been active in promoting anti-democratic sentiments in cooperation with secret agents of the German Government and in addition was a convicted thief. (Shortly after Slap-Happy Eddie, as he was known around Boston because of his convictions on drunkenness, lined up with the Nazis, he got six months for a little stealing.) Before going on with the Congressional Committee's strange

19 Formerly known as J. Parnell Feeney. He changed his name because he thought he could get along better in the business world with a name like Thomas than with a name as potently Irish as Feeney.

attitude toward suspected spies and known propagandists in constant communication with Germany, it might be well to review a meeting which the Congressional Committee's investigator addressed in the Nazi stronghold in Yorkville.

On the night of Tuesday, June 5, 1934, at eight o'clock, some 2,500 Nazis and their friends attended a mass meeting of the Friends of the New Germany at Turnhall, Lexington Ave. and 85th Street, New York City. Sixty Nazi Storm Troopers—attired in uniforms with black breeches and Sam Brown belts, smuggled off Nazi ships—were the guard of honor. Storm Troop officers had white and red arm bands with the swastika superimposed on them. Every twenty minutes the Troopers, clicking their heels in the best Nazi fashion, changed guard in front of the speakers' stand. The Hitler Youth organization was present. Men and women Nazis sold the official Nazi publication, *Jung Sturm,* and everybody awaited the coming of one of the chief speakers of the evening who was to bring them a message from the Boston Nazis.

W. L. McLaughlin, then editor of the *Deutsche Zeitung,* spoke in English. He was followed by H. Hempel, an officer of the Nazi steamship "Stuttgart," who vigorously exhorted his audience to fight for Hitlerism and was rewarded by shouts of "Heil Hitler!" McLaughlin then introduced Edward Francis Sullivan of Boston as a "fighting Irishman." The gentleman whom the Congressional Committee chose as one of its investigators into subversive activities, gave the crowd the Hitler salute and launched into an attack upon the "dirty, lousy, stinking Jews." In the course of his talk he announced proudly that he had organized the group of Nazis in Boston who had attacked and beaten liberals and Communists at a meeting protesting the docking of the Nazi cruiser "Karlsruhe," in an American port.

The audience cheered. Sullivan, again giving the Nazi salute, shouted: "Throw the goddam lousy Jews—all of them—into the Atlantic Ocean. We'll get rid of the stinking kikes! Heil Hitler!"

The three suspected Nazi spies were subpoenaed on August 23, 1938. They were:

Walter Dieckhoff, Badge No. 38117, living at 2654 E. 19th Street, Sheepshead Bay.

Hugo Woulters, Badge No. 38166, living at 221 East 16th Street, Brooklyn.

Alfred Boldt, Badge No. 38069, living at 64-29 70th Street, Middle Village, L. I.

Boldt had worked in the Navy Yard since 1931. Dieckhoff and Woulters went to work there within one day of each other in June, 1936.

The three men were kept in the Committee's room from one o'clock on the day they were subpoenaed until five in the afternoon. When it became apparent that the Congressmen would not show up until the next day, the men were dismissed and told to come back the following morning.

Not a word was said to them as to why they had been subpoenaed. Nevertheless Dieckhoff, who was with the German Air Corps during the World War, instead of going to his home in Sheepshead Bay, drove to the home of Albert Nordenholz at 1572 Castleton Ave., Port Richmond, S. I., where he kept two trunks. Nordenholz, a German-American naturalized citizen for many years, is highly respected by the people in his neighborhood. When Dieckhoff first came to the United States, the Nordenholzes accepted him with open arms. He was the son of an old friend back in Bremerhafen, Germany. Dieckhoff asked permission to keep two trunks in the Nordenholz garret; he stored them there when he went to work in the Brooklyn Navy Yard.

During the two years he worked in the Yard, he would drop around every two weeks or so and go up to the garret to his trunks. Just what he did on those visits, Nordenholz does not know.

On the night Dieckhoff was subpoenaed he suddenly appeared to claim the trunks. He told Nordenholz that he planned to return to Germany. Just what the trunks contained and what he did with them I do not know. They have vanished.

I called upon Dieckhoff in the two-story house in Sheepshead Bay where he lived. He had no intimate friends, didn't smoke, drink or run around. The life of the German war veteran seemed to be confined to working in the Navy Yard, returning home unobtrusively to work on ships' models and making his occasional visits to Nordenholz's garret.

So far as I could learn, Dieckhoff became a marine engineer, working for the North German Lloyd after the World War. In 1923 he entered the United

The Commonwealth of Massachusetts

MIDDLESEX, ss.
AT THE FIRST DISTRICT COURT OF EASTERN MIDDLESEX, holden at Malden, in the County of Middlesex, for the transaction of criminal business, on the fourth day of February in the year of our Lord one thousand nine hundred and ~~twenty~~ thirty-two

Edward Francis Sullivan , defendant, is brought before said Court, in due ~~~~ THE COMMONWEALTH OF MASSACHUSETTS, on a complaint, duly made under oath, a true copy of which is herewith transmitted.

Which complaint is read to the said defendant, and he is asked by the Court whether he is guilty or not guilty of the offence charged against him in said complaint, and said defendant pleads and says that he is ~~not~~ guilty, ~~and the further consideration of said complaint is there from time to time continued to the~~ ~~day of~~ ~~then next ensuing,~~ and after hearing the witnesses in the case duly sworn, and fully hearing and understanding the defence of said defendant, it appears to said Court that said defendant is guilty of the offence aforesaid.

IT IS THEREFORE CONSIDERED AND ORDERED BY THE COURT, that the said defendant, for the offence aforesaid,

~~pay a fine of~~ ~~dollars, or the sum prescribed by law, and that he stand committed until said sentence be complied with~~

Billerica
be committed to the House of Correction, in ~~Cambridge,~~

there to be kept and governed according to law and the rules and regulations thereof, for the term of six ~~days,~~ months, from said last mentioned day. ~~And the said defendant is~~ thereupon notified by said Court of his right to appeal from said conviction and sentence.

ATTEST:— *Wilfred B. Tyler*
Clerk.

From which sentence the said defendant appeals to the SUPERIOR COURT, next to be holden at Cambridge, within and for the County of Middlesex, for the transaction of criminal business, on the first Monday of March next, and he is ordered to ~~be held on his own recognizance,~~ recognize to the Commonwealth,—in the sum of Two thousand ~~hundred~~ dollars,—with sufficient surety,—to prosecute said appeal there as the law directs—and stand committed to abide the sentence of said Court thereon, until he so recognizes.

With which said order the said defendant refuses to comply and is committed.

ATTEST: *Wilfred B. Tyler* Clerk.

A true copy, Attest:
(L. S.)
Wilfred B. Tyler, Clerk.

6-28-31-1000

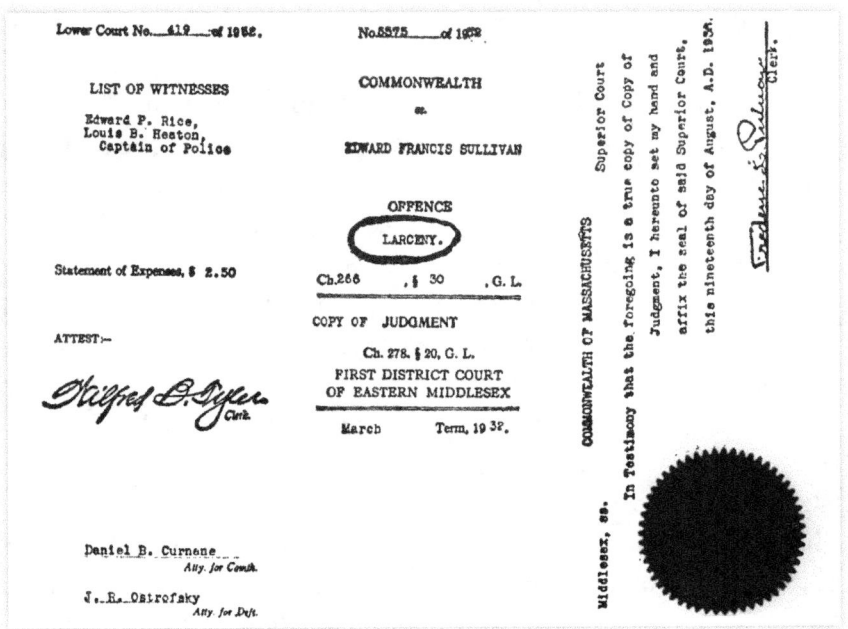

*Reproduction of a document showing that Edward Francis
Sullivan, at one time chief investigator for the Dies Committee,
was convicted of larceny and sentenced to prison.*

States illegally and remained for two years. Eventually he returned to Germany, but came back to the United States, this time legally, applied for citizenship papers and became a naturalized citizen five years later.

Before he went to work on American war vessels, he worked in various parts of the country—in automobile shops, in the General Electric Co. in Schenectady and as an engineer on Sheepshead Bay boats. Even after Hitler came into power, he worked on Sheepshead Bay boats. After the Berlin-Tokyo axis was formed (1935), Germany became particularly interested in American naval affairs, for the axis, among other things, exchanged military secrets. Shortly before the agreement was made, Dieckhoff suddenly went to work for the Staten Island Shipbuilding Co., Staten Island, which was building four United States destroyers, numbers 364, 365, 384 and 385. He worked on these destroyers during the day. Until late at night he pursued his hobby of building ships' models, which he never made an attempt to sell.

Dieckhoff weighed his words carefully during our talk.

"Why did you apply for a transfer from Staten Island to the Brooklyn Navy Yard?" I asked.

"I don't know," he said. "I guess there was more money in it."

"How much were you getting when you were working on the destroyers?"

"It was some time ago," he said slowly. "I do not remember very good."

"How much are you getting now at the Navy Yard?"

"Forty dollars and twenty-nine cents a week."

"You went to Germany last year for a couple of months and before that you went to Germany for six months. Were you able to save enough for these trips on your wages?"

"I do not spend very much," he said. "I live here all alone."

"How much do you save a week?"

"Oh, I don't know. Ten dollars a week."

"That would make five hundred dollars a year—if you worked steadily, which you didn't. You traveled third class. A round trip would be about two hundred dollars. That would leave you three hundred to spend provided you did not buy clothes, etc., for these trips. How did you manage to live in Germany for six months on three hundred dollars? Did you work there?"

He hesitated and said, "No, I did not work there. I traveled around. I was not in one place."

"How did you do it on three hundred dollars for six months?'

"My brother gave me money."

"What's your brother's business?"

"Oh, just general business in Bremerhafen. He's got a big business there."

"Perhaps I can get a report from the American Consul—"

"Oh," he interrupted. "His business isn't that big."

"Have you a bank account?"

He hesitated again and then said, "No, I do not make enough money for a bank account."

"Where do you keep your money for trips to Germany? In cash?"

"Yes, in cash."

"Where? Here? In this room?"

"No. Not in this room. I have it locked up."

"Where?"

"Oh, different places," he said vaguely.

"Where are those places?"

"I have my money with a friend."

"Who?"

"Nordenholz, Albert Nordenholz."

"You work in Brooklyn, live in Sheepshead Bay and save ten dollars a week in Port Richmond with a friend? Isn't that a long distance to go to save money?"

He shrugged his shoulders without answering.

"What's Nordenholz's business?"

"I think he's retired. I think he used to be a butcher."

"You don't know very much about a man's business and you travel all this distance to give him money to save for you when there are banks all around? Why do you do that?"

"Oh, I don't know. It seems to me that it is better that way."

Later when I asked Nordenholz, he denied that Dieckhoff had ever given him any money to hold.

Dieckhoff had worked on turbines, gear reductions and other complicated mechanical parts on the cruiser "Brooklyn." The moment I asked him if he handled blueprints he answered in the affirmative, but quickly added that the blueprints were returned every night and locked up by the officers. A capable machinist could, he admitted, after careful study remember the blueprints well enough to make a duplicate copy.

"When you went to Germany after working on the destroyers did anyone ever question you about them over there?"

"No," he said quickly. "Nobody."

"My information is that you did talk about structural matters."

He looked startled. "Well," he said, "my brother knew I worked in the Brooklyn Navy Yard. We talked about it, naturally."

"My information is that you talked about it with other people, too."

He stared out of the window with a worried air. Finally he said, "Well, my brother has a friend and I talked with him about it."

"A minute ago you said you had not talked about it with anyone."

"I had forgotten."

"This is the brother who gave you money to travel around in Germany?"

He didn't answer.

"I didn't hear you," I said.

"Yes," Dieckhoff said finally, "he gave me the money."

I called upon the second of the three suspected spies subpoenaed by the Dies Committee. Alfred Boldt had done very responsible work on the U. S. cruiser "Honolulu." Though he had not been in Germany for ten years, he suddenly got enough money last year to go there and to send his son to school at a Nazi academy. Boldt, too, has no bank account. He needed a minimum of seven hundred dollars for his wife and himself to cross third class, but the Dies Committee was not interested in where the money for the trip had come from.

Boldt left for Germany on August 4, 1936, and returned September 12. On the evening I dropped in to see him, he was tensely nervous. He had heard that someone had been around to talk with Dieckhoff.

"I understand your only son, Helmuth, is going to school in Langin, Germany?" I asked.

"Yes," he said, "I sent him there two years ago."

"No schools in the United States for a fifteen-year-old boy?"

"I wanted him to learn German."

"What do you pay for his schooling over there?"

He hesitated. His wife, who was sitting with us and occasionally advising him in German, suddenly interrupted in German, "Don't tell him. That's German business."

I assume they did not know that I understood, for Boldt passed off her comment as if he had not heard it and said casually, "Oh, twenty-five dollars a month."

"You earn forty dollars a week at the Navy Yard, pay for your son's schooling in Germany, clothes, etc., and you and your wife took more than a month's trip to Germany last year. How do you do it on forty a week?"

His wife giggled a little in the adjoining room. Boldt shrugged his shoulder without answering.

"The cheapest the two of you could do it, third class, would be about seven hundred dollars. Where do you have your bank account?"

"No. No bank account," his wife interrupted sharply.

"All the money is kept here, right here in this house," he laughed.

"You saved all that money in cash?"

"Yes; in cash, right here."

"No banks?"

"We like it better like that—in cash."

Boldt, like Dieckhoff, had been a marine engineer on the North German Lloyd. He went to work in the Brooklyn Navy Yard in 1931. When the cruiser "Honolulu" made its trial run in the spring of 1938, Boldt was on board.

Like Dieckhoff and Boldt, Harry Woulters, *alias* Hugo Woulters, the third of the three subpoenaed men, is a naturalized citizen of German extraction. He went to work in the Navy Yard within one day of Dieckhoff. Before that, both had worked on the same four American destroyers at the Staten Island Shipbuilding Company.

The house where Woulters lives has a great many Jews in it, judging from the names on the letterboxes, and since Hugo sounded too German, he listed his first name as "Harry."

"You and Dieckhoff worked on the same destroyers on Staten Island and you say you never met him there?" I asked.

"No, I never met him until the second day after I went to work in the Navy Yard."

"How many people work on a destroyer—a thousand?"

"Oh, no. Not that many."

"About one hundred?"

"About that," he said uncertainly.

"And you worked with Dieckhoff for six months on the same warships and never met him?"

"Yes," he insisted.

"How come that if you never met him both of you applied for jobs at the Brooklyn Navy Yard at about the same time?"

He shrugged his shoulders. "I don't know. It's funny. Sounds funny, anyway."

"When you worked on the cruiser 'Honolulu' you handled blueprints?"

"Yes, of course, but they were never left in my possession overnight," he added quickly. I couldn't help but think that Dieckhoff, too, had been very quick in protesting that the blueprints had never been left in his possession overnight. They seemed worried about that even though I had not said anything about it.

"Were they *ever* left in your possession overnight?"

"No. They guarded the blueprints—"

"My information is that they were left in your possession."

"Wells, sometimes—blueprints—you know, when you work from blueprints sometimes, yes, sometimes blueprints were left in my possession overnight. I was working on reduction gears on the cruiser 'Brooklyn' and I kept the blueprints overnight."

"How often?"

"I can't remember how often. Sometimes the blueprints were kept overnight in my tool box."

"You also worked on turbines and other complicated and confidential structural problems on the warship?"

"Yes."

"And you kept those blueprints overnight, too?"

"Sometimes—not often. Sometimes I left them in my tool box overnight."

Woulters, during the latter period of construction on the "Brooklyn" and the "Honolulu" had got two jobs which most workers do not like. He had the four to midnight and the midnight to eight A.M. watches. Normally Woulters likes to stay at home with his wife.

"While you had these watch duties you had pretty much the run of the ship?"

He hesitated and weighed his words carefully before answering. Finally he nodded and added hastily, "But no one can get on board."

"I didn't ask that. Did you have the run of the ship while everybody else was asleep when you were on watch?"

"Yes," he said in a low voice.

"How did you happen to work in the Brooklyn Navy Yard?"

"Oh, I don't know. I like to work for the Government."

"Have you a bank account?"

"Yes."

"What bank?"

"Oh, I don't know, it's some place on Church Avenue."

"You have about 2,400 dollars in the bank, a nice apartment, and you and your wife went on a trip to Germany last year. Did you save all that money in so short a time on wages of forty dollars a week?"

He shrugged his shoulders.

"Your bank account does not show withdrawals sufficient to cover the trip to Germany—"

"Say," he interrupted excitedly as soon as he saw where the question was leading, "when I was called before the Dies Committee, the Congressman there shook hands with me and asked me if I knew anything about un-American activities in the Navy Yard. I told him I didn't and he told me to go back to work and not to say anything about having been called before them. Now I do not understand why you ask me all these questions. The Congressman told me not to talk and I am saying nothing more. Nothing."

The Dies Congressional Committee was not interested in these three men whom they had subpoenaed and then, oddly enough, refused to question. Besides this very strange procedure by a Committee empowered by the Congress to investigate subversive activities, the Dies Committee withheld for months documentary evidence of Nazi activities in this country directed from Germany. The Committee obtained letters to Guenther Orgell and Peter Gissibl, but quietly placed them in their files without telling anyone about the existence of these documents. They did not subpoena or question the men involved.

The letters the Committee treated so cavalierly are from E. A. Vennekohl in charge of the foreign division of the *Volksbund für das Deutschtum im Ausland* with headquarters in Berlin, letters from the foreign division headquarters in Stuttgart, and from Orgell to Gissibl.

Gissibl was in constant touch with Nazi propaganda headquarters in Germany, receiving instructions and reporting not only on general activities, but especially upon the opening by the Nazis here of schools for children in which Nazi propaganda would be disseminated.

The letters, freely translated, follow. The first is dated October 29, 1937, and was sent by Orgell from his home at Great Kills, S.I.:

Dear Mr. Gissibl:

Many thanks for your prompt reply. My complaint that one cannot get an answer from Chicago refers to the time prior to May, 1937.

I assume from your writing that it is not opportune any more to deliver further books to the *Arbeitsgemeinschaft,* etc.

The material which Mr. Balderman received came from the V.D.A.[20] It has been sent to our Central Book distributing place (Mirbt). If he wishes he can get more any time; that is, if you recommend it.

The thirty books for your Theodore Koerner School, which arrived this summer (via the German Consulate General in Chicago), also came from the V.D.A. If you need more first readers or study books, please write

20 Nazi propaganda center for foreign countries with headquarters in Germany.

directly to me. Your request then goes immediately—without the official way via the Consulate and Foreign Office—to our Central Book distributing place. Please say how many you need and what else beside the first readers and primers[21] you need. I will take care that it will be promptly attended to. Fritz Kuhn, of course, has to be informed of your request and has to give his okay. . . .

    With German greetings,

CARL G. ORGELL.

Five days earlier Orgell had written to Gissibl: "You may perhaps remember that I am in charge of the work for the *Volkbund für das Deutschtum im Ausland*[22] for the U.S.A."

On March 18, 1938, Gissibl, who had been taking instructions from Orgell, received the following letter from Stuttgart:

Dear Peter:

    From your office manager, Comrade Möller, I received a letter dated February 15. He informed me among other things that an exchange of youth is out of the question for this year. I regret this very much. I would like to see, in the interests of our common efforts, if we would have had youth all ready this year, especially also from your district. Perhaps it is still possible with your support. The time, of course, which is still at our disposal, is very limited. This I can see clearly.

    I will write to you again in greater detail soon. In the meantime you can perhaps send me more detailed information about the development of your school during the past weeks; I recommend again the fulfillment of your justified wishes wholeheartedly. Let us hope that the result might be achieved very soon towards which we in common strive.

    Hearty greetings from house to house.

In loyal comradeship,

Yours,

G. MOSHACK.

---

21 The notorious Nazi Primer teaching children songs of hate against Jews and Catholics.

22 People's Bund for Germans Living Abroad.

SECRET ARMIES × **131**

Great Kills, 'S.I./NY 24.10.37

Herrn Peter Gissibl
3853/57 North Western Ave.
Chixago, Ill.

Lieber Herr Gissibl;

      Sie werden sich vielleicht erinnern, dass ich
die VDA (Volksbund fuer das Deutschtum im Ausland, Berlin)
Arbeiten fuer USA erledige.
      Unsere Buecherstelle in Berlin moechte nun gerne

2541 Sunnyside Ave. Chicago um Buecher fuer seine "Organisation "(?) gebeten. Kennen Sie ihn ? Welche Organisation
leitet er ?
           Deutschen Gruss

                    Carl G. Orgell
                    Great Kills, S.I./NY

*A letter the Dies Committee shelved—Carl G. Orgell identifying himself to
Peter Gissibl as a representative of the People's Bund for Germans Living Abroad.*

On May 20, 1938, E. A. Vennekohl, of the People's Bund for Germans Living Abroad, wrote to Gissibl as follows:

Dear Comrade Gissibl:

We wrote you yesterday that the 3,000 badges for the singing festival would be sent to you via Orgell; for various reasons we have now divided the badges in ten single packages of which two each went to the following addresses: Friedrich Schlenz, Karl Moeller, Karl Kraenzle, Orgell and two to you.

Please inform your co-workers respectively and take care that in case duties have to be paid they should be laid out; please see to it that Orgell refunds the money to you later; this was the simplest and the only way by which the badges could be sent in order to arrive on time.

With the German people's greetings,

E. A. Vennekohl.

Deutsches Ausland-Institut Stuttgart
Fernsprecher 26237-26239 ✦ Telegramme: Auslandinstitut ✦ Postscheckkonto: Stuttgart 7640
Bankverbindung: Deutsche Bank und Diskonto Gesellschaft, Abt. Gymnasiumstr. Stuttgart

Haus des Deutschtums

Unser Zeichen:AV - Kb/Vi.   Stuttgart-S, den 18. März 1938

            Herrn
            Peter Gissibl
            Amerika-Deutscher Volksbund
            3855 N.Western Avenue

            C h i c a g o , Ill.

            U.S.A.

            Lieber Peter!

            Von Deinem Amtsträger, dem Kameraden Möller, erhielt ich unter
            dem 15. Februar ein Schreiben. Er teilte mir u.a. mit, dass
            ein Austausch von Jugendlichen für dieses Jahr nicht mehr in
            Frage kommt. Ich bedaure das sehr. Ich hätte es im Interesse
            unserer gemeinsamen Bestrebungen sehr gerne gesehen, wenn wir
            bereits in diesem Jahre, gerade auch aus Eurem Kreise, Jugendliche
            hier gehabt hätten. Vielleicht lässt sich mit Deiner Unter-
            stützung diese Möglichkeit doch noch schaffen. Die Zeit, die
            noch zur Verfügung steht, ist allerdings sehr knapp bemessen.
            Darüber bin ich mir durchaus im klaren.

            Ich werde Dir demnächst wieder ausführlicher schreiben. In der
            Zwischenzeit kannst Du mir vielleicht nähere Angaben über die
            Entwicklung Deiner Schule während der letzten Wochen übermitteln.
            Eine Erfüllung Deiner berechtigten Wünsche habe ich erneut aufs
            wärmste befürwortet. Hoffentlich lässt sich auch sehr bald das
            Ergebnis erzielen, um das wir gemeinsam bestrebt sind.

            Herzliche Grüsse von Haus zu Haus
                                    in treuer Kameradschaft
                                    Dein G. Wohack

Another letter connecting Gissibl with a German propaganda agency.
This letter, translated in the text, was hardly noticed by the Dies Committee.

Volksbund für das Deutschtum im Ausland
Hauptgeschäftsstelle

Bankkonten: Deutsche Bank, Depositenkasse C 1, Berlin W 62, Kleiststr. 27; Bank der Deutschen Arbeit, Berlin SW 19, Wallstr. 61–65, Postscheckkonto: Berlin NW 7, Nr. 114 67, Drahtanschrift: Deutschtum Berlin.

Unser Zeichen: Vol/Gr.　　　　Ihr Zeichen:　　　　Berlin W 30, den 20. Mai 1938
In der Antwort anzugeben　　　　　　　　　　　　　Martin-Luther-Str. 97
Betrifft:　　　　　　　　　　　　　　　　　　　　Fernruf 259186

Herrn
Peter Gissibl
3855 North Western Ave.
Chicago, Ill.
U.S.A.

Lieber Kamerad Gissibl!

Wir schrieben Ihnen gestern, dass die 3.000 Sängerfestplaketten
über Orgell an Sie geleitet würden. Aus verschiedenen Gründen
haben wir die Plaketten jetzt in zehn Einzelpakete verteilt,
von denen je zwei anfolgende Anschriften gingen:
Friedrich Schlenz, Karl Moeller, Karl Kraenzle, Orgell und zwei an
Sie.
Bitte informieren Sie Ihre Mitarbeiter entsprechend und tragen
Sie Sorge, dass die etwaigen Zollspesen verauslagt werden. Diese
wollen Sie sich später von Herrn Orgell zurückvergüten lassen.
Es war dies der einfachste und einzigste Weg, auf dem die Plaketten
versandt werden konnten, um rechtzeitig drüben einzutreffen.

Mit volksdeutschem Gruss
i.A.
E.A. Vennekohl

Further evidence of Gissibl's tie-up with the People's Bund for Germans Living Abroad. This letter, a translation of which appears in the text, was also long withheld by the Dies Committee.

These documents in the hands of the Dies Committee show definite tie-ups between German propaganda divisions and agents in the United States (some of them came through the Nazi diplomatic corps), yet these documents were put aside. The letters from True, Allen, and others quoted in the previous chapter were also placed before the Congressional Committee. It refused to call the men involved.

CONCLUSION

THE ACTIVITIES OF THE FEW agents and propagandists described in the foregoing chapters do not, as I said in the preface, even scratch the surface of what seem to be widespread efforts to interfere in the internal affairs of the American people and their Government; but a few basic conclusions can reasonably be drawn from what little is known of the Fifth Column's operations.

Berlin-directed agents in foreign countries sometimes combine propaganda and espionage, frequently using the propaganda organizations as the bases for espionage. In the United States, so far as I have been able to ascertain, agents of the Rome-Berlin-Tokyo axis are just beginning to cooperate. In the Central and South American countries, however, the axis has apparently agreed to a division of labor, each of the fascist powers assuming a specific field of activity.

Germany, Italy and Japan have already shown the extent to which they will go in their drive for raw materials vital to their industries and war machines. In Spain, the German and Italian Fifth Column organized and fomented a bloody civil war in order to establish a wide fascist area to the south of France, for Germany and Italy, of course, consider France a potential enemy in the next war. In France itself, German and Italian agents, aided by their Governments, built an amazing network of steel and concrete fortifications manned by at least 100,000 heavily armed men—all this before France awoke to the treason within her own borders.

The strategy pursued by the Fifth Column in different countries falls into like patterns. In Austria, before it was swallowed, Nazi agents first established propaganda organizations as the bases from which to work. When, after the abortive attempt to seize the Austrian Government, the Nazis were made illegal, they went underground but continued to get aid from Germany. Eventually Berlin ordered *Standarte II* organized as a specific body prepared to provoke disturbances. When the Austrian police quelled them, the provocations enabled Germany to protest that German citizens were being attacked and mistreated. The activities of *Standarte II,* directed by the Gestapo, continued with increasing intensity until the unfortunate country was absorbed.

In Czechoslovakia the same strategy was followed: first the establishment of propaganda centers to which Nazis and Nazi sympathizers could gravitate—under the cloak of bodies seeking to improve relations between the Sudeten Germans and the Czech Government; then the utilization of propaganda headquarters and branches as centers for espionage. Shortly before the Munich Pact, *Standarte II* again came into being, creating disorders which, when Czech police tried to suppress them, enabled Germany to raise the cry that Czech subjects of German blood were being cruelly mistreated.

Invariably the aggressor nation raises a moral issue to cover up proposed acts of aggression. Italy wanted to "civilize the Ethiopians" by dropping bombs on defenseless women and children. Germany and Italy openly sent aid to Franco "to keep Spain from being Bolshevized." And so on. The broad "moral issue" on the international field to cover up aggressions by the Rome-Berlin-Tokyo axis is "Communism." The axis, announced as having been formed "to exchange information about Communism," is really a military alliance now generally recognized. With the same issue, the axis is now boring into the Western Hemisphere. Actually the reasons seem to be military and not missionary.

Germany, especially, has sent and is sending agents not only to carry on espionage but to organize groups for political pressure upon the American republics. I very much doubt, from all I have been able to learn, if the motive is primarily to win the Americas over to the joys of totalitarian government or to the theory of Aryan supremacy. The money and the effort seem to be expended for more practical reasons. The Bunds can exert not only political pressure, but can develop natives with fascist leanings into the spies and *saboteurs* so badly needed in war time; for this reason it is worth the enormous effort and money it is costing the aggressor nations.

When the long expected war breaks, neither Europe nor the Far East will be in a condition to supply war materials and foodstuffs to the warring countries. The chief sources of raw materials will be the Western Hemisphere. A strong foothold in the Americas means a tremendous advantage in the coming struggle, since materials are as important to an army as is man power.

And, should the fascist powers be unable to get these raw materials for themselves, secret agents can at least sabotage shipments to enemy countries—as did German agents in the United States during the first years of the World War, while we were still neutral.

Mexico, because of its enormous oil supplies, plays an important part in fascist military strategy. Consequently, we find intensive efforts by the axis, and especially Germany, to overthrow the Cárdenas Government because it is avowedly antifascist. A fascist government, helped into power by the Rome-Berlin-Tokyo axis, could be depended upon to supply much needed oil in war time.

The United States, as one of the world's greatest sources of raw materials and foodstuffs, is an even more important factor. Germany has not forgotten that its armies had the Allies on their knees when American supplies and American man power turned their imminent victory into defeat; should America be on the side of the democracies as against the fascist powers, sabotaging shipments of supplies and men will be as important as crushing an enemy line.

The tactics utilized in the Western Hemisphere by the Fifth Column are similar to those used in Europe. Propaganda machines, masquerading as organizations designed to promote better relationships between a fascist and an American nation, are set up. Fascist movements are organized, usually from across national boundaries. In Mexico, Nazi agents operating out of the United States organized the Gold Shirts; subsequently, as in Austria, a Putsch was attempted (in 1935 and again in 1938). The storing of arms in Sonora by General Yocupicio, who is working with Nazi agents, promises another rebellion when the time seems ripe.

In Central America, the axis is presenting small republics with gifts of arms in efforts to win their friendship. Agents sent from Germany are establishing Nazi centers and the home Government is supplying them with propaganda. In Panama the situation is somewhat more sharp. There Japan has always had an intense interest in the Canal. In the axis, Germany has become a co-worker since she has large colonies in Brazil and Colombia, next door to the Panama Canal. These colonies are now being organized at a feverish pace while the countries themselves are deluged with propaganda over special short-wave beams. In Brazil, a Nazi-directed abortive Putsch took place in 1938.

These activities point to an objective which certainly is not calculated to be in the interest of the United States and our Monroe Doctrine. From all indications the efforts appear directed toward ringing the United States with fascist countries, or at least countries with fascist bodies capable of giving the United States a headache should she ever be involved in a war with one or all of the axis powers.

In the United States itself we find that the strategy is the same as that followed in Austria, Czechoslovakia and in countries of the Western World. The German-American Bund functions "to promote better relations between the United States and Germany," but the efforts consist of persistent anti-American and anti-democratic propaganda and, within the past year or two, of serving as a base for military and naval spies.

With Germany directing the strategy, her agents in all countries raise the issue of the "menace of the Jew and the Catholic," with especial emphasis upon the Jew; the Catholics are still too strong for the Nazis to come to grips with at this time.

The Federal Government, of course, has ample legal machinery for prosecuting spies, but espionage is only part of the broad Nazi campaign against this democratic Government. So far as the Western World is concerned, the Federal Government has already taken steps to try to counteract the short-wave broadcasts by German and Italian government-controlled stations. Counter broadcasts are being employed as a defensive measure, and though of value, will probably not completely counteract fascist "news" agencies supplying propaganda in the guise of news, free of charge, to the Central and South American newspapers as well as printed propaganda sent from Germany and distributed by the bunds. Outside of military action, economic pressure seems to be the only language the fascist governments understand, and a little of that pressure by the American Government would probably make them understand our resentment at their invasion far more than broadcasts and general talk about a family of nations in the Western Hemisphere.

Our laws and courts provide a machinery which can be used to prevent any infringement upon the democratically constituted rights of the people. It is of vital importance, however, that preparations for fascist lawlessness be vigilantly uprooted. The Italian and German people made just this fatal mistake of tolerating the activities of Mussolini's and Hitler's gangs until they grew strong enough to seize power and crush every sign of democracy.

There is no reason why a great people, attacked by a pernicious ideology, cannot counteract such propaganda with greater and more intelligent propaganda to educate our people to the advantages of democracy—to what fascism really means to everyone, including the big industrialists and financiers, some of whom have been flirting with fascism. The Government, however, can and should be instructed by the representatives of the people, to take proper steps to stop the infiltration of Nazi agents and propagandists into this country.

There are various other and perhaps more practical and useful steps which can be taken, but those can be worked out once the people awake to the danger of permitting fascist propaganda to go on, and sentiment becomes strong enough to put an end to foreign-directed activities here.

— THE END —

THE
GERMAN SPY
IN AMERICA

JOHN PRICE JONES

Foreword by
THEODORE ROOSEVELT

Introduction by
ROGER B. WOOD

CONTENTS

432 Fourth Avenue, New York
Office of Theodore Roosevelt
February 27, 1917

My dear Mr. Jones,

I have read the galley proofs of your book, and I wish to say, with all emphasis and heartiness, that you are doing this country a great service in publishing it.

Your statements are evidently for the most part based on official Government records, happening in the course of prosecuting the various criminals, who by the direct instigation of the German Government, have for the last two and one-half years been using this country as a base for war against the Allies, and more than this, have in effect been waging war on us within our own boundaries, no less than on the high seas. Our people need to know certain of the facts that you set forth. They need to understand that Germany has waged war upon us, and has waged war against our property, and has waged war against the lives of non-combatants, including women and children, and therefore a far more evil war than one waged openly. Our people also need to understand what you so clearly set forth that very much of the pacifist movement has been directly instigated by German intrigues, and paid for by German money, and that the entire pacifist movement in this country, during the past two and a half years, has really been in the interest of German militarism against the rights of small nations, and against our own honor and vital national interests.

You have done a capital work, and I wish it could be put in the hands of all good Americans.

Sincerely yours,
THEODORE ROOSEVELT

Mr. John Price Jones,
The Sun, New York

FOREWORD

THERE HAVE BEEN TWO KINDS of German propaganda. One, devoted to setting before the American people Germany's side of the war, may be classed as legitimate. The other has been illegal and criminal. While both are set forth in this narrative, the greater space has been devoted to illegal activities.

The author claims for this book no other distinction than a plain unvarnished statement of facts—vital, dramatic, absorbing facts of the manner in which secret agents of the Teutonic governments, acting under orders of authorized directors, have attacked the very integrity of our national life, commercial, social and politic. It contains facts arranged from an American viewpoint by an American who considers it his duty to present them to his fellow Americans.

These facts were obtained by the writer as a reporter on the *New York Sun* who devoted a year to no other work. *They were derived by a painstaking investigation and where flat statements are made they are based on knowledge obtained by the author from various authorities and from the examination of documents some of which have never been published.* They show how German agents sought to subvert the aims of our government to the advantage of the Central Powers. They furnish a glimpse of the manner in which these men and women sought to make America the hinterland for the European War; how they planned and executed bribery, arson, felonious assaults; how they plotted destruction of property and even murder on American territory.

These facts emphasize the need of a new kind of preparedness. They prove that not only does the nation need preparedness in arms on both land and sea against a foreign foe but also defense against those within our bounds, who are eager to betray us. No true American, whether he be pro-Ally, pro-German, or strictly neutral, can read this book without realizing the thoroughness and the perfection of the German espionage system and being convinced of the way in which Germany's spies have overrun the entire country, nor can anyone doubt the necessity for preparedness to cope with these men and this system in a different guise in the event of still graver issues.

John Price Jones

INTRODUCTION

WHEN THE GERMAN NOTE ANNOUNCING that the Imperial German Government intended to resume with greater vigor its ruthless submarine warfare was handed to the Secretary of State of the United States, a crisis in the affairs of this nation was abruptly precipitated. The President met that crisis with courage, with promptness and in a way that merits, and has, the unqualified support of every American who is proud of his citizenship.

After the receipt of such an insulting note it was unthinkable that the United States could longer remain on friendly terms with a nation that deliberately returned to wanton murder of innocent non-combatants, including women and helpless children.

The conduct of the Imperial German Government in striving to win a war by means (which barbarians would hesitate to use) begun by that Government without just cause and pursued by riding rough-shod over a much smaller and much weaker nation, has been condemned by every civilized country, and it will be many years before the German people recover from the shame and degradation into which they have been plunged.

Germany will have to repent in sackcloth and ashes for a long, long time before it is received again into the Family of Nations.

In prosecuting the war, Germany and her allies have proceeded from the beginning upon the theory that "the end justifies the means" and acting upon that theory have held in supreme contempt the rights of neutral nations.

From the beginning of the war, subjects of Germany, resident in the United States, have continuously violated our laws in the most outrageous and flagrant manner.

At the very threshold, they sought to use the United States as a base from which to supply the German raiders in the South Atlantic, and to that end, by fraud, obtained from the collectors at various ports of the United States legal clearances, thus subjecting every ship which lawfully cleared from any United States port to seizure by the Allies.

Next, they sought and obtained, by fraud, and false swearing, passports to be used by German reservists in returning to Germany, traveling under the guise of American citizens; thus placing in danger the lives and liberty of honest Americans traveling with legitimate passports and entitled to the protection of this Government.

Because the Allies were able to purchase in the United States munitions of war, foodstuffs and all other supplies they might need, and were able to transport them, and because the United States did not at the behest of the Imperial German Government, stop the sale and transportation of the supplies, which its citizens had a perfect right to sell and transport, German residents devised the inhuman scheme of making chemical fire bombs and infernal machines to be placed on ships carrying passengers and supplies, with the deliberate intent and purpose that the ships should be crippled or sunk in mid-ocean—it mattered not to them that all on board might find a watery grave.

Numerous attempts have been made to equip men of the most desperate character with necessary explosives and other implements of death and destruction and have them go from the United States into Canada, our friendly and respected neighbor, to destroy railroads, canals, ships, warehouses and factories without regard to human life.

Agents have been sent to the United States with unlimited money at their command to engage gunmen and thugs to blow up our munition plants and factories—many explosions have occurred—many lives have been lost—much damage has been done—I cannot say who caused such wholesale murder to be committed, but I have the right as you have, to suspect.

It is a matter of record that the German Military Attaché, Captain Franz von Papen, and the German Naval Attaché, Captain Boy-Ed, knew of and sanctioned some of the conspiracies above referred to—*perhaps* the German Ambassador did not know of them; but it will be hard to convince a hard-headed, common-sense American citizen that he did not know what his right hand and his left hand were doing in such a crucial period.

Murder has followed murder on the high seas, one crime came fast upon another in the United States, and now we are told that this Government must do as the Imperial German Government directs; or murder on a more

THE GERMAN SPY IN AMERICA × **149**

colossal scale will be the result. The people of the United States have not taken orders from any Government since 1776, and the German murderers ought to have known we would take none now, least of all from a Government that had forfeited its right to the respect of any civilized nation.

"The German Spy in America" will give you some small conception of what the Germans in the United States have been doing since August 1, 1914. Its author has followed their nefarious plots very closely and he has an intimate knowledge of his subject.

Its purpose is to let the American people know the danger that lurks within; to sound the alarm so that every man may be on his guard; to show the grave necessity for preparedness against a foreign foe, and particularly numerous alien enemies within our borders.

If it serves in a small measure to accomplish its high aim, its author will be amply repaid because he will have rendered a great service to humanity, and above all to our country, which we love more than all else, save God.

Roger B. Wood

I

AMERICA: The BACKGROUND of the WAR

AMERICA HAS BEEN THE GREAT background of the European War. Though far removed from the trenches with the play of artillery and the heroic charges, this country has been the scene of an equally dramatic, though silent struggle—a battle not visible to the eye. It has been a conflict of wits, of statesman pitted against statesman, of secret agent striving to outdo his opponent of a belligerent nation; for in America, agents of Germany have been striving for a two-fold aim. They have sought to enmesh the United States in an international conspiracy and to use this country as the means of a rear attack on the Entente Allies.

And New York has been the center of it all. In several of the huge office buildings that make the thoroughfares of the city seem like canyons, Germany had, and still has, the headquarters of a vast nerve-like system radiating throughout the country. The nerve coils are composed of thousands of secret agents located in every city and town. These men have worked under orders from Berlin in the execution of a series of campaigns designed to be of service to the Teutonic Allies. Against these men have been pitted agents of the American government, all aiming to detect the schemes and frustrate any plans for the violation of our neutrality laws.

A diplomat, famed for his finesse and grace of manner, was at a reception given to distinguished statesmen, talented business men and attractive women. The conversation was turned to the topic of spies. One woman wished to know if the diplomat had encountered any spies.

"Well," remarked the diplomat, "I used to stop at the Hotel Grandeur, but Count—" (mentioning the name of a diplomat of a nation with which his country was at war) "persisted in having my baggage searched every day. So I moved to the Hotel Excellency; but I found things no better there."

"Didn't you complain to the management?"

"Ah, no," answered he gravely, "but every time the Count stops at the Hotel Elaborate, I have his baggage searched, too."

Perhaps the diplomat was not serious, but in days when the destiny of nations was at stake, it was likely that he was speaking none too lightly of a game that had doubtless cost him many an hour of the keenest anxiety.

Of all the secret service systems, the German is the most elaborate and machine-like. It has been organized not merely to gather information, but to trample upon the laws of the United States, in order to hinder any project of the Entente Allies. Constructed in the hours of peace with the utmost care and foresight, it was easily expanded in the United States at the outbreak of the war into such a vast network that if a representative of the Allies suddenly retraced his steps or halted suddenly when around a corner, he was almost sure to bump the shins of a German spy. Germany, always methodical and thorough, possessing a genius for molding a multitude of details into an effective whole, had prepared her secret service system with the same efficiency with which through scores of years she had equipped her military forces for battle; indeed, her secret service was a part of her military forces.

The system is based on the principle of "Lass die linke Hand nicht wissen was die rechte tut"—"let not the left hand know what the right is doing." *So thoroughly is this maxim followed that two German spies may be working side by side and not be aware of the fact.* Though groups of Germans may engage in some activity with a thorough understanding of the aims of another, still the order of silence is rigorously enforced. The agents hand their information to a superior, who in turn transmits it to somebody higher up. *One spy knows only the person or group of persons with whom he directly deals, sending information along devious and hidden routes up to the final assembling point.*

Germany's spy system has been the sword hand of her statesmen and her diplomats. When this war is over and the world learns of the moves, counter-moves, and Machiavellian methods of German diplomats, with their intrigues, secret understandings, and their daring attempts to force this country into dangerous situations, people will realize more clearly than to-day what a marvelous system has been behind many seemingly casual developments in this country. It will be shown how German agents have violated our laws in order to gain secret information for the benefit of Germany; how her secret agents have committed crimes in order to coerce diplomatic negotiations.

RAMIFICATIONS OF UNDERGROUND PLOTS

So perfectly organized and so responsive to the slightest suggestion from Berlin is the American branch of the Kaiser's secret service that vast undertakings—some legitimate, many in violation of American laws—were carried out.

The magician, who invented the wireless, enabled the German General War Staff to move to New York. The splash and splutter of electricity over oceans and continents virtually transported Germany's leading statesmen, tacticians, and scientists at will to hold sessions in Manhattan on matters arising in America and bearing on the battle-front in the many theaters of actual warfare. For instance, how many people know that the secretary to one of the generals on the Western Line was a brother to one of the most notorious woman plotters in America? Germany had foreseen the possibilities of the wireless in war and had developed secret methods of sending code messages by radiogram, when apparently only ordinary messages were being transmitted, and she had also, some way or other, got possession of the code ciphers of other nations. Every night messages have been sent out from Germany, apparently blindly, addressed to no one and have been picked up by hidden receiving stations in America and other countries.

While Germany calls her spy system "a bureau of intelligence," its purpose is confined not merely to the gathering of information, but to the carrying out of any campaign that will be harmful to her enemies. In the United States, Germans—reservists, army officers, representatives of the German Government—have been indicted for crimes against Federal laws. These violations were committed without doubt in a self-sacrificing spirit with the aim of helping the Fatherland. Germans, or German influences, have been behind schemes in violation of neutrality laws and restraint of trade. *They have attempted arson, bribery, forgery, engaged in military enterprises, caused explosions in ships and factories, resulting in many deaths, and have set fires in ships and factories.*

They have participated in plots against Canada, Ireland and India, all developed in the United States under the supervision of the German representatives of Berlin, though often ostensibly carried out by anarchist tools. *The activities of the German agents,* multitudinous in detail and variety, *all have been designed to hinder the Allies* in their prosecution of the war, *to cause a breach between the Allies and the United States, to embroil this country in a war and to accomplish other secret aims of the General War Staff.* In all the propaganda, German secret agents and official representatives of the German Government have not only worked with utter disregard to American laws, but have endeavored to place the United States in a position of being secretly unneutral.

But the German Government has officially denied that she ordered any of her subjects to undertake any act in violation of American laws. Shortly after President Wilson in his message to Congress bitterly attacked the activities of Germans and German-Americans in America, accusing the latter of treason, the German Government authorized the statement that it:

"Naturally has never knowingly accepted the support of any person, group of persons, society or organization seeking to promote the cause of Germany in the United States by illegal acts, by counsels of violence, by contravention of law, or by any means whatever that could offend the American people in the pride of their own authority. If it should be alleged that improper acts have been committed by representatives of the German Government they could be easily dealt with. To any complaints upon proof as may be submitted by the American Government suitable response will be duly made. . . . Apparently the enemies of Germany have succeeded in creating the impression that the German Government is in some way, morally or otherwise, responsible for what Mr. Wilson has characterized as anti-American activities, comprehending attacks upon property in violation of the rules which the American Government has seen fit to impose upon the course of neutral trade. This the German Government absolutely denies. It cannot specifically repudiate acts committed by individuals over whom it has no control, and of whose movements and intentions it is neither officially or unofficially informed."[1]

To this official disavowal of German propaganda in America, there are two answers that stand out with dramatic force. First, the extent to which the subjects of Germany are expected to go in war time is shown by excerpts from Germany's War Book of instructions to officers, which says in part:

"Bribery of the enemy's subjects with the object of obtaining military advantages, acceptances of offers of treachery, reception of deserters, utilization of the discontented elements in the population, support of the pretenders and the like are permissible; indeed, international law is in no way opposed to the exploitation of the crimes of third parties (assassination, incendiarism, robbery and the like) to the prejudice of the enemy. Considerations of chivalry, generosity and

---

1 Berlin despatch in the New York *Sun,* Dec. 19, 1915.

honor may denounce in such cases a hasty and unsparing exploitation of such advantages as indecent and dishonorable, but law, which is less touchy, allows it. The ugly and inherently immoral aspect of such methods cannot affect the recognition of their lawfulness. The necessary aims of war give the belligerent the right and imposes upon him, according to circumstances, the duty not to let slip the important, it may be decisive, advantages to be gained by such means."[2]

Secondly, since Germany sent out that semi-official proclamation from Berlin concerning propagandists, many steps have been taken by the American Government, both administrative and judicial. Captains von Papen and Boy-Ed, military and naval attachés respectively, have been dismissed from this country for "improper activities in military and naval affairs."

There was no favoritism in the German secret service. Every German, high or low, was open to assignment, disagreeable and dishonorable, in getting information, and to orders to commit crimes—for Germany stops at no crime—that may be necessary to circumvent the enemy.

Captain von Papen showed his feeling keenly one night at a dinner of a few men where the wine flowed freely.

"My God, I would give everything in the world," he exclaimed, "to be in the trenches where I could do the work of a gentleman." In his work, there was no public reward for work well performed according to the war code. That man's sentiments were echoed by von Rintelen, who, when among friends, fairly shook with emotion at the thought of the work in which he was engaged.

"How loathsome I feel," he said. "How this dirty work sticks to me! When this war ends, I shall take a bath in carbolic acid."

THREE EXECUTIVES IN THE UNITED STATES

Over all the thousands of reservists, trained agents, and other spies were the men in charge of the centres of information to whom they made their report; and the three or four chief lieutenants in charge of the various and distinct line of activities into which these matters of war, finance and commerce automatically were divided. There were practically, outside of the Chief Spy, three important executives in this country, supervising respectively the commercial, military and naval lines of information and activity. Each one

2 The War Book of the German General Staff, translated by J. H. Morgan, M.A., pp. 113–114.

of these men was surrounded by a group of experts who had charge of a subdivision of the work. All had their legal advisers, their bankers, and every sort of an expert that their special work required. Upon them fell the task of sifting and analyzing the mass of facts gathered by the spies and making reports to Berlin. Upon each one of them also fell the duty of carrying out any orders that might come from the General War Staff in Germany.

First and foremost of the three lieutenants was Dr. Heinrich F. Albert, Privy Councilor to the German Embassy in America and Fiscal Agent of the German Empire. He directed the gathering of a huge mass of information of value to Germany concerning the financial, industrial and commercial activities of this country, and was the chief instrument through whom money reached the army of spies. Though he was the director of many activities, nothing criminal, it must be asserted in justice to him, has been traced to him.

The military agent was Captain Franz von Papen, the attaché of the German Embassy. His work was confined specifically to the procuring of information that would be of aid to the Imperial German army and to the military tasks that might be peculiarly helpful to the army.

The naval expert was Captain Karl Boy-Ed, another attaché of the German Embassy. He had under him experts who made a speciality of various lines of naval matters, fortifications, coast defenses and explosives.

The headquarters of the entire system were and are yet in New York. Dr. Albert had his offices in the Hamburg-American Steamship Company's building, and he utilized at times a good part of the Hamburg-American Company's staff—a concern in which the Kaiser himself owns a large percentage of the stock. In the same building was the office of Paul Koenig, the business manager of part of Germany's spy system in America, though nominally the Superintendent of Police for the Hamburg-American line. Captain Boy-Ed had his headquarters in Room 801 of 11, Broadway, and Captain von Papen had his on the twenty-fifth floor of 60, Wall Street.

This narrative seeks to show as definitely as possible the work of these three agents of Germany in America and of others co-operating with them. It sets forth the enterprises that they plotted and the ramifications of their organization. It reveals how countless agents, unaware that they were parts of a vast system and often innocent of any intentional wrongdoing, acted their parts. It shows how that part of the machinery engaged in legitimate propaganda was linked at places with the machinery executing illegal acts.

While the conspiracy has been manipulated, the American Government has been very active. To the skill of the United States secret service, headed by Chief William J. Flynn, always alert and apparently unruffled in the most trying crises, and to A. Bruce Bielaski, head of the special agents of the Department of Justice, and William M. Offley, Superintendent of the New York Bureau of the special agents, has fallen the task of seeing that the representatives of the different countries followed the American maxim, "Play fair; play according to the rules of international law and the laws of this country." Upon Police Commissioner Woods, his deputy, Guy Scull, of New York, and his enthusiastic and clever aid, Police Captain Thomas J. Tunney, has devolved also the hazardous and difficult task of combating the schemes of those spies. Those men, by courageous and skillful detective work have unearthed and foiled some of the most daring bomb plots of the Germans.

To Messrs. Flynn and Bielaski, at times, have come secrets of intrigue and conspiracy that must have made them, even as it has the President, almost tremble with the import of impending events that had to be forestalled.

II

CAPTAIN FRANZ VON PAPEN, DIRECTOR of GERMANY'S MILITARY ENTERPRISES on the AMERICAN FRONT

"I ALWAYS SAY TO THESE idiotic Yankees they had better hold their tongues."

So wrote Captain Franz von Papen, German military attaché in America, to his wife in Germany—a letter which he entrusted to Captain James F. J. Archibald, American newspaper correspondent and bearer of secret and confidential messages from Teutonic representatives. The German word which the Captain used was "bloedsinnig," meaning silly, stupid, idiotic. It has a sneering ring, truly typical of the Prussian warrior's contempt for Americans. It suggests the disdainful feeling which the military attaché had for the loyalty of Americans. One can imagine his sly laugh as he handed to an American that letter and code messages to the War Staff. With a similar feeling of contempt for the British, when dismissed from this country and assured of safe conduct as to person, he carried on board the steamer *Noordam* a portfolio of papers from friends reflecting the same disgust for America and outlining his own unlawful and criminal acts in America. But in both instances his arrogant self-confidence brought exposure.

This attitude of arrogance was Captain von Papen's chief characteristic. Joined to it was the brother trait, bluntness. He believed that the American people were not only stupid but also weak-sighted and that he could do anything he wanted without detection. So he put his heart and soul into military and criminal enterprises upon American soil. The Captain apparently thought that the American authorities would not suspect his machinations, for, unlike Captain Boy-Ed, he made comparatively few efforts to cover up the trails of his activities. That carelessness proved his scorn for American detective methods, for with all his haughtiness and bravado he had been trained in a school of craft. He had been drilled under instructors who placed a prize on cunning, deceit, intrigue, reckless disregard of the rights of others, and the destiny of Prussia as a conqueror. The Captain presumably believed that craft and cunning were not necessary in America.

CONTEMPT FOR DEMOCRACY

Confident that he was eluding the watchful eye of the United States author-ities with more skill than his associates, he sent a telegram one day to Cap-tain Boy-Ed, warning him to be more careful. Whereupon the latter, smiling cheerfully to himself, wrote this letter: "Dear Papen: A secret agent who returned from Washington this evening, made the following statement: 'The Washington people are very much excited about von Papen and are having a constant watch kept on him. They are in possession of a whole heap of incriminating evidence against him. They have no evidence against Count B. and Captain B.-E. (!)'" Boy-Ed, a little too optimistically, added: "In this connection I would suggest with due diffidence that perhaps the first part of your telegram is worded rather too emphatically."

Wrapped in that sense of contempt the military attaché began immedi-ately upon the outbreak of war, even as he had planned before it, to make the United States "the hinterland" of the European battlefield. In the Embassy at Washington, the German consulate in New York, the Hamburg-American Building, an office in 60, Wall Street—which he secretly leased—and on board German merchantmen tied up in New York Harbor, he gathered about him German officials and German reservists, outlining plots in violation of Amer-ican law, all designed to injure the Allies and help the cause of Germany. In those conferences, *his arrogant disregard of America* and his determination *overruled the hesitating dissenters.* His was the Prussian spirit of aggression. In those gatherings, he was both the dominating and the domineering factor: tall and broad-shouldered, with a commanding attitude, energetic in speech, and lightning-like in the development of bold plans. He has the strong fore-head, the long, firm nose, and the heavy underjaw of a commander, but the large ears that denote recklessness and eyes blue and hard as steel.

UNDER ORDERS FROM BERLIN

He had been selected in his youth for secret work because of an aptness which he early displayed. He had been trained especially for the work which he undertook in other countries under direction of the German General Staff and for the tasks that devolved upon him in America both before and after the war. As a young officer he was sent out from Germany, traveling as a civilian, making special studies of the sentiment of the people, the topography of the country, and getting in touch with other secret workers. One of the countries which he studied with remarkable care was Ireland. He tramped and rode every foot of the land and knew it thoroughly. He displayed something of the knowledge he had acquired when riding in Central Park, one day after the war started, he stopped to chat with an acquaintance who had bought a mare. Waxing enthusiastic over the animal he quickly showed his acquaintance with Ireland by giving the breed of the mare and telling exactly the counties in Ireland where that breed could be found.

How well he disguised himself in those various expeditions when he rode horseback simply as a sightseer, is indicated by his horsemanship. Though he was trained in a riding school at Hanover, where ostensibly they teach the French method, nevertheless in Central Park, where many a morning he could be observed, he displayed perfect English form. They say that when one learns the French style, one invariably clings to it above all others. Naturally, a horseman traveling through Ireland revealing every characteristic of the French school would attract attention.

As the military attaché of the German Embassy, Captain von Papen was under orders, not of Count von Bernstorff, but of the military head in Germany. Appointed personally by the Kaiser as the representative of the German Army in America and Mexico, he had the commission that falls to every military attaché of a foreign government, namely, to make a study of the army of the nation to which he is accredited.

Captain von Papen, always striving for praise and preferment from the Kaiser, was a most enthusiastic gatherer of military information. Knowing that no phase of military activity throughout the world escapes the watchful eye of the Chief Spy or the German General Staff, von Papen was always on the alert for any invention, new method of warfare, or germ of an idea that might be developed into an important advantage for Germany; just as the War Staff got their suggestion for the modern trench warfare from the Indians and later from the Civil War. For instance, shortly before the great war started, Captain von Papen, addressed as "Royal Prussian Captain on the General Staff of the Army," was directed by R. von Wild, of the Ministry of War's office, to proceed to Mexico and there investigate the attacks on railroad trains by means of mines and explosives. He made a thorough investigation and though he reported: "I consider it out of the question that explosions prepared in this way would have to be reckoned with in a European war," he nevertheless sought to utilize that method in blowing up tunnels and railroads in Canada.

AT WORK IN MEXICO

How well von Papen, as an organizer and military investigator, acquitted himself in the interest of the Kaiser is set forth in Rear Admiral von Hintze's own language in a report which he made from Mexico to the Imperial Chancellor recommending von Papen for a decoration. That letter is striking; for it suggests the work which von Papen afterwards did in America, if he had not already made the arrangements for it prior to the outbreak of the European conflict. The admiral wrote that von Papen "showed special industry in organizing the German colony for purposes of self-defense and out of this shy and factious material, unwilling to undertake any military activity, he obtained what there was to be got."

While von Papen had a staff of experts and of secret agents prior to the war, he did not then have the perfectly developed system at his command which he used afterwards. That he had his plans well mapped out for any contingency and that he knew the situation thoroughly is vividly illustrated in a draft of a cable message which he sent to Captain Boy-Ed from Mexico City on July 29, 1914, saying:

"If necessary, arrange business for me too with Pavenstedt. Then inform Lersner. The Russian attaché ordered back to Washington by telegraph. On outbreak of war have intermediaries located by detective where Russian and French intelligence office." The latter part of the message, referring to intermediaries, is open to two interpretations: first, that Boy-Ed was to have detectives locate the Russian and French intelligence offices; second, Boy-Ed was to place spies in the Russian and French intelligence bureaus.

Hurrying to Washington, the military attaché immediately took charge of the military part of Germany's spy system. He began to weld together into a vast organization scientists, experts, secret agents and German reservists who would gather information for him and who would be ready at the command of the General War Staff, to undertake any military enterprise. The entire organization of German consuls and representatives in America work in unity in war as in peace. How quickly von Papen got his staff together is shown in a statement made by Franz Wachendorf, alias Horst von der Goltz, alias Bridgeman Taylor, who became one of Papen's aids in spy work and military enterprises. Wachendorf, who was a major in the Mexican army at the outbreak of war, said under oath: "The 3rd of August, 1914; license was given me by my commanding officer to separate myself from the service of the brigade for the term of six months. I left directly for El Paso, Texas, where I was told by Mr. Kuck, German consul at Chihuahua, Mexico, who stayed there, to put myself at the disposition of Captain von Papen."

CALLING RESERVISTS

The military attaché also had help from Germany and from German reservists coming from other countries. The War Office in Berlin sent him men. Captain Hans Tauscher, the husband of Mme. Gadski, was in Germany when war was declared. A reserve officer of the German Army, he immediately offered himself for duty. His order was to return to America at once and report to Captain von Papen. Likewise, soldiers and secret agents with special equipment, who were in different parts of the world and who had no definite work, were ordered by wireless or through secret channels to hasten to Captain von Papen's assistance. After a time, the Chief Spy in Germany detailed some of his aids to America to help in the upbuilding of a still more effective system of espionage.

Though remarkably skilled and trained to a high degree in a number of different lines, Captain von Papen made it his business to gather around him experts on every phase of military affairs, giving definite assignments to each and thus dividing the work so that greater speed and efficiency were obtained. He chose Captain Tauscher, agent of the Krupps and other big and small gun manufacturers in Germany and Austria, as one of his aids in gathering information. Captain Tauscher is an expert on ordnance and as such he was of invaluable assistance to Captain von Papen in obtaining facts regarding the manufacture of heavy ordnance and explosives for the Allies. *Tauscher was on most friendly terms with U.S. Ordnance officers.*

Von Papen selected George von Skal, a German journalist and former Commissioner of Accounts of New York, as a paid assistant in his office; and as a matter of fact every one of the big German agents in America had on his staff at least one trained newspaper man. He took as his secretary Wolf von Igel, a young man of distinguished appearance, and through him secretly rented a suite of offices in Wall Street "for advertising purposes."

Another man upon whom he could call for help was Paul Koenig, lent by the Hamburg-American Steamship Company. Through Koenig, von Papen could reach out to countless Germans and select men for any sort of task. Sometimes, however, von Papen met with a refusal. He asked Captain

Tauscher to perform a certain piece of work of questionable character and received in substance this answer: "I am ready to do anything within the law but I will not attempt this task." Experts in the chemistry of explosives, scientists of various sorts, lawyers and other advisers were on the military attaché's staff, all having special tasks and all working for the Kaiser with or without pay.

FOREIGN ARMY ON U.S. SOIL

Von Papen sought to protect his Wall Street suite of offices from public investigation by installing therein a safe bearing the seal of the Imperial German Government. That safe, protected by timelocks and by electrical devices against the curiosity of other secret agents or the prying eyes of policemen, is said to have contained the plans of the military phases of German propaganda. When the Federal agents suddenly descended upon the office one day to arrest von Igel, they found the safe open and the documents neatly laid out on the table preparatory to shipment to Washington. From those papers the State Department and the Attorney-General have learned much of the history of von Papen's activities—the inner workings of the German spy system. In that office von Papen kept the full list of his various secret agents, German and American, working for him, their addresses and telephone numbers; various code books for the deciphering of messages sent to him and for sending word to agents in this country or making reports.

Accordingly, when von Papen's plan for espionage was perfected, he had not only a staff of experts at his elbow, but thousands of reservists and the help of German and Austro-Hungarian consuls and channels of information. He had men at his disposal for dangerous and delicate missions to other countries. The ramifications of the system, the collecting agency and activities which he supervised for the good of the Fatherland were so finely organized and so comprehensive that von Papen in reality was the head of the military division of the German spy system of the entire world, outside of the countries belted by the Allies with a ring of steel.

Facts to prove the details of von Papen's organization and deeds were obtained from the von Igel papers, from the letters and secret documents taken from Captain Archibald; from documents and check stubs found in von Papen's possession when searched at Falmouth, England; from von der Goltz's confession; from scores of witnesses and from facts dug up by the

Secret Service and the Department of Justice. The trials of various offenders against neutrality laws have given the public more evidence. United States District-Attorney H. Snowden Marshall, in New York, his assistants, Roger B. Wood, in charge of the criminal division; Raymond H. Sarfaty, John C. Knox, and Harold A. Content, all set forth before the public many phases of the ingenious underground methods of spying and violating the law. Upon the evidence found by those officials and by United States District-Attorney Preston, of San Francisco, the following facts are presented:

Once the spies were selected and assigned to their duties, von Papen sought first, to glean information bearing on the great war. He was interested, naturally, in the amount of shrapnel shells and high explosives which the Allies were purchasing. He was eager to ascertain what American Army officers were learning about the military operations on the Continent and what the American Government was doing to develop its army to cope with the new problems arising from the war. He was watching the officers of the Allies in this country. He was seeking lines of communication with the racial elements in America that were allied with the insurrection forces in the colonies of the Entente Powers. The varied results of his investigations are shown by extracts from reports which he sent to Berlin by Captain Archibald. One letter told, for instance, that the Norwegian and Dutch governments were in the market for war materials. Von Papen asked if there were any objection by Germany to the sale to those governments of war products purchased by him in America, adding:

"I could probably dump on the Norwegian Government a great part of the Lehigh Coke Company's toluol which is lying around useless."

In a cipher dispatch to the chief of the General Staff in Berlin, he noted a conversation overheard in Philadelphia between two Englishmen. One British army officer, he said, was explaining a method for conveying military information by photographs. Likewise he gathered news of the Spanish Government seeking supplies, and sifted the facts assembled from factories, banking houses, diplomatic sources and transportation offices about the Allied war orders.

SECRET AGENTS BLOCK OUT AMERICA

Captain von Papen's cheque counterfoils are a veritable diary of some of his criminal—or if you please, military—activities in America. They give the names and the aliases of his secret agents; and day after day are recorded therein the payments made by von Papen to the persons working for or with him. The counterfoils tell the story of the purpose of the payment and by means of the endorsements on the cheques one can gather in skeleton form the story of a part—but not all—of the propaganda which the military attaché supervised. The stubs show the receipt of money, almost immediately after the beginning of the war marked for "War Intelligence Office." The interesting thing is that money for war intelligence work came from von Bernstorff and that funds for salary and expenses came from Dr. Fr. Adler, the Ambassador's secretary. To the fact that Captain von Papen kept such an accurate diary—an instance of German efficiency—is due in part the exposure of his varied activities in this country.

To Anton Kuepferle, another German spy captured in England and suspected after a confession to have shot himself, he gave $100. To Wachendorf he gave funds that the latter might go both to Berlin and England in the service of the Kaiser. To Paul Koenig, he handed many accounts for secret service work, paying also the expenses of Koenig's agents on trips to Montreal and Quebec in hunting information about enlistments of soldiers in Canada and the shipments of supplies from Canadian ports. The stub book also shows that he sent agents to investigate ammunition factories in different parts of the country, and that he paid the expenses of von Skal in getting "photographs for the War Intelligence Office." He constantly was sending checks to consuls in various parts of the country to pay the expenses of reservists and agents.

TO INVADE CANADA

The diary, too, tells us of Captain von Papen's plan to invade Canada. Scarcely had he arrived in this country from Mexico, a few days after the Germans had invaded Belgium, than, as general-in-chief of the German reservists, he began to mobilize his forces for a military enterprise in Canada. If you look at the Captain's diary you see these entries: "September 1, 1914, Mr.

Bridgeman Taylor, $200;" "September 16, for Buffalo, Taylor, Ryan, $200;" "September 22, for Ryan, Buffalo, $200;" "October 14, for Fritzen and Busse, Buffalo, $40,00."

These are the earmarks of an unsuccessful military enterprise; for just as soon as Captain von Papen saw reservists gather in New York and assembling in other points he laid his plans for a concerted move on Canada. He discussed the details with his majors, captains and lieutenants assembling in New York. He met them in secret at night in the German Club and with maps and other detailed plans he set forth his mode of attack.

Captain von Papen's scheme—as they talked it over at the German Club— was to create such a reign of terror among Canadians that the provincial governments would deem it absolutely necessary to keep all the troops in Canada for defense rather than hurry them to the European battle-front. The plan, while it entailed explosions and fighting, was largely for psychological effect. One part of the scheme was to send an expedition to blow up the Welland Canal, a waterway that runs around Niagara Falls on the Canadian side and is a most important avenue of transportation for freight and passengers. *The second part was to have an invasion by German reservists upon various parts of the Canadian border.*

Captain von Papen aimed to create a panic among the Canadians, to put such fear into them that they would say to England, "We need our troops for self-protection against the Germans in the United States"—thereby putting the United States in a position of being unable to preserve its neutrality. The destruction of the canal by a tremendous explosion, or the detonation of a carload of dynamite on some railroad, or any sort of explosion in the Dominion, believed to have been supervised by Germans, would have had a tremendous effect upon the people. Doubtless this was what Captain von Papen sought; for that was the way he outlined the scheme to his assistants.

It has been stated that Wachendorf was one of the men whom von Papen gathered for secret conference in the German Club. "Von der Goltz" in a confession made to the Federal authorities said that he was asked to give his opinion about a proposal made to the German Embassy, the writer of which, a certain Schumacher, had asked for financial support in order to carry out a scheme by which *he would be able to make raids on towns situated on the coast of the Great Lakes. He proposed to use motor-boats armed with machine-guns.* Though the proposal was rejected on account of the Embassy receiving unfavorable information about the writer, "von der Goltz" next was requested to aid in a scheme of invasion of Canada with a small armed force recruited from the reservists in the United States. The scheme, which was proposed by von Papen and Boy-Ed, was abandoned as objections to it were made by Count von Bernstorff. "Von der Goltz" says he was told so by Captain von Papen.

BLOWING UP CANALS

Captain von Papen next asked "von der Goltz" to see at his hotel two Irishmen, prominent members of Irish associations, both of whom had fought in the Irish rebellion and who had proposed to Captain von Papen to blow up the locks of the canals connecting the Great Lakes, main railway junctions and grain elevators. "Von der Goltz" says he received the gentlemen at his hotel, the men bringing with them a letter of introduction written by Captain von Papen. After having taken them to his room he got further details of the matter, maps and diagrams evidently cut out of books.

"Von der Goltz" also tells of going to Baltimore to enlist a number of German reservists who were staying on a German vessel there. In that scheme, he says, he had the aid of Karl A. Luederitz, German consul. He brought them to New York, but believing that his movements were being watched by Federal agents, he sent them back. Continuing his story of the conspiracy, von der Goltz writes:

I saw Mr. Tauscher and he gave me a letter of introduction to the Dupont Powder Company, recommending B. H. Taylor, and the company supplied me with an order to the bargeman in charge of the dynamite barges lying on the New Jersey side near the Statue of Liberty. Captain Tauscher told me he would send the automatic pistols by messenger to Hoboken, to be delivered there to one of my agents at a certain restaurant, as he would be liable to punishment if he delivered them in New York without having seen my permit. The reasons why I did not apply to the police for a permit are obvious.

SCATTERING DYNAMITE

"In order to get the dynamite it was necessary for me to hire a motor-boat at a place near 146th Street, Harlem, and to put the dynamite on board in suit-cases. After returning to the dock, where I had hired the boat, I went in a taxicab, having two suit-cases with me, to the German Club to see von Papen, who told me to call for the generators and then wire again at the club. I took the dynamite to my rooms, where I kept also a portion of the arms packed in small portmanteaus ready to be moved, the rest of the dyna-mite and arms being in the keeping of two of my agents, one of whom was Mr. Fritzen, discharged from a Russian steamer, where he had acted in the capacity of purser; the other one being Mr. Busse, a commercial agent, who had lived for some time in England. The only other agent I employed was C. Covani, who attended to me personally, Tucker not being entrusted with any of those things."

Going to Buffalo with his men and equipment, "von der Goltz" was unable for some reason to receive definite instructions from von Papen, who was supposed to communicate with him under the name of "Steffens." He says:

> Being thrown on my own discretion, I determined to reconnoiter the terrain where I wanted to act first, but to do nothing further till I should receive orders.
>
> On 25th September received notice from Ryan to come to Buffalo. Having meantime received private information that the 1st Canadian Contingent had left Valcartier Camp, I knew that I should be recalled, the object of the enterprise being removed. I received from Ryan the tele-gram agreed upon in that case, but as I had spent most of the money furnished to me I asked whether Ryan had not received money to enable me to pay off the men. Ryan said he had not, but gave me some of his own initiative, and said he would wire 'Steffens.' On the 26th September I received telegram from 'Steffens' telling me to do what I thought best, and asking whether I had received the $200. Thinking it best to return to New York, all the more as funds were insufficient, I discharged Busse and Fritzen, who went to Buffalo, left dynamite and other materials in the keeping of an aviator who was manager of a restaurant at Niagara Falls, to be used again when necessary, and left with Covani for New York by way of Buffalo.

The trial of Captain Tauscher on the indictment charging him with conspiring with von Papen, von Igel and others to blow up the Welland Canal resulted in the acquittal of the German reservist; but it was admitted that von Papen and von der Goltz had developed a plot to destroy the Canal.

The evidence presented by Prosecutor Wood made a case, corroborated by details of testimony and documents, that delighted legal experts. The jurors, several of whom were of foreign birth, acquitted the captain apparently on the theory that, though he had furnished the dynamite, fuses and automatic revolvers to von der Goltz, he knew nothing about the plot, but simply had followed the orders given him by his superior officer, Captain von Papen.

OBEDIENCE IN AMERICA EXACTED

Captain Tauscher, in the witness-box, testified that he was in Germany at the outbreak of the war; that he had proffered his services as a reservist officer and that he had been directed to return to America and report to Captain von Papen. He said he knew von Papen as the head of the German secret service and that he was compelled to obey him. He protested, however, that he had exacted a promise from von Papen to the effect that he would not be asked to do anything contrary to American laws. He said he was an ordnance expert under von Papen.

Many documents, revealing the manner in which von Papen and his assistants worked, had been taken from von Igel's office, formerly von Papen's New York headquarters, and were presented as evidence by Prosecutor Wood. One document was a piece of paper in von Papen's own handwriting directing that a cheque in payment of the ammunition, pistols and dynamite, be drawn in favor of Captain Tauscher and that the same be charged to the account of William G. Sichols. Still another document was a copy of a letter written to a preacher in March, 1916, saying that Tucker, one of the witnesses in the Canal expedition, must be sent away for a time and remain quiet. The amount, $100, was enclosed for that purpose. Tucker was arrested in Texas. Although Captain Tauscher was freed, practically every charge of the prosecution was admitted except that Captain Tauscher had any knowledge of von Papen's criminal intentions.

RECKLESS ADVENTURERS HIRED

Without doubt, according to facts gathered by the Federal authorities and developed in Canada, Captain von Papen and reservist German army officers in the country did plan a mobilization of German reservists to attack Canadian points. Hundreds of thousands of rifles and hundreds of thousands of rounds of ammunition that were to be available for German reservists were stored in New York, in Chicago, and different places along the border. While the Canadian and the American officials developed evidence concerning this plan of invasion, Max Lynar Louden, known to the Federal authorities as "Count Louden," a man of nondescript reputation, who had secret communications with the Germans in the early part of the war, has confessed that he was party to the scheme for quick mobilization and equipment of an army of German reservists. Many persons insist that Louden is a fabricator, nevertheless his secret activities were of such a character that he was under suspicion by the Federal authorities. At one time, he succeeded in getting himself invited to a Government House Ball, when the Duke of Connaught was the host. His bizarre costume attracted attention. The moment it was rumored that he was supposed to have two or three wives, a State investigation was commenced, which resulted in the imprisonment of Louden. His story, therefore, is interesting.

Through German–American interests the plans were made in 1914, he said, and a fund of $10,000,000 was subscribed to carry out the details. Secret meetings were held in New York, Buffalo, Philadelphia, Detroit, Milwaukee, and other large cities, and at these meetings, Louden asserted, it was agreed that *a force of* 150,000 *men, German reservists, was available to seize and hold the Welland Canal,* other strategic points and munitions centers.

"We had it arranged," said Louden, "to send our men from large cities following announcements of feasts and conventions; and I think we could have obtained enough to carry out our plans had it not been for my arrest on the charge of bigamy. *The troops were to have been divided into four divisions, with six sections. The first two sections were to have assembled at Silvercreek, Michigan. The first was to have seized the Welland Canal. The second was to have taken Wind Mill Point. The third was to have gone from Wilson, N.Y., to Port Hope, Canada. The fourth was to have proceeded from Watertown, N.Y., to Kingston, Canada. The fifth was to have assembled near Detroit and land near Windsor. The sixth section was to leave Cornwall and take possession of Ottawa."*

After the enterprise on the Welland Canal failed and Count von Bernstorff, according to von der Goltz, disapproved of the Canadian invasion, there was a lull in any concerted move upon Canada.

By referring again to Captain von Papen's diary it is evident that he had other matters to absorb his attention. The counterfoils of the check-book record payments such as the following payment dated July 10, 1915, "H. Tauscher (Preleuther's bill for 'Res. Picric Acid') $68." The busy attaché, fighting here in the interests of the Fatherland had other plans.

BUYS UP EXPLOSIVES

Captain von Papen was keenly alive to the production of explosives in America for sale to the Allies. He was watching closely the product of the different ammunition factories. He was locating the source of the ingredients for such explosives, and he was naturally concerned in any method for preventing the export of arms and ammunition to the Allies. He possessed an unusual mind for economic data—a quality which aroused the admiration of Dr. Albert. The two men were much in conference over industrial matters that might be managed in the interest of the Teutonic Allies. Under Dr Albert's guidance he took up the project of acquiring a monopoly in toluol, a constituent of the deadly explosive T. N. T., and for buying picric acid, and liquid chlorine.

How he made recommendations on these things to Dr. Albert was shown in connection with the fiscal agent's activities. Other secret letters and reports prove that he and his associates had control of the Lehigh Coke Company, which turned out a large amount of toluol, and that he was studying to control the supply of picric acid in this country. Still further, he devoted much time to the Bridgeport Projectile Company in Bridgeport, Connecticut. This company was organized shortly after the outbreak of the war, and its promoters were prevailed upon to sell out to German buyers who, after an exposé of their activities, disposed of their holdings to still another group. Carl Heynen, an able German organizer and expert in Mexican affairs, had charge of the plant and supervised construction work and the placing of contracts for steel, ammunition and presses. The money was furnished by Hugo Schmidt and Dr. Albert.

Von Papen, Heynen, Dr. Albert, frequently in conference, planned, as excerpts from memorandum prepared by them prove, to utilize the company in several ways: (1) *to turn out supplies that could be used by Germany and her*

Allies, or by countries planning to make trouble for the United States; (2) to take the Allies' orders and fail to fill them; (3) to use the company as a means of getting information from the War Department.

One of Captain von Papen's own letters reveals the importance of these enterprises. Writing to his wife about the so-called Albert papers, he says:

> Unfortunately they stole a fat portfolio from our good friend, Dr. Albert, in the elevated. The English secret service, of course. Unfortunately, there were some very important things from my report, among them such as buying up liquid chlorine and about the Bridgeport Projectile Company, as well as documents regarding the buying up of phenol and the acquisition of Wright's aeroplane patent. But things like that must occur. I send you Albert's reply, for you to see how we protect ourselves. We composed the document to-day.

STOPPING SHIPMENTS FROM AMERICA

This search for information of military value and these plans for acquiring monopolies on certain ingredients for high explosives, carried on during the winter and spring of 1914-15, were but preliminary to a much more extensive campaign in which, as will be shown later on, Dr. C. T. Dumba, the Austro-Hungarian Ambassador, assisted by von Papen and Boy-Ed, worked with the idea, first, of controlling the arms and ammunition factories in this country, and next, of preventing the shipment of such products from America.

Naturally, during the winter and spring, Captain von Papen, Captain Boy-Ed, Dr. Albert and Count von Bernstorff, all along various lines, had been struggling to help the Fatherland, each eagerly hoping for success and some preferment extended by the Kaiser as a reward for tasks well performed.

Attacks were planned upon the Canadian Pacific Railway in the east, the Welland Canal, the St. Clair tunnel, running under the Detroit River from Port Huron, Michigan, to Sarnia, Ontario, and tunnels of the Canadian Pacific Railroad in the Selkirk mountains. It is also stated in indictments handed down by a Federal Grand Jury in San Francisco that *the conspirators in the West planned also to blow up trains carrying munitions of war, horses, arms and the like, and also to attack trains carrying soldiers.* By a study on the map of the points thus mentioned it will be observed that these enterprises were planned with the utmost care to break into sections of the Canadian transcontinental railway system and to paralyze it absolutely. It can be seen at a glance that such plots, if carried out, would have prevented soldiers and munitions of war from traveling East to ship for the Western front, or from going West to cross the Pacific, thence through Siberia to the Eastern front. *To this land scheme was added the additional plots of destroying docks by incendiarism, ships by explosions and fire.* Furthermore, *agents* on land under the direction of other men *were studying the munition factories in the western part of the United States preparatory to causing explosions and fires.*

For the execution of these campaigns against munition industries and railroads in the West and North-west, Captain von Papen had special lieutenants. The persons who have been convicted in San Francisco on the charge of conspiring to blow up railroads and to wreck the transcontinental railway system in Canada are: Franz Bopp, German consul in San Francisco; Baron Eckhart H. von Schack, German vice-consul; Lieutenant Wilhelm von Bricken, attaché of German consulate; Charles C. Crowley, detective for German consul; and Mrs. Margaret W. Cornell, secretary to Crowley. They were sentenced to two years' imprisonment each.

The question may justly be asked: "Why is it asserted that von Papen was behind and directed all these enterprises?" The Federal authorities have established a connection between von Papen's headquarters in 60, Wall Street, and the German Consulate in San Francisco, whence, according to United States District-Attorney Preston of that city, ramifications led out to the different angles of the conspiracy in the West. So strong is the evidence that the San Francisco officials have accused the defendants of using the mails to incite murder, arson and assassination. It is stated that the defendants planned to destroy munition works at Aenta, Indiana, at Ishpeming, Michigan, and at Gary and other places in the West. Among the evidence is one letter among several which has to do with the question of the price which would be paid for the destruction of a powder plant at Pinole, California, and in it reference was made to "P." The letter follows:

DEAR S.,—Your last letter with clipping to-day, and note what you have to say. I have taken it up with them and 'B.' (which the Federal officials say stands for Franz Bopp, German Consul) is awaiting decision of 'P.' in New York, so cannot advise you yet, and will do so as soon as I get word from you. You might size up the situation in the meantime.

While this and other letters show, in the opinion of the Government officials, that von Papen was concerned with the defendants mentioned in the western indictment, still other facts have been gathered against von Papen. He has been traced from Washington and New York to a number of points in the United States, his visits coinciding with remarkable closeness to the time that meetings of the alleged conspirators were being held. Captain von Papen sauntered from the Ritz-Carlton Hotel in New York one afternoon about 3.30, down Madison Avenue to 42nd Street, where he wavered for a moment as if deciding whether he would turn over for a jaunt on Fifth Avenue or drop into the Grand Central Station to buy a magazine.

After a moment he walked slowly into the station, glancing casually at his watch, and moving just before the gate closed toward the entrance to the track where stood the Twentieth Century Limited, was soon safely on board. The next day he was observed in Chicago, where he announced that he was on his way to Yellowstone National Park—and he disappeared. For several weeks he was lost to the sight of the zealous agents who were hunting him; but one day he was observed sauntering through the lobby of the Palace Hotel, San Francisco. In the course of his absence, he is said to have swung down along the Mexican border, where he caught up with Captain Boy-Ed, conferred with a number of secret agents from Mexico, with spies scattered throughout the country, and then hurried up to San Francisco, where he was busy before the agents of the Department of Justice picked him up again.

CONSPIRACIES ON LAND AND SEA

One indictment against the five defendants, phrased in legal terms, is vivid and forcible though barren of details. *It accuses the German representatives and their hirelings of plotting to blow up railway tunnels, railroads, railroad trains, and bridges, already mentioned.* Over this vast system of transportation, the indictment explains, supplies were being shipped westward for transportation on the ships *Talthybius* and *Hazel Dollar*. The defendants, it is stated, hired Smith to help them gain information about the sailings and the cargoes of ships leaving Tacoma bound for Vladivostok; that after Smith went to Tacoma, Crowley sent him money. Crowley and Smith came to New York, where they had conference with Germans who were in touch with von Papen. They next went to Detroit, where they were working out plans for the blowing up of the tunnel when they were arrested. Smith, who was working on the shipping and the tunnel end of the scheme, confessed, while van Koolbergen also has made a statement to the authorities which is of great interest, showing the workings of the defendants.

"On different occasions in his room," says van Koolbergen, "von Brincken showed me maps and information about Canada, and pointed out to me where he wanted the act to be done. This was to be between Revelstoke and Vancouver on the Canadian Pacific Railway, and I was to get $3,000 in case of a successful blowing up of a military train, or bridge, or tunnel.

"There are many tunnels and bridges there, and military trains pass every three or four days; he also knew when a cargo of dynamite would pass. He then informed me how I could get hold of dynamite, and explained to me that on the other side of the river on which the Canadian Pacific ran (I believe it was the Fraser River) the Canadian Northern Railway was in course of construction, and they had at intervals powder and dynamite magazines and that it would be very easy to steal some of the dynamite."

Several ships were blown up on the Pacific; others were disabled under circumstances that suggested conspiracies. There were schemes also to destroy docks on the Pacific coast. In view of these plots, it is striking to observe in von Papen's check counterfoils this entry: "May 11, 1915, German Consulate, Seattle (for Schulenberg), $500." An explosion in Seattle Harbour occurred on May 30, 1915.

Another excerpt from the counterfoil is dated February 2nd, 1915, recording the payment of $1,300 to the Seattle, Washington, German Consulate marked "C. Angelegenheit," a very vague word for "affair." He also paid to A. Kalschmidt, of Detroit, who is accused by the Canadian authorities of plotting to blow up armories and factories in Canada, $1,000 on March 27, 1915, and $1,976 on July 10, 1915.

While this enterprise was being mapped out in the West, a second project against the Welland Canal was in the making in New York. Paul Koenig, the intermediary between von Papen and reservists and others, had charge, it is alleged, of selecting assistants who would carry dynamite, fuses, and other equipment to the Canadian waterway. Koenig selected as his assistants Richard Emil Leyendecker, retailer of art woods, a naturalized German-American, Fred Metzler, Koenig's stenographer, George Fuchs, a German, who after a quarrel with Koenig turned State's evidence; as also did Metzler, and one or two other men. The party went to Buffalo and to Niagara Falls, being trailed all the time by agents under direction by William M. Offley, chief of the Federal investigators of New York.

EXPLOSIONS IN FACTORIES

While these plots in the West were developed in vain and some of the culprits have been convicted, still other enterprises were conceived and set in motion in the East. A great number of explosions and fires have occurred in factories in the eastern part of the country. Though many of them were due to natural causes, yet suspicions seem to show that bombs were manufactured and placed in various plants and that incendiary bombs were hidden in other factories. The men believed to have committed the crime have been traced. They invariably proved to be Germans who, under assumed names, had obtained work in the factory; and then, shortly after the fire or explosion, had disappeared. But Federal agents following them learned that they had hurried back to Germany or skipped away to Mexico or South America. Bombs for their purposes were manufactured in various places in New York and Brooklyn; and in fact the authorities have obtained statements from men who made the bombs, but thus far they have not located the chief man. A German officer skilled in the manufacture of explosives spent a number of months in New York, living on board one of the German merchantmen and conferring frequently with Germans. He disappeared one day and was not heard of until a wireless message announced his arrival in Berlin.

Into this general scheme for preventing supplies from going to the Allies fits the conspiracy of Robert Fay and his associates. Fay, a tall, military-looking man, who has told many stories, some of which are true, some of which are lies, fought in the trenches for Germany and then obtained leave of absence and a passport to come to America. He had an inventive bent, and *he conceived the idea of manufacturing high explosive mines which could be attached to the rudder posts of ships, and which would be so regulated by a detonating device that explosions would occur far out at sea.* Fay says that he sought to blow off the rudder, disable the ship, but not to sink the vessel or injure her passengers.

His aim was to frighten steamship owners, and insurance underwriters, so that the insurance on munition ships would be raised to an almost prohibitive rate. Experts, however, have testified that so great was the amount of high explosive in the mines, that it would have blown off the stern of the ship, and detonated the cargo of explosives. In other words, had Fay's scheme worked, nothing of the cargo and ship would have remained but a few chips floating upon the waves. But through the vigilance of Chief Flynn, of the secret service, and Captain Tunney, of the bomb squad of the New York Police Department, Fay's plan was detected and John C. Knox, Assistant United States District Attorney, presented the evidence so thoroughly that Fay and his brother-in-law, Walter Scholz, and Paul Daeche, a German reservist, were found guilty. They were sentenced respectively to eight, four and two years in the penitentiary. Fay admitted on the witness stand that he laid his plan before Captain von Papen and Captain Boy-Ed, that he had more than one conference with Captain von Papen; but he asserted that both men warned him not to undertake the scheme. It will be remembered that Fay escaped from the Atlanta Penitentiary within a short time after his sentence, and he is believed to be either in Mexico or back in the trenches. He undoubtedly secured aid from German sympathizers.

FIRE BOMBS

Another part of this vast conspiracy against the export of arms and ammunition was the scheme to manufacture the so-called fire bombs, which could be placed in the holds of ships and which, exploding after a certain time, would set fire to the cargoes. *By this means, thirty-three ships were stealthily attacked, with New York as a basis of operation, and damage of* $10,000,000 *was done.* Vessels sailing not only from New York, but from Boston, Galveston, and even from Pacific ports, carried these bombs stowed away in their holds. Sugar ships especially were an object of attack, for sugar forms an ingredient of a certain explosive. These ships especially were adapted to this method, because once a fire started, the bomb itself would be destroyed, and as water had to be poured into the hold, the sugar would be destroyed.

Several bombs would be placed in the same hold, as has been shown by the fact that one fire was started in a vessel before she had left port. The fire was extinguished and more sugar loaded on the boat. Scarcely had the boat got out of port when another fire started. Among the ships attacked by bombs were *La Touraine,* of the French line, the *Minnehaha,* of the Atlantic

Transport Line, the *Rochambeau,* the *Euterpe, Strathtay, Devon City, Lord Erne, Lord Ormonde, Tennyson* and many others.

The man accused of having charge of these bombs is a chemist, named Dr. Walter T. Scheele, formerly of Brooklyn, later of Hoboken, and still later a resident of some foreign country, whither he fled. He developed—or it was suggested to him by German officers—a scheme for taking a small metal container divided into two parts. Into one part would be put sulphuric acid; into another part, chlorate of potash. The sulphuric acid eating through the partition between the two sections made of aluminum, would unite with the chlorate of potash, causing combustion. Thus started, a fire so intense would be created that the container made of lead would be destroyed, and the cargo would be set on fire. Dr. Scheele, it is charged, made hundreds of these bombs, and received a large amount of money from German sources. One story is that von Rintelen paid him $10,000. Another story is that Wolf von Igel, von Papen's assistant, paid him money after von Papen left the country. Still further, Captain Otto Wolpert, Pier Superintendent of the Atlas Line, is charged with having received some of these bombs. The metal containers were manufactured on board the steamship *Friedrich der Grosse,* tied up in the North German Lloyd pier in Hoboken. The chief engineer, Carl Schmidt, who spent some time in collecting money for a monument to commemorate the part Germans have taken in the present war, is said to have been directed by a German officer to turn over the workshop of the ship as a bomb factory. At any rate, Ernst Becker, chief electrician, who has turned State's evidence, and three assistant engineers have been arrested as co-conspirators in this ship plot. Dr. Scheele's assistant, Captain Charles von Kleist, also has been arrested. It was through information unwittingly supplied by him that Captain Tunney and Detective George Barnitz, assisted by extremely keen members of the bomb squad, unearthed the whole conspiracy.

Captain von Papen, as an organizer of a part of Germany's secret service in America, as the schemer who sought to control a monopoly in certain high explosives and as a director of military enterprises—has been revealed by the Federal authorities as an extremely able servant of the Kaiser. These activities, however, were only a part of the task assigned to him by the German General Staff. He had still other plans which will be set forth in the following chapter.

III

CAPTAIN von PAPEN, BUYER of PASSPORTS and PROMOTER of SEDITION

THREE OTHER PHASES OF CAPTAIN von Papen's campaigns against the Allies upon American territory as a base of operations remain to be set forth. They are his supervision of a bureau for obtaining fraudulent passports for German reservists ordered home to fight for the Fatherland, the fomentation of insurrections in the colonies of the Allies and of war between Mexico and the United States.

PASSPORT FORGERIES

The passport bureau is a striking instance of Germany's disregard of the rights and laws in a neutral country. With the sending of Great Britain's ultimatum to Germany, the cable between Germany and the United States had been cut. The United States forbade the use of wireless for the transmission of messages in code to Germany, or the use of the cable for cipher dispatches to the warring countries. The Allies' war vessels began at once to search all passenger ships for German citizens, taking them off and sending them to concentration camps. Meantime, von Papen, Boy-Ed and the other German officials realized the utmost necessity of transmitting to their respective home offices information concerning the developments in America. They knew also the vital necessity of sending back to Berlin, army and naval officers who had been selected and trained for special commissions in the event of war.

But they had been taught in their early days the value of fraudulent passports, and to these they turned at once. The Germans had at first no regular passport bureau for the aid of German reservists. Every German, left to his own resources, did the best he could under the circumstances. Carl A. Luederitz, German consul in Baltimore, has been indicted on a charge of conspiracy in connection with obtaining a fraudulent passport for Horst von der Goltz under the name of Bridgeman Taylor. The young German has confessed that with the aid of Herr Luederitz he applied for a passport and on August 31, 1914, obtained one bearing the signature of William J. Bryan, then Secretary of State. To get that document von der Goltz took an oath that he was born in San Francisco.

But this method was rather loose, and upon Captain von Papen devolved the necessity of establishing a regular system. The military attaché, always resourceful and daring, selected for the work Lieutenant Hans von Wedell. Von Wedell had been a newspaper reporter in New York, later a lawyer; but when he received orders from Captain von Papen, he gladly undertook the work in New York, bureaus being started in other cities. He opened an office in Bridge Street, New York, and began to send out emissaries to Germans in Hoboken, directing them to apply for passports. He sent others to the haunts of hobos on the Bowery, to the cheap hotels, and other gathering places of the downs-and-outs, offering ten, fifteen and twenty dollars to men who would apply for passports. He spent much time at the Deutscher Verein, at the Elks clubhouse, where he would meet his agents, give them instructions and receive passports. His bills were paid by Captain von Papen, as revealed by the attaché's checks and counterfoils. These show that on November 24, 1914, von Papen paid him $500; that on December 5, he gave him $500 and then $300, the latter being for journey money; that he paid von Wedell's bills at the Deutscher Verein, amounting in November, 1914, to $38.05. Meantime, he was using Mrs. von Wedell as a courier, sending her with messages to Germany. On December 22, 1914, he paid Mrs. von Wedell, by his own account, $800.

BUYING PASSPORTS WHOLESALE

The passports which von Wedell, and later on his successor Carl Ruroede, Sr., obtained, were used for the benefit of German officers whom the General Staff had ordered back to Berlin. American passports, then Mexican, Swiss, Norwegian and the passports of South American countries, were seized eagerly by various reservists bound for the front. Stories were told in New York of Germans and Austrians, who had been captured by the Russians, sent to Siberia as prisoners of war, escaping therefrom, and making their way by caravan through China, embarking on vessels bound for America, arriving in New York and thence shipping for neutral countries. Among them was an Austrian officer, an expert observer in aeroplane reconnaissance, who lost both his feet in Siberia, but who escaped to this country. He was ordered home because of his extreme value in reconnoitring. The British learned of him, however, and took him off a ship at Falmouth to spend the remainder of the war in a prison camp.

Captain von Papen used the passport bureau to obtain passports for spies whom he wished to send to England, France, Italy and Russia. Among these men were Kuepferle and von Breechow, both of whom were captured in England, having in their possession fraudulent passports. Kuepferle and von Breechow both confessed.

But so reckless was von Wedell's and Ruroede's work that the authorities soon discovered the practice. Two hangers-on at the Mills Hotel called upon the writer one day and told him of von Wedell's practices, related how they had blackmailed him out of $50, gave his private telephone numbers and set forth his haunts. As a result of this and other information reaching the Department of Justice, Albert G. Adams, a clever agent, started out one day, got into the confidence of Ruroede and offered to get passports for him for $50 each. Meantime, von Wedell had gone on a trip to Cuba, apparently on passport matters, and Adams, posing as a pro-German, got into the inner ring of the passport-buyers. He was informed by Ruroede as to what was wanted.

CHANGING OFFICIAL STAMPS

Though in the early days of the war it had not been necessary for the applicant to give to the Federal authorities anything more than a general description of himself, the reports of German spies in the Allies' countries became so insistent that the Government directed that the document, bearing the United States seal, must have the picture of the person to whom it was issued. The Germans, however, were not worried. It was a simple matter to give a general description of a man's eyes, color of hair, age and so forth, that would fit the man who was actually to use the document and then forward the picture of the applicant, who, getting the passport, would sell it. Even though the official stamp was placed on the picture, the Germans were not dismayed. Federal Agent Adams rushed into Ruroede's office one day waving five passports which had been issued to him in a batch by Uncle Sam. Adams seemed proud of his work. Ruroede was delighted.

"I knew I could get these passports easily," boasted Ruroede. "Why, if Lieutenant Hans von Wedell had kept on here, he never could have done this. He always was getting into a muddle."

"But how can you use these passports with these pictures on them?" asked the agent, curiously.

"Oh, that's easy," answered Ruroede. "Come into the back room and I'll show you." The agent followed the German, who immediately soaked one of the passports with a damp cloth and with adhesive paste fastened a photograph of another man over the original upon which the imprint of the United States seal had been made.

"We wet the photograph," said Ruroede, "and then we affix the picture of the man who is to use it. The new photograph also is dampened, but when it is fastened to the passport, there still remains a sort of vacuum in spots between the new picture and the old, because of ridges made by the seal. Well, turn the passport upside down, place it on a soft ground made with a silk handkerchief, and then, taking a paper cutter with a dull point, just trace the letters on the seal. The result is that the new photograph looks exactly as if it had been stamped by Uncle Sam. You can't tell the difference."

Through the work of Adams, four Germans, one of them an officer of the German reserves, were arrested on the Norwegian-America liner *Bergensfjord,* outward bound to Bergen, Norway. They had passports issued to them through Ruroede's bureau under the American names of Howard Paul Wright, Herbert S. Wilson, Peter Hansen and Stanley F. Martin. Their real names were Arthur Sachse, Pelham Heights, N.Y., who was returning to Germany to become a lieutenant in the German Army; Walter Miller, August R. Meyer, and Herman Wegener, who had come to New York from Chile, on their way to the Fatherland. Ruroede pleaded guilty and was sentenced to three years in Atlanta, Ga., prison. The four Germans, also pleading guilty, protested they had taken the passports out of patriotism and were fined $200 each.

Von Wedell, himself, was a passenger on the steamer *Bergensfjord,* but when he was lined up with the other passengers, the Federal agents, who did not have a description of him, were deceived, and let the vessel proceed. He was taken off the ship by the British and placed in prison.

The arrest of Ruroede exposed the New York bureau, and made it necessary for the Germans to shift their base of operations; but it did not put an end to the fraudulent passport conspiracies, as will be shown. In the face of the exposures, so daring were the German agents that they continued to commit fraud upon the United States, and to put in danger every honest American traveling in Europe with an American passport.

FOMENTING REVOLTS

Captain von Papen was a supervisor and a promoter of sedition. His headquarters in Wall Street were the centre of lines running out to British and French colonies, where Germany planned at critical moments to start revolutions, if it would help her interests.

One of the enterprises which Captain von Papen, acting under orders from Berlin, supervised in the United States, was a revolt against British rule in India. Preparations for this insurrection had been in the making for years, and, in the course of all of them, German agents were working with the Hindus and also with the German-Irish in America, the latter organization being really headquarters for many Hindus traveling from Germany to England, then to United States, on their way back to India. There has been for years a sort of understanding between pro-German Irish and certain members of an American society interested in India. In this organization, prior to the war, were men who were plotting a revolution in India, who were in touch with German agents and who received German money.

Immediately after the outbreak of the war, von Papen and his agents poured more money into Hindu pockets, and made arrangements to supply arms and ammunition to Hindus. For the promotion of this German-Hindu conspiracy, two other centers were established. One was fathered by Germans in San Francisco, and another was at Shanghai, China. Confessions by men, who were active in the enterprise, tell how Hindus in sympathy with the sedition plots conferred with certain German officials in Berlin, that they came to New York—this in the course of the war—where they met certain pro-German-Irishmen and were aided financially. From New York they journeyed to Chicago, where more money was handed to them, and then to San Francisco, where they had talks with Hindu revolutionists—whose openly avowed aim is in rousing the people of India to celebrate the year 1917, "the diamond jubilee of the mutiny of 1857," by a general and universal rising against British rule in India.

HINDUS LAUNCH BOMB CAMPAIGN

Many Hindus, who were assembled in the West, also had an opportunity to study the fine art of explosive and bomb making at a bomb factory up in the state of Washington. On several occasions groups of Hindus equipped with money and carrying secretly arms with them sailed from San Francisco for the Philippines, planning thence to go to India. Furthermore, ships were chartered by German agencies to carry arms and ammunition to India and Ceylon. The American schooner *Annie Larsen* and the ship *Maverick,* both owned by a man named Fred Jebsen, a German naval officer, were chartered on the Pacific coast to sail for India in June, 1915. The *Annie Larsen* was seized by the United States officials at Hoquiam, Washington, and on board was found a cargo of rifles and ammunition. The *Maverick,* however, got away also equipped with rifles and cartridges, carrying a number of Hindus. The good ship had a most eventful voyage, the sailors and the passengers suffering many hardships, and finally reached Batavia, where she was seized by the Dutch authorities.

In the early stages of his plans, Captain von Papen had an opportunity to send a rather detailed report of events in India to the secret office in Berlin. The chance came through Captain Archibald, who was about to sail from this country, and Captain von Papen, accordingly, prepared in code a long message. This document, which has been translated, is illuminating. Here it is:

Since October, 1914, there have been various local mutinies of Mohammedan native troops, one practically succeeding the other. From the last reports, it appears that the Hindu troops are going to join the mutineers.

The Afghan army is ready to attack India. The army holds the position on one side of the Utak River. The British army is reported to hold the other side of the said river. The three bridges connecting both sides have been blown up by the British.

In the garrison located on the Kathiawar Peninsula, Indian mutineers stormed the arsenal. Railroad and wireless station have been destroyed. The Sikh troops have been removed from Beluchistan; only English, Mohammedans and Hindu troops remain there.

The Twenty-third Cavalry Regiment at Lahore revolted; the police station and Town House were stormed. The Indian troops in Somaliland in Labakoran are trying to effect a junction with the Senussi. All Burmah is ready to revolt.

In Calcutta, unrest is reported with street fighting; in Lahore, a bank was robbed; every week at least two Englishmen are killed; in the northwestern district many Englishmen killed, munitions and other material taken, railroads destroyed; a relief train was repulsed.

Everywhere great unrest, in Benares a bank has been stormed.

Revolts in Chitral very serious; barracks and Government buildings destroyed. The Hurti Mardin Brigade, under General Sir E. Wood, has been ordered there. Deputy Commissioner of Lahore wounded by a bomb in the Anakali Bazaar.

Mohammedan squadron of the cavalry regiment in Nowschera deserted over Chang, southwest Beshawar. Soldiers threw bombs against the family of the Maharajah of Mysore. One child and two servants killed, his wife mortally wounded.

In Ceylon a state of war has been declared.

THE REVOLT IN IRELAND

The extensive conspiracy on the part of Germany to start a revolt in Ireland has been thoroughly set forth in the public prints in connection with the arrest and trial of Sir Roger Casement as a rebel. Sir Roger worked openly among the Irish prisoners in Germany, traveling backwards and forwards between Ireland and Germany by means of a German submarine. Nevertheless, a very large and important American phase of this whole revolution occupied von Papen's attention prior to his recall. German agents here were in touch with the Irishmen in America, who were actively co-operating with Patrick H. Pearse.

German funds were poured into Irish hands in America, the money being used for the purchase of arms and the printing of seditious papers and leaflets. More than $100,000 was collected in America for Ireland between September, 1914, and April, 1915. Plans also were worked out with the aid of Germans in America to ship arms and supplies to the Irish rebels.

There also have been vague reports of dramatic schemes in America to arm the Arabs in northern Africa and start an uprising against British rule. There have been signs of dramatic plottings to stir up trouble in Afghanistan and in Egypt. It is a fact that various attempts have been made to ship rifles and cartridges from the United States to South America and then from South America to Africa. Some of these have proved successful. In other cases, the shipments have been stopped.

FORCING WAR IN THE UNITED STATES

Throughout all the crises arising between the United States and Germany over the submarine campaign, German agents constantly kept in view the possibility of a war between their country and this nation. They prepared for it.

"Before I left New York," confesses von der Goltz, "I had some conversation with Captain von Papen about the war, and while speaking of the end of the war Captain von Papen said: *'Should things start to look bad for us, there will be something happen over here.'* In connection with other statements of his, he speculated on America joining Germany, or on a possible uprising." The significance of that remark was shown two years and a half later when on January 31, 1917, three days before the break between the United States and Germany, an order went forth from the German Embassy in Washington. Immediately the machinery of every German merchantman interned in American ports was wrecked. The damage was $30,000,000.

Here again Captain von Papen's and Captain Boy-Ed's advice and orders were involved. *It devolved* upon Captain von Papen not only to keep in thorough touch with the development of American military affairs, but also *to study constantly the topography of the United States, the plan of cities and their surroundings from a military viewpoint. Upon him fell the task of stationing German reservists in the various cities and towns where, in case of hostilities, they would be valuable to the German cause.* German efficiency and foresight came to the front in connection with these plans. *There were under consideration at one time when the crisis between the United States and Germany was acute, military plans to start a reign of terror in America.*

First of all, Captain von Papen and Captain Boy-Ed *supervised the purchase of ground near New York and Boston, which was to be used for the construction of concrete bases for big guns in the same manner in which the Germans prepared in Belgium, England and France prior to the war.* There is absolute proof that German representatives spent money for this purpose, and that they caused to be built foundations that could be used for big guns for the purpose of making an attack upon New York City, for instance. But that was only a part of the scheme.

When von Papen and his colleague Boy-Ed were recalled, it was announced by the State Department that the reason was "improper activities in military and naval affairs." A brief summary of Captain von Papen's activities shows that he violated the courtesies extended to him as a diplomatic agent in secretly sending code messages by couriers; that he handed out money for fraudulent passports; that he schemed in military enterprises against Canada; that he plotted with Ambassador Dumba to start strikes in American factories; that he plotted in connection with other criminal activities in this country, such as blowing up factories; that he was a promoter of seditious enterprises; and that he and his associates schemed to start war between the United States and Mexico.

When he set foot upon the gangway of the steamship *Noordam,* homeward bound, he said: "I leave my post without any feeling of bitterness, because I know full well that when history is once written it will establish our clean record, despite all the misrepresentations spread broadcast." But at the moment he handed out that statement he was carrying under his arm a portfolio which was a veritable diary of his payments to law-breakers. Again he gave proof of his expression about "stupid Americans," because he thought he could make those "stupid Americans" believe him, and that he could sneak the proofs of his law-breaking past the British at Falmouth. Again the stupidity was on his side.

IV

Von IGEL AND KOENIG, TWO of the KAISER'S FAITHFUL WORKERS

WOLF VON IGEL, VON PAPEN'S MAN FRIDAY and custodian of his secret documents, was hustling about his private office on the twenty-fifth floor of 60, Wall Street, on the morning of April 19, 1916. He was hurried. His full, gray eyes glistened with excitement and he curled his stubby mustache as he glanced upon heaps of papers carefully arranged on the long council table and on the floor. Then squaring his stocky shoulders, he turned again to the big safe, bearing the seal of the Imperial German Government, and swinging back the heavy doors, extracted another bundle of papers which he ranged among the other sheets with military precision.

"It's eleven o'clock and Koenig should be here now," he said in German to another employee of von Papen's who was with him. "These papers must be packed up at once."

He paused and then began a mental inventory of each stack of papers to make sure none was missing. All these documents—there were hundreds of them, and their weight, as revealed by a government agent, was seventy pounds—had belonged to von Papen. They revealed the inner workings of the German spy system in America and a great part of the world. They told many of the details. Those papers, connecting the German Government with violators of law in America, were a vast responsibility for any officer of von Igel's age. Naturally, the young man was keyed to a high pitch of excitement; for hitherto they had come from the safe only piecemeal, and to permit daylight to reach so many at one time was almost a little more than von Igel's nerve could stand.

Perhaps he had a presentiment. In fact, secret agencies had been at work to instill in him a feeling of uneasiness. Von Igel, stopping again and again to twirl his mustache, knew that von Papen and Captain Tauscher had been indicted on a charge of plotting to blow up Welland Canal. Word also had come to him that still more ominous events were portending and the idea—by stealthy prearrangement—had been given to him to ship all the documents to Washington, where they would be absolutely safe. Therefore von Igel was both busy with his packing and intensely perturbed.

"A man to see you, Herr von Igel," announced a stout German attendant. "He refuses to tell his business except that it is important."

Von Igel was gruffly directing his agent to make the stranger specify his name and mission when the door was flung open. In dashed Joseph A. Baker, of the Department of Justice, in charge of Federal Agents Storck, Underhill and Grgurevich.

"I have a warrant for your arrest!" shouted Baker, who had a warrant charging the German with complicity in the Welland Canal enterprise. Von Igel eyed the intruders for the fraction of a second. With one spring he reached the safe, and swinging the doors shut, was turning the combination when Baker leaped upon him bearing him to the floor. Then followed a battle of four Americans against two Germans, the attendant having been quieted by the flash of revolvers.

"This means war," yelled von Igel. "This is a part of the German Embassy and is German territory. You've no right here."

"You're under arrest," said Baker soothingly, as he pulled a revolver.

"You shoot and there'll be war," answered von Igel, while Storck and Underhill grappled with a third. "I'm connected with the Embassy and you can't arrest me." The first skirmish was quickly ended by von Igel, realizing the importance of the documents entrusted to his care and straining every resource to outwit his captors, he fought again and again, facing revolvers and braving fists to reach the telephone to call for the help of the German Ambassador and prevent the officers from gathering up the documents. But he was unsuccessful. As the agents led him from the office, they met Koenig, von Igel's associate, and von Papen's agent in many enterprises just entering. Koenig, who was already facing three charges growing out of his activities, was rendered speechless by the sight of von Igel in custody and some of his documents in possession of the government.

The mass of documents—it makes no difference whether the Secretary of State, for reasons of State or of law, orders their return—not only set forth the secrets of Germany's activities in this country; but they also told what part von Igel and Koenig played in the invisible war in America. They show how both men were errand boys, carriers of cash and of messages for von Papen and Boy-Ed.

WHO WAS VON IGEL?

Concerning young von Igel there is much mystery. At the outbreak of the war he was reported to be wandering around looking for a job, willing to work for any wages. Then von Papen picked him up, paying him a salary of $238 a month. There is a rumor, too, that he is a grandson of Graf von Waldersee, one time Germany's Chief of Staff. That he is a man of importance is indicated by the manner in which he was trusted by von Papen, Boy-Ed, and Dr. Albert. When in an automobile ride from Captain Tauscher's home on Long Island with von Papen and Dr. Albert, he met with an injury, he was hurried secretly to a hospital. Every effort was made to hide his identity; but Dr. Albert and von Papen visited him frequently. Von Papen paid the hospital bills and charged them up to "War Intelligence."

Almost immediately upon beginning service under von Papen, he leased the offices in Wall Street, putting down in the contract "advertising" as the purpose to which the rooms were to be devoted and never making any statement as to his connection with the German Embassy. He quickly gave von Papen every reason to trust him fully and won the respect of the reckless attaché. Though he did not begin work for von Papen until September, 1914, he had, it is charged, a hand in the first Welland Canal enterprise.

HANDLING MONEY FOR EVIL ENDS

Von Igel also handled money for von Papen. For instance, on March 27, 1915, the latter gave to his secretary a check payable to his order for $1,000 and on the counterfoil of his check-book he wrote "for A. Kaltschmidt, Detroit," who since has been accused by the Canadian authorities as an accomplice in the project against Canadian armories and munition factories. It was von Igel, furthermore, who cashed many checks for von Papen, the proceeds of which were to go to secret agents starting on missions to the enemy's country. He carried confidential messages which von Papen would not put in writing. He handled the code books in compiling and deciphering messages. He carried orders to Koenig, conferring with him and directing him when to meet von Papen.

When von Papen was preparing to leave the country at the request of President Wilson, he began to turn over his documents to von Igel for safe keeping. He gave him instructions as to the custody of the papers and the cleaning up of work left undone. In his regard, he undoubtedly followed Dr. Albert's instructions put in a letter from San Francisco: "If you should leave New York before my return, we must try to come to some agreement about pending questions by writing. Please instruct Mr. Amanuensis Igel as precisely as possible. You will then receive in Germany the long-intended report of the expenses paid through my account on your behalf."

So von Igel, as a trusted clerk, took unto himself the duties of confidential man for von Papen and for other big Germans who began but were obliged to leave unfinished certain projects in this country. There were many lines of information and activities converging to von Papen, afterwards to von Igel. After von Rintelen left this country, part of his schemes were entrusted to von Igel, who saw men with whom von Rintelen or his assistants had dealt. For instance, he has been indicted jointly with Dr. Scheele, Captain Gustave Steinberg, von Rintelen's aid, for complicity in a plan to ship articles abroad under fraudulent manifests and thus deceive the Allies. One of these schemes was to export lubricating oil, much needed in Germany, to Sweden as fertilizer. Some of the payments for this purpose were made after von Rintelen sailed for home.

With von Papen gone and Koenig arrested, von Igel became a somewhat important person, taking upon himself the attaché's prestige and a lot of Koenig's work after the latter's arrest. Many, many checks were cashed by von Igel in the four months intervening between the attaché's departure and the former's arrest. He carried on von Papen's work in a miniature way, conferring with many secret agents, giving orders and preparing reports in code for dispatching to Germany.

While von Igel, in point of family, education and confidential association with the big German agents in America, is an important link in the Teutonic spy chain, Paul Koenig ("P. K."), is more striking because of his rough activities, his underground connections and his associations with law-breakers. He was a sort of business manager of Germany's secret service in the eastern part of America.

"P. K."

"P. K.," as his hirelings called him, was a sort of boss, an unmerciful autocrat in the lower world, physically fearless, trusting no man and driving every man to work by the use of violent abusive language, boastful of his skill, physical prowess and his craft. In appearance, he gives this impression. A tall, broad-shouldered man, he has bony fingers and arms long and powerful reaching almost to his knees. His dark, sharp eyes dart suspiciously at you from beneath black, arching eyebrows, showing defiance and yet a certain caution. A truly typical person he is for the work for which he was selected, and though perhaps a little too boastful, such supreme confidence undoubtedly is a necessary attribute of any man who would acquire any degree of success in such undertakings.

Koenig is another product of the Hamburg-American Steamship Line— the Kaiser's very own. Prior to the war he was superintendent of the company's police, having a half-score men under him and keeping watch on the pier workers or investigating complaints received by the management. He had grown to that task from similar training in the Atlas Service, a subsidiary corporation. He had spent years among 'longshoremen, bossing them and cursing them. He knew wharf rats, water-front crooks, and was thoroughly acquainted with their schemes—as naturally such a man would be. He understood thoroughly how to handle men of the rough type.

When the war started and von Papen was searching for an assistant organizer, he found in Koenig's little police force a splendid nucleus of just what he needed. At his request the *Hamburg-American Line* quickly put Koenig at von Papen's disposal and straightway von Papen began to link up to Koenig's police a number of channels of information, to supply him with reservists for special assignments, to suggest to him how to spread out and install spies in various places to gather important facts. Koenig accordingly became the business manager of a part of Germany's secret service, not only gathering information, but acting as a link in the labyrinth system employed by von Papen in communicating with the reservist or agent selected to do certain work in behalf of the Fatherland.

How varied and steady was his work for von Papen is revealed by the latter's checks. Here are a few excerpts: "March 29, 1915, Paul Koenig (Secret Service bill), $509.11; . . . April 18, Paul Koenig (Secret Service bill), $90.94; . . . May 11, Paul Koenig (Secret Service), $66.71; . . . July 16, Paul Koenig (compensation for F. J. Busse), $150; . . . August 4, Paul Koenig (5 bills Secret Service), $118.92," and so on. Remember also that von Papen only paid from his check account for a part of Koenig's expenses, other German officials who employed him receiving a bill for the special work.

KEEPING WATCH ON SPIES

"P. K." also kept a most carefully prepared note-book of his spies and of persons in New York, Boston and other cities who were useful in furnishing him information. In another book he kept a complete record of the assignments on which he sent his men, the purpose and the cost. In this book of names were several hundred persons—German reservists, German-Americans and American clerks, scientists and city and Federal employés—showing that his district was very large and that his range for picking facts and for supervising other pro-German propaganda was broad. For his own hirelings or reservists, over whom he domineered, he had specially worked out a system of numbers and initials to be used in communicating with them. These numbers were changed at regular intervals and a system of progression was devised by which the agent would know when his number changed. He also employed suitable aliases for his workers. These men likewise had codes for writing letters and for telephone communication, and they knew that *on fixed days these codes changed.*

Always alert for a listening ear or a watchful eye—because playing the eavesdropper was his job—he looked for spies on himself. He believed that his telephone wire was tapped and that he was overheard when he spoke over the telephone. Accordingly, he instructed his men in various code words. For instance, if he told an agent to meet him at five o'clock at South Ferry that meant: "Meet me at seven o'clock at Forty-second Street and Broadway."

His wire was not tapped, but P. K. kept the men who were spying on him exceeding busy and worried. He would receive a call on the telephone and would direct the man at the other end of the wire to meet him in fifteen minutes at Pabst's, Harlem. Now from Koenig's office in the Hamburg-American Building to 125th Street, it is practically impossible to make the journey in a quarter of an hour; but his watchers learned that Pabst's, Harlem, meant Borough Hall, Brooklyn. Just as he eluded espionage for days and months, this man, skilled in shadowing others and in doing the vanishing act whenever necessary, boasted that the Federal authorities or the police never would get him. "They did get Dr. Albert's portfolio," he said one day, "but they never will get mine, for I won't carry one."

SHADOWS FOLLOWING SHADOWS

He sought likewise to elude Americans trailing him. He never went out in the daytime that he did not have one or two of his agents trailing him to see whether he was being shadowed. He used to turn a corner suddenly and stand still so that a detective following came unexpectedly face to face with him and betrayed his identity. Koenig would laugh heartily and pass on. He loved to jibe the American authorities and oft-times he would dodge around a corner and then reappear to confront the detective with a merry jest and pass on. By that means he came to know many agents of the Department of Justice and many New York detectives. When he started out at night he used to have three of his own men follow him, and by a prearranged system of signals inform him if any strangers were following him.

The task, consequently, of keeping watch of Koenig's movements was most difficult and required clever guessing and keen-headed work on the part of the New York police. So elusive did Koenig become that it was necessary for Captain Tunney to evolve a new system for shadowing Koenig and yet not betray to him the fact that he was under surveillance. One detective, accordingly, would be stationed several blocks away and would start out ahead of Koenig. The "front shadow" was kept informed by a series of signals whenever Koenig turned a corner so that the man in front might dart down the street beyond and by a series of manœuvres again get ahead of him. If Koenig boarded a street car, the man ahead would hail the car several blocks beyond, thus avoiding any suspicion from Koenig. In other instances, detectives, guessing that he was about to take a car would board it several blocks before it got abreast of Koenig. Because of his alertness, he kept Detectives Barnitz, Coy, Terra and Corell always on the edge; but they finally ran him down.

It was never possible to overhear any conversation between Koenig and any man to whom he was giving instructions. Koenig always made it a point to meet his agents—some of his workers he never permitted to meet him at all—in the open, in parks in broad daylight, in the Pennsylvania Station, or the Grand Central Station. There, as he talked to them, he could make sure that nobody was eavesdropping. In the open he met many a man for the first time, talked with him and then said:

"Be at Third Avenue and Fifty-ninth Street at 2:30 tomorrow after-noon beside a public telephone booth there. When the telephone rings, you answer it."

The man would obey the request. Promptly at the minute named, the telephone rang and the man answered the telephone. A strange voice spoke to him and told him to do certain things, perhaps to be at a similar place on the following day and receive a message, or he would receive instructions as to what he should do and where he should go to meet another man, who would give him money and instructions as to what he should do. The voice at the other end of the wire was speaking from a public telephone booth and was thus reasonably sure also that the wire was not tapped.

Koenig trusted no man. *He never sent an agent out on a job without detailing another man to follow that man and report back to him the movements of the agent and the person whom that man met.* He was severe with his men when they made their reports to him, and always insisted that they do exactly what he told them and never permitted them to use their own initiative. So stubborn was he in sticking to his own ideas that some of his men used to call him "the Westphalian, bull-headed Dutchman."

As to the outline of Koenig's activities, his book of spies, the great mass of information gained by trailing him, and by study of the documents seized in his office, show that *he had spies along the water front on every big steam-ship pier. He had eavesdroppers in hotels, telephone switchboards, among porters, window-cleaners, among bank clerks, corporation employees and in the Police Department.*

To Roger B. Wood, formerly assistant United States District-Attorney in New York, is due the credit for the unfolding of the intricate and varied schemes charged against Koenig. He studied the evidence for months as it was developed by Federal agents under Superintendent Offley of the New York office and Captain Tunney, and prepared for trial the cases against the German agent.

One of Koenig's spies was listed in his book as "Special Agent A. S.," namely Otto F. Mottola, a detective in the warrant squad of the New York police force whom he paid for special work. The note-book revealed Mottola as Antonio Marino, afterwards changed to Antonio Salvatore. Evidence was produced at Mottola's trial at Police Headquarters that Koenig paid him for investigating a passenger who sailed on the *Bergensfjord;* that he often called up Mottola, asked questions and received answers which Koenig's ste-nographer took down in shorthand. In other words, Koenig sought to keep closely informed as to the developments at Police Headquarters, and to be advised, perhaps, of the inquiry being made by the police into the activities of the Germans. Mottola was dismissed from the force because of false state-ments made to his superiors when asked about Koenig.

STARTING TROUBLE IN CANADA

"P. K." also dispatched men to Canada to gain information concerning the Canadian preparations for war, and facts that could be used by the Germans here in planning attacks upon munition factories, railroads and transporta-tion facilities in the Dominion. An Irish employee of the *Atlas Line* has been arrested on a charge of planning with Koenig to start a "military enterprise" against the Dominion. The employee, named Justice, is accused of going to Quebec to ascertain the number of troops which were being transported by the Dominion of Canada to ports in France and Great Britain; the names of the steamships on which said troops were being transported; the kind and quantity of supplies which were being shipped from the Dominion to France and Great Britain, and other information which would or might be of value to the German Government, and which would assist the military operations of the German Government.

The complaint stated that the undertaking was one of hazard, and came within the purview of the statute forbidding the undertaking of any military venture with this country as a basis of operation. It says, further, that Justice and Metzler, Koenig's secretary, left New York on September 15, 1914, and went to Quebec; that Koenig left New York on September 18 and met Metzler in Portland, Me., and that he went to Burlington, Vt., where on September 25 he conferred with Justice. The authorities also say that Metzler and Justice gained a varied assortment of information in Quebec; that they inspected the fortifications there, went to the training camps, observed the number of men, the condition of the men and estimated the time when they would be sent to the front.

VARIOUS ALIASES

In his meetings with various persons who had been picked for some daring enterprise, Koenig is accused of having employed various names. The Federal authorities give him at least thirteen, among which are Wegenkamp, Wegener, Kelly, Winter, Perkins, Stemler, Rectorberg, Boehm, Kennedy, James, Smith, Murphy and W. T. Munday.

After indictments had been returned against some of the Hamburg-American officials for conspiring to defraud the United States of legal clearance papers, Koenig, assisted by a private detective in the pay of Captain Boy-Ed, developed a scheme to get affidavits from tugboat captains to the effect that they had supplied English war vessels patrolling off Sandy Hook with provisions.

The plan was to turn sentiment against the British by proving that the British were doing the same thing that had been charged to the Germans. Accordingly, Koenig called a number of tugboat captains to a room in the Great Eastern Hotel, New York, and offered them a contract to haul provisions to the English cruisers. He told them that the captains were extremely suspicious of boats approaching the war vessels, and the affidavits were necessary to allay their fears that the tugboats might have a few Germans with bombs on board. So, in return for sworn statements from them to the effect that they already had been carrying supplies out to other English cruisers, he, Koenig, was to give them a monthly contract to do the work. Many of the tugboat captains signed the affidavits; but the scheme was exposed before the Germans really made any use of the documents. So carefully did Koenig work that he made the stenographers who took the statements transcribe the notes in his presence, give him the shorthand notes and he immediately destroyed them.

SPIES IN BANKS

Through the arrest of Koenig and the facts obtained thereby, one of the mysteries concerning the Germans' method of getting information about the shipment of munitions of war to the Allies was cleared. *They knew the number of the freight car rushing to the Atlantic seaboard and its exact contents.* They knew the ship's hold into which that product was to be placed; but how they got this data was a mystery until Koenig was caught. Then Metzler, Koenig's secretary, made a confession that cleared the mystery. Agent Adams got the confession.

Besides having spies in some of the factories throughout the country, the Germans had one great fountain of information in the foreign department of the National City Bank, an institution that has carried hundreds of millions of dollars in financing the purchase of supplies for the Entente Powers. That source was Frederick Schleindl, a German who has since been convicted of selling stolen information and sentenced to three years in a New York State prison.

Schleindl, only twenty-three years old, came to this country from Germany several years ago, obtained work with a private banking firm, and after the war started was shifted to the National City Bank. He had influence to get the position, and, incidentally, it may be said, that for years prior to the war German agents, trained financiers, have been stationed in New York, making friends and learning conditions, so that at the critical time they could, by underground means, succeed in getting positions for such men as Schleindl who would betray their trust.

SECRET INFORMATION ON BANKS

When the war started Schleindl registered with the German Consul, giving his address and his place of business. One day word reached him that a German wished to see him, and going to the Hotel Manhattan he was approached by a man who introduced himself as Koenig. The latter sounded him thoroughly as to his sentiments on the war, and then outlined the scheme by which Schleindl was to help Germany and make $25 a week. Schleindl was to keep his eyes open for all letters and cable messages bearing on the deposits of the Allies with the bank, the payments of orders and other facts bearing on the war.

The bank clerk succumbed, either through patriotism or love of money. And Koenig had placed his finger on exactly the right spot; so accurate was he that there seems no doubt that he received guidance from a master spy higher up, who knew banking operations thoroughly, and where to go for information. It quickly developed that Schleindl could obtain information of two very important kinds.

First, he received in his department cable messages bearing on war orders and deposits by the Allies. The day he was arrested he had in his pocket certain messages and letters addressed to the National City Bank. One had come from the Banque Belge pour Etrangers in regard to a shipment of two million rifles that was being handled through the Hudson Trust Company. Another message that he picked up and handed over to Koenig had come from the Russian Government, directing the bank to place at the disposal of Colonel Golejewski, a Russian naval attaché, a large amount of money for the purchase of war materials.

Secondly, the bank paid for orders of goods as soon as they had been inspected and delivered on board ships at the seaboard. The manufacturers sent their bills of lading to the bank, showing the carload shipments and the vessel to which they were consigned. *Thus accurate information was obtained as to every item, the railroad route of shipment and the name of the vessel.* All this information was turned over to Koenig, who passed it along for dissemination to the proper persons. Consequently, *the Germans knew exactly what ships to attack; in what vessels to place their fire bombs or other explosives.*

Schleindl was accustomed to meet Koenig almost every night and hand him papers. Sometimes he would go to Koenig's office, where "P. K.," Metzler and Schleindl would spend many hours copying the documents. Other times Schleindl would give the papers to Koenig and receive them on his way to work, so that they would be in their proper place the moment any bank official desired them. *Koenig pleaded guilty in the Court of Special Sessions to an information charging him with having corrupted the boy to sell such information. Koenig was set free on a suspended sentence.*

The National City Bank leak is only one of a hundred channels through which Koenig and his agents received information. Koenig compiled it with the aid of his secretary, conferred with von Papen or Boy-Ed. He would spend a few weeks gathering facts, and then he would pack hundreds of papers into a trunk and run down to Washington. Arriving there, he would take a taxi to a rooming house, where he would unpack his trunk, and put the contents into another trunk in an adjoining room.

As weeks went by and Koenig believed he was escaping police and Federal espionage, he grew bolder, more defiant of the authorities, and louder in his talk. He treated his employés with less consideration. He always followed a principle of never hiring the same reservist for a second job. Then he quarreled with George Fuchs, a relative whom he had employed to go to Buffalo with him. The police heard of that quarrel, and quickly got into the confidence of Fuchs, obtained his confession, and enough information on which to arrest Koenig. He has been indicted by the Federal authorities twice on charges that may get him six years, if convicted.

The two men were active workers for a time. Koenig continues in New York, but von Igel sailed with Count Bernstorff when the latter was dismissed from this country.

V

CAPTAIN KARL BOY-ED, the EMPEROR'S SOCIAL DANDY and von TIRPITZ'S TOOL

IN THE DAYS BEFORE THE Kaiser booted his spur through the treaties of Europe, you could observe, almost any afternoon, a faultlessly-attired man—well built, his big round head resting firmly on a powerful neck—sauntering down Connecticut Avenue, the Rotten Row or Fifth Avenue of Washington. Jauntily swinging his cane and puffing at his inevitable cigarette, he would bow gracefully in greeting the members of the capital's smart set. He could be seen later at tea at the Chevy Chase Club, then among government officials and diplomats at the Metropolitan Club, or a guest at the Army and Navy Club. He was much desired at the most brilliant functions in New York in the winter, or at the resorts where, in the summer, the wealthiest and most exclusive Manhattanites gathered. One always found him graceful, suave, clever at repartee, effervescing natural humor—the object of admiration on the part of matchmaking mothers, and the reported seeker after an American heiress—but always mingling with the persons in official, diplomatic and navy circles who knew the innermost government secrets.

He was Germany's Beau Brummel, Captain Karl Boy-Ed, the Kaiser's naval attaché, seemingly more interested in the frills, foibles and gaieties of society than in the supremacy of the German Navy. Very much like an American in appearance, Oriental in his sense of luxury, and possessing the French quality of subtlety in rapid-fire wit, he lacked apparently every vestige of the much vaunted Teutonic efficiency. He would occasionally, however, drop out of the scenes of beauty and charm, traveling about the country, visiting warships, tramping over coast country, scrutinizing fortifications, or places where Uncle Sam would have coast defenses, until finally it began to be whispered that Captain Boy-Ed knew as much about the American Navy and coast forts as did the naval officers themselves. Under the veneer of lightness

206 × MEIN SPY

and graceful ease, the naval attaché hid with the craft to which that Turkish part of his ancestry made him heir, the persistent methodical thoroughness of his German ancestry.

And, when the Kaiser set the dogs of war loose, Boy-Ed shunted aside the cloak of frivolity, disappeared almost entirely from festive gatherings, settled down by day to room 801, No. 11, Broadway, New York, receiving code messages as "Nordmann," and by night to his suite in the German Club, where he delved into records, conferred with associates and elaborated plans for activities on the seven seas. From a hale, jolly fellow he became—as if by the shift of the magic wand of a Turkish sorcerer—a veritable machine, mind and body, working for the Kaiser. A man of great brain power, erudite, fertile in schemes, for long an aid to Admiral von Tirpitz, he assumed charge in America of all enterprises dealing with the naval phases of the Teutonic warfare in this country and in or near American waters. These were activities which, despite his boast: "They haven't got any evidence against B. E.," caused his dismissal from America by President Wilson.

BOY-ED'S CAREER

Born of a Turkish father and German mother—the latter, Ida Boy-Ed, a novelist much loved in Germany—he possessed an unusual combination of traits, a mingling of Oriental subtlety, the brutal frankness of the Prussian, and the artistic genius of his mother. He elected for the navy, and early displayed qualities that attracted von Tirpitz's attention. The admiral took him up and made him one of his "Big Six," young German officers who were admitted to the naval lord's most secret councils and trained for just such executive work and such emergencies as the great war produced. Having both a literary and constructive ability, in addition to unusual qualities as a tactician and naval officer, he was selected by Grand Admiral von Tirpitz as his chief lieutenant, and was made the head of the news division. As such, he had charge of propaganda enlightening the German people and arousing a demand for a bigger navy. He prepared articles for the newspapers and compiled pamphlets arguing for many battleships, in all of which he cleverly instilled a distrust of England. Prior to each appropriation for an increase in the German fleet, Boy-Ed carried on a Press campaign designed to educate the public as to the urgent necessity for more Dreadnoughts and submarines. By this means, an appropriation equal to a hundred million dollars was obtained in 1910.

For five years, prior to his arrival in Washington in 1911 as the Kaiser's naval representative, he served under von Tirpitz, making trips around the world, observing and working out the details of Germany's plans for breaking Great Britain's sea-power. Because of the work which he performed, the unusual ability which he displayed, and because Germany was seeking to surpass the naval power of the United States, then the second only to Great Britain, he was sent to this country. When he arrived here, he impressed Americans by his knowledge of America and American ideas. With ample tact and keen insight into American customs, he began immediately to make himself almost an American. Speaking English fluently and possessing an unusually attractive personality, he made himself extremely popular.

NAVAL STUDENT IN TIMES OF PEACE

His duties in peace times, naturally, were to study the American Navy and gain whatever facts he could about American war vessels, the personnel of the navy, the government's plans for increasing the fleet's power and building up coast defenses; also to pick up whatever he could, openly or stealthily, about the secret plans of America in the use of her battle-fleet. When the war started, a thousand and one more tasks devolved upon him. As von Papen was in Mexico, he had for a time to look after the military attaché's secret service, and, after being relieved of that, he devoted himself to the manifold details peculiar to naval intelligence. Like von Papen, he, too, had a staff of experts. They began, under his direction, delving into every phase of American naval activities, seeking information about the naval plans of the Allies, striving to exert their influence to prevent the shipment of arms and ammunition from this country. Boy-Ed's work lay also in supervising the registration of naval reservists with the German consuls, providing for the return of as many as possible of them to the Fatherland, assigning spies to the country's enemies, and collecting all naval information bearing upon the war.

WATCHING BRITISH VESSELS

Seated in his room 801, Captain Boy-Ed gathered a great mass of facts of value to Germany from enemy sources and from neutral nations. From his room, which was stacked with maps of the sea and steamer routes, he sent directions to his spies. He forwarded information about ships—English merchantmen and British warships—that could be utilized by the German Government in raids on Allied commerce. He also gave directions for provisioning the German raiders scouring the Seven Seas for enemy ships—an enterprise just as romantic—though in violation of American laws—as the spectacular dashes of the *Karlsruhe, Emden* and the *Prince Eitel Friedrich.*

Here was a project in which before the war and in preparation for it, the German Admiralty and the *Hamburg-American Steamship Company* participated; and after hostilities began, it was simply necessary for the captain through his staff of assistants or in person to issue orders. The Atlantic phase of the enterprise, its financing, its spectacular features and its illegality were presented to a Federal court in New York by Roger B. Wood, the Assistant United States Attorney, at the trial and conviction of several *Hamburg-American Line* officials: Dr. Karl Buenz, its general representative in America, George Koetter, supervising engineer, Adolf Hachmeister, purchasing agent, and Joseph Poeppinghaus, second officer and supercargo, on the charge of conspiring to obtain from the collectors of the ports false clearances for ships in connection with the coaling and provisioning of raiders. The Pacific phase of the scheme has been unearthed by United States District Attorney Preston in San Francisco.

SMUGGLING SUPPLIES TO RAIDERS

Two years before Germany sent a declaration of war to England, and just when a crisis in European affairs was impending, Dr. Karl Buenz, who never before had engaged in steamship business, came to New York as the American head of the *Hamburg-American Line.* Prior to that he had been a judge in Germany, a consul in Chicago and New York, and a minister to Mexico. One of the first things which came to his attention was the completion of a contract between the Admiralty Division of the German Government and the steamship company for the provisioning, during war, of German warships at sea from America as a base. Arrangement also was made for communication between these ships and the company by the Admiralty's code. The documents dealing with this agreement were kept locked up in the German Embassy in Washington, and the *Hamburg-American* officials declined to produce them at the trial, "because in that agreement," Prosecutor Wood asserted, "I venture to say the whole plan whereby false clearances should be obtained is worked out in detail."

When Germany stood on the brink of war and England stood ready to pen her in by a blockade, the Admiralty Division sent its orders to make ready to provision the raiders. Dr. Buenz himself, on July 31, 1914—before the war—received a cable which he read, and then at once sent to the German Embassy for safe-keeping. Straightway Boy-Ed was in and out of Dr. Buenz's office, giving directions as to the warships needing supplies and whither the provision ships should proceed by routes outside the regular freight lines. He kept urging upon Dr. Buenz the necessity of haste, and even before the German Government advanced the cash, the ships were chartered—others purchased—under bonds that guaranteed payment to the owners in the event of seizure. Twelve or more ships in all set forth from Atlantic ports, carrying coal and food supplies bought with Hamburg-American cash.

The steamship *Berwind,* which had been chartered and loaded in a hurry, was the first to sail. When some of the conspirators met in Dr. Buenz's office, there was hesitancy as to who should apply for clearance papers—documents of which Dr. Buenz testified he knew nothing. They finally told G. B. Kulenkampf, a banker and exporter, that the *Berwind* was loaded with coal—she had coal and provisions—and told him to get the clearance papers. He did so, swearing to a false manifest, as he afterwards admitted. In getting such clearance papers, Germany's agents aimed to prevent the Allies from learning about the supply ships. Germany desired, naturally, to carry on this work secretly in order to deceive her enemies and prevent her adversaries from knowing where the German cruisers were.

Such a ruse may be a legitimate trick in war, but the German Government or her agents had no right to use the American Government in such an enterprise. So men employed by the *Hamburg-American Line* went to the collector of the ports from which these ships sailed, making affidavits as to the cargo—generally false—and the destination for which they sailed—also false. On board these ships—the *Berwind* and the *Lorenzo,* sailing from New York presumably for Buenos Aires on August 5 and 6, 1914, respectively; the *Thor* from Newport News for Fray Bentos, Uruguay; the *Heina* from Philadelphia in August, for La Guayra; the *Mowinckle, Nepos* and others—the officials put supercargoes bearing secret instructions. These men had authority to give sailing orders to the captains once they were outside the three-mile limit. They knew that the ships were not bound for the ports designated, but to lonely spots on the high seas, where they would lie in wait for the arrival of the German cruisers, whose captains would receive the "tip" by wireless.

210 × MEIN SPY

RISKY WORK FOR SKIPPERS

Very few of the supercargoes, however, accomplished their aims. The *Berwind* reached a point near Trinidad where Supercargo Poeppinghaus directed the ship to lie to. Presently five German ships, the *Cap Trafalgar, Pontus, Elinor Woerman, Santa Lucia* and *Eber* appeared, and after the task of transferring the supplies to them was begun, the British converted cruiser *Carmania* came up. A brisk fight ensued between the *Carmania* and the *Cap Trafalgar,* lasting for two hours, and ending when the German ship sank.

One representative of the *Hamburg-American Line* sought to use bribery to effect his purpose. One of the ships chartered was the *Unita,* in charge of Eno Olsen, a Canadian citizen of Norwegian birth. The German supercargo made a mistake in thinking that Olsen was friendly to Germany. When, however, the supercargo explained to him after they had got out to sea, what the purpose of the cruise was, Captain Olsen baulked.

"'Nothing doing,' I told the supercargo," Captain Olsen testified, with a Norwegian twist to his pronunciation. "So the supercargo offered me $500 to change my course. 'Nothing doing—nothing doing for a million dollars,' I told him.

"The third day out he offered me $10,000. 'Nothing doing.' So," concluded Captain Olsen with finality, "I showed him my citizenship paper. I said the *Unita* cleared for Cadiz; and to Cadiz she goes. After we got there I sold the cargo and looked up the British Consul."

The provisions for each ship were ordered under directions from the *Hamburg-American* officials who eventually provided the money. The *Hamburg-American Company* received three payments of $500,000 each from the Deutsche Bank in Berlin. In addition, $750,000 was sent to Boy-Ed by exchange through Kulenkampf's firm, Wessels, Kulenkampf & Company, from the Deutsche Bank, making $2,225,000 in all. Telling of the receipt of the money, Kulenkampf testified:

> Some time after that, Captain Boy-Ed came to me and asked if I had received money from Berlin. I said, 'Yes,' and he told me that it was for him. I asked him to obtain instructions, and a little later I was telephoned to hold the money at the disposal of Boy-Ed. I followed the instructions of Captain Boy-Ed. He instructed me at different times to pay over certain amounts, either to banks or to firms. I transferred $350,000 to the

Nevada National Bank in San Francisco, $150,000 to the *North German Lloyd,* $63,000 to the *North German Lloyd.* That left a balance of approximately $160,000, which was placed to the credit of the Deutsche Bank with Gontard & Company, successors of my former firm. That amount was reduced to about $57,000 by payments drawn by Captain Boy-Ed's request to the order of the *Hamburg-American Steamship Company.*

MONEY SPENT FREELY

How part of the money was spent is shown by the following account of payments through the *Hamburg-American Line:*

STEAMER	TOTAL PAYMENT
Thor	$113,879.72
Berwind	73,221.85
Lorenzo	430,182.59
Heina	288,142.06
Nepos	119,037.60
Mowinckel	113,867.18
Unita	67,766.44
Sommerstad	45,826.75
Fram	55,053.23
Graecia	29,143.59
Macedonia	39,139.98
Navarra	44,133.50
Total	**$1,419,394.49**

But Boy-Ed's supervision of supplies to the raiders covered both the Atlantic and the Pacific Oceans. While the *Hamburg-American* took charge of handling the supplies in the North and South Atlantic, another German agency is accused of doing similar work on the Pacific. That accounts for Boy-Ed's transfer of money to the West, where his cash also was used in the purchase of at least one ship. Boy-Ed's funds, amounting to more than $600,000, have been traced to the Pacific. In following these payments it is important to observe how differently and more cleverly Boy-Ed handled his money than von Papen. Unlike the military attaché, he paid out little money by personal cheque; but he had accounts with various commercial firms to whom he gave orders for payments. Working with the ingenuity of an adept in covering up his tracks, he caused money in large amounts to be shifted from one bank to another, from one firm to another, through various cities until after myriad devious turnings and twisting it finally reached its destination. He used various commercial concerns as his bankers.

Out on the Pacific Coast, Boy-Ed employed members of the German consulate to distribute the money and supervise provisioning. Two indictments returned against Germans and others in San Francisco charge that an effort was made to employ that port as a "naval base" for provisioning the German raiders; that false manifests were filed for the succouring of merchantmen; that supplies were transferred to the German raiders. More than $150,000, it is specifically charged, was paid out for this purpose by the German consulate.

The outfitting of the steamships *Sacramento, Olsen and Mahoney, Mazatlan* and the barque *Retriever* are said to be charged to the defendants. One device employed in San Francisco Bay to outwit the Government officers watching for violations of the neutrality laws was to fill the *Retriever* with coal, and then announce that the vessel would be used for an expedition on the high seas to take cinema pictures of a stirring sea drama. But the officials were not hoodwinked. The steamer *Sacramento,* formerly the German-owned *Alexandria,* which, after the war started, was bought by the *Northern and Southern Steamship Company* and which flew the American flag, left port piled high with supplies of all sorts, including sauerkraut and beer, and reached Valparaiso, Chile, empty. All her supplies were transferred to German cruisers and a German supply ship at Masefuero Island, near the Chilean coast.

Captain Fred Jebsen, a lieutenant in the German naval reserve, took a cargo of coal south on his boat, the *Mazatlan,* for delivery at Guaymas, Sonora, Mexico. He transferred it to lighters, which carried it to the German cruiser *Leipzig.* Jebsen also is said to have planned to pilot a ship to India, and being frustrated, made his way in disguise to Germany, where he is reported to have been drowned by the sinking of a submarine. The *Olsen and Mahoney,* a steam schooner, was loaded with supplies, but after considerable controversy with customs officials, was unloaded. In the early days of the war, the cruisers *Leipzig* and *Nürnberg* lay off San Francisco. The *Leipzig* put to port for supplies which were granted in quantities permissible under international law. Efforts to supply still further quantities are alleged by the Government.

One of the picturesque incidents of the provisioning, which reveals how minutely Captain Boy-Ed looked after finances and sets forth other phases of his work on the high seas, as directed from No. 11, Broadway, is revealed in the piratical cruise of the good ship *Gladstone,* rechristened under German auspices *Marina Quezada.* Her owner, when she bobbed into the view of Captain Boy-Ed, was a Norwegian syndicate; but what money was behind that group it has not been possible to learn. Under the name of *Gladstone,* the ship had plied between Canada and Australia; but shortly after the outbreak of the war she put into Newport News. Then Captain Hans Suhren, a sturdy German formerly of the Pacific coast, appeared in New York, called upon Captain Boy-Ed, who took most kindly interest in him, and then departed for Newport News. Here he assumed charge of the *Gladstone.*

"I paid $280,000 in cash for her," he told First Officer Bentzen. After making arrangements for his crew, he flitted back to New York, where he received messages in care of "Nordmann, Room 801, 11, Broadway, N. Y. C." Meantime, in consultation with Captain Boy-Ed, the captain received instructions to erect a wireless plant on his ship—the equipment having already been shipped to the *Marina Quezada*—and to hire a wireless operator. Boy-Ed handed Suhren a German naval code book, gave him a map with routes marked out and sailing instructions that would take him to the South Seas, there to await German cruisers. Food supplies, ordered for a steamer which had been unable to sail, were waiting on the piers at Newport News and Captain Boy-Ed ordered them put on the *Marina Quezada.* Two cases of revolvers also were sent to the boat. In a like manner, it may be observed, ships on the Pacific had been equipped secretly with arms and wireless.

Again Suhren went back to his boat, kept the wireless operators busy, hurried the loading of the cargo, which was under the supervision of an employé of the *North German Lloyd,* and needing more money before sailing in December, 1914, he drew a draft for $1,000 on the *Hamburg-American Line,* wiring Hachmeister, the purchasing agent, to communicate with "Room 801, 11, Broadway," the office of our friend Boy-Ed.

Prior to his departure, the skipper had difficulty with the registration of his ship. Though he insisted he owned her, a corporation in New York whose stockholders were Costa Ricans were laying claim to ownership, for they really christened her, and got provisional registration for her from the Costa Rican minister in Washington. It was necessary, however, in order for the ship to get permanent registration, to go to Port Limon, Costa Rica, and register there. So hauling down the Norwegian flag, that had fluttered over the ship as the *Gladstone,* Captain Suhren ran up the Costa Rican emblem.

Then, having loaded his ship and having obtained false clearance papers stating his destination as Valparaiso, based upon a false manifest, sailed for Port Limon. But the Costa Rican authorities declined to give Suhren permanent papers, and, accordingly, being without authority to fly any flag and in such status not permitted under international law to leave port, Suhren was in a plight. He waited, however, until a heavy storm came up one night, then quietly slipping his anchor, he sped out into the high seas, a veritable pirate. Finally, as he neared Pernambuco, he ran up the Norwegian flag, put into port and got into such difficulties with the authorities that his ship was interned. His supplies never reached the raiders, and Boy-Ed, at No. 11, Broadway, learned from Suhren of another fiasco. Suhren is supposed to have been taken prisoner to Canada.

Had the *Hamburg-American* officials carried out their part of the enterprise by means of the false clearance papers—and the same applies to Boy-Ed—a guest of the nation and to others engaged in the project—they would have put the American Government in the position of officially endorsing their work of deceit and stealth. "Is it a nice thing," asked Prosecutor Wood, "to have this Government endorse the lies of these defendants?"

Boy-Ed, furthermore, violated the clause of *The Hague Conference of 1907, which says: "Belligerents are forbidden to use neutral ports and waters as a base of naval operation against their adversaries."*

QUEER WIRELESS CODES

Another operation that appealed to Captain Boy-Ed's ingenuity was the use of the wireless to frustrate the enemy. He had given implicit instructions to Skipper Suhren in regard to the use of the wireless. Members of the crew of the *Sacramento* are accused of breaking the Government seal and using the radio plant. The Government officials also found such extensive misuse of the German-owned wireless plants in America that they were obliged either to close them down or take them over. The Sayville, Long Island, plant, finally was taken over and operated by the government.

CUTTING IN ON MESSAGES

But Boy-Ed delighted in circumventing the Federal authorities. A few instances have been published, but there remain hundreds of cases which the Federal radio inspectors have un-covered. To Chief Flynn of the Secret Service and Charles E. Apgar, an inventor, much credit is due for detecting one ingenious method used by Boy-Ed and others for sending out wireless messages. Apgar, an enthusiastic wireless operator, spent much time "listening in" to the messages sent every night from the wireless plants at Sayville, Long Island, to Germany. Finally he hit upon the scheme of recording the splash and splutter of the radio in a phonograph. After perfecting his device he began to "can" the Berlin messages—coming and going—every night. Then reeling off these messages on his phonograph, he would study again and again the dots and dashes of each word. He observed that messages had been repeated by the Sayville operator, that numbers were thrown in at intervals and finally that between words there were gaps of varying lengths—all means undoubtedly of sending messages in code—a new language of science invented by the Germans. Many messages were sent by Boy-Ed, himself. It was after a thorough study of these canned messages that the government began to operate the Sayville plant itself.

FRAUDULENT PASSPORTS

Like von Papen, Boy-Ed was under orders to send spies to the adversaries' countries, to make arrangements for naval reservists to return to Germany, all of which required the use of fraudulent passports. While there have been charges that Germany had a factory for forging passports and while the *New York World* charged, at the time of Boy-Ed's recall, that he had dealings with a gang of forgers and counterfeiters, who made passports, there is evidence that the naval attaché did pay money to German reservists, who procured passports fraudulently. One of these men was Richard Peter Stegler, a Prussian, thirty-three years old, who had served in the German Navy, and afterwards came to this country to start on his life work. Before the war he had applied for his first citizenship papers; but his name had not been removed from the German naval reserve list.

"After the war started," says Stegler, a well-dressed young man with rather stern features, "I received orders to return home. I was told that everything was in readiness for me. I was assigned to the naval station at Cuxhaven. My uniform, my cap, my boots and my locker were all set aside for me, and I was told just where to go and what to do. But I could not get back at that time and I kept on with my work."

Stegler then became a member of the German secret service in New York. "There is not a ship that leaves the harbor, not a cargo that is loaded or unloaded, but that some member of this secret organization watches and reports every detail," he said afterwards. "All this information is transmitted in code to the German Government." In January, 1915, if not earlier, Stegler was sent to Boy-Ed's office, and there he received instructions to get a passport and make arrangements to go to England as a spy. Boy-Ed paid him $178, which he admits, but denies that it was to buy a passport. Stegler immediately got in touch with Gustave Cook and Richard Madden, of Hoboken, and made use of Madden's birth certificate and citizenship in obtaining a passport from the American Government. Stegler has pleaded guilty to the charge and the two men were convicted of conspiracy in connection with the project. Stegler paid $100 for the document. Stegler, Cook and Madden each served a term on Blackwell's Island.

"I was told to make the voyage to England on the *Lusitania,*" continued Stegler. "My instructions were as follows: 'Stop at Liverpool, examine the Mersey River, obtain the names, exact locations and all possible information concerning warships around Liverpool, ascertain the amount of munitions of war being unloaded on the Liverpool docks from the United States, ascertain their ultimate destination, and obtain a detailed list of all the maritime ships in the harbor.'"

NEW YORK, THE CENTER FOR SPIES

"I was to make constant, though guarded inquiries, of the location of the Dreadnought squadron which the Germans in New York understand was anchored somewhere near St. George's Channel. I was to appear as an American citizen soliciting trade. Captain Boy-Ed advised me to get letters of introduction to business firms. He made arrangements so that I received such letters and in one letter were enclosed some rare stamps which were to be a proof to certain persons in England that I was working for the Germans.

"After having studied Liverpool, I was to go to London and make an investigation of the Thames and its shipping. From there, I was to proceed to Holland and work my way to the German border. While my passport did not include Germany, I was to give the captain of the nearest regiment a secret number which would indicate to him that I was a reservist on spy duty. By that means, I was to hurry to Eisendal, head of the secret service in Berlin."

Stegler did not make the trip because his wife learned of the enterprise and begged him not to go. He also had been detected by Federal Agent Adams and was placed under arrest in February, 1915, shortly after he decided to stay at home. In his possession were all the letters and telegrams exchanged between him and Boy-Ed, none of which, however, said anything about passports. There was one telegram from "Winko," who was Captain Boy-Ed's servant.

LODY SENT TO DEATH

Stegler also said that he had been told that Boy-Ed previously had sent to England Karl Hans Lody, the German who in November, 1915, had been put to death as a spy in the Tower of London. Lody also had been in the navy, had served on the Kaiser's yacht and then had come to this country and worked as an agent for the *Hamburg-American Line,* going from one place to another.

Still another man who had a fraudulent German passport was a German naval reservist, who had shipped as a hand on the freighter *Evelyn* carrying horses to Bermuda. On one trip that he took, practically all of the horses were poisoned and were lost. He, however, was arrested by Federal authorities on the charge of using the name of a dead man in order to get an American passport.

In passport matters and the handling of spies, Captain Boy-Ed was more acute and more subtle than his colleague, von Papen. Nevertheless, the Government officials succeeded in getting a clear outline of his activities. It seems quite likely that after the arrest of Ruroede in December, 1914, when suspicion was directed to von Papen as the superintendent of the passport bureau, the management thereof was switched to Boy-Ed. The exposure of Boy-Ed's connection with Stegler made it necessary for the German Government to change its system once more.

Boy-Ed, as has been shown, had supervision of naval affairs and matters pertaining to the sea. He issued information to the Press bearing on

Germany's conduct of her naval warfare. He made pleas for an embargo on the export of arms and ammunition. He received from Count von Bernstorff all information which the Ambassador obtained bearing on that question, and, on one occasion, the Count sent him a list of the countries which had forbidden the export of war supplies.

The conviction throughout the country has been steadily growing, since the exposure of von Papen's methods, that Boy-Ed was not an innocent associate of the military attaché. The Federal authorities, in fact, have unearthed a large amount of evidence to show active participation by Boy-Ed in these enterprises, for to him they simply were a part of the war of Germany on her enemies. Colonel Roosevelt, who has made a special study of Germany's crimes on neutral territories, has expressed the sentiment of Americans in a speech at the Academy of Music, Brooklyn, on January 30, 1916, in these words:

> The German and Austrian Governments through their accredited representatives in the embassies here have carried on a campaign of bomb and torch against our industries. The action our government should have taken in view of this campaign was not action against Dumba, von Papen and Boy-Ed, but the holding of the German and Austrian Governments themselves responsible for every munition plant that was blown up or damaged.

The roll of Boy-Ed's associates, as indicating his knowledge of plots of violence, is illuminating. He employed Paul Koenig for a series of secret activities. He was said to have known Captain Eno Bode, dock superintendent of the *Hamburg-American Steamship Line* in Hoboken, and Captain Otto Wolpert, another dock superintendent, both of whom, it is charged, were involved in a bond conspiracy.

Boy-Ed and von Papen, in many secret conferences on board the *Vaterland* in Hoboken, where they were sure of no eavesdroppers, developed details of their war on America and the campaign of violence on land and on sea to stop the carrying of munitions of war to England, France and Russia. Von Papen superintended the campaigns on land and projected his work upon the seas. The moment, however, the schemes, as papers found in von Igel's possession prove, had anything to do with the sea, he consulted Boy-Ed.

INVOLVING AMERICA IN THE MEXICAN MUDDLE

One of the causes for the summary dismissal of both Boy-Ed and his confrère, von Papen, from America, was their schemes to involve this nation in a conflict with Mexico, to bring about American intervention in that country and thus prevent America's supply of explosives and rifles from being used exclusively against Germany. Boy-Ed, prior to the war, had opposed the suggestion of intervention, but he changed his mind when he began to appreciate the fact that America in arms would take the powder, high explosives and rifles that Europe was buying. He always was a warm supporter of General Huerta, for, when von Papen was in Mexico, getting acquainted with Huerta, Boy-Ed, addressing his colleague there, wrote: "I was especially pleased by what you wrote about Huerta, the only strong man in Mexico. In my opinion, Admiral von Hintze was not quite right in his estimate of him. For Huerta can scarcely be such a drunken ruffian as Hintze often implies, if only because a chronic drunkard could hardly have kept so uncertain a position under such uncommonly difficult circumstances. I met a number of people in Mexico City who were in close touch with Huerta, and without exception they all spoke very highly of the President's patriotism, capacity and energy."

PLANNING WAR WITH THE UNITED STATES

Of Boy-Ed's schemes to do his share in preparing, from a naval standpoint, for war between Germany and the United States, of the plots to create disorganization in the American seaports and to render the German merchantmen useless to Americans, much evidence has been gathered by Federal investigators. Of his methods in getting information secretly from the Navy Department and from battleships, of his placing spies, ready for any deed of daring, on the warships, a greater amount of information has been learned than ever will be made public by the Government. Suffice it to say precautions already have been taken against those schemes. All these formed the basis for the decision to hand Boy-Ed his passport. Summing up Boy-Ed's work for the Kaiser in America, accordingly, we have his supervision of the shipment of supplies to the German raiders, his activities in fraudulent passports and his co-operation with Dr. Dumba. When President Wilson requested the Kaiser to recall his military and naval representatives, he made the announcement that his action was due to "their improper activities in military and naval affairs," a double-barreled assertion applying to both men.

Captain Boy-Ed, on his return home, received from the Kaiser the decoration of the Order of the Red Eagle, third class, with sword, in "recognition of his services in the United States." He would undoubtedly, for "those services," except for the immunity granted him as a member of a diplomat's official family, be facing prison in the United States with Dr. Karl Buenz and other officials of the Kaiser's own steamship line.

VI

CAPTAIN FRANZ von RINTELEN, GERMAN ARCH-PLOTTER

WHEN THE GERMAN SPY SYSTEM was working smoothly and giving gleeful satisfaction to its builders, the War Staff in Berlin sent to America a masterly schemer who threw sand into the machinery. He was Franz von Rintelen, a finished product of the Prussian war-mold. He had been born with a supreme confidence in the conquering destiny of Germany. He had been trained for his work in that order of things and he had subordinated to the needs of the Empire, his business, wealth, brains, energy—yes, his very soul. *He had been ordered here to undertake, with the aid of Germany's agents, the enormous task of isolating commercial and financial America, as a base of war supplies, from Europe.* In trying to accomplish his aim, *he sought to wreck American institutions and to use the United States as a battlefield in a rear attack on the Allies.*

Highly imaginative, keen of foresight, a master of detail, a superb organizer, and conscienceless in the execution of his plans, he seemed like a man so perfectly trained for the emergencies of war that under no circumstances would he lose his poise. And yet when put face to face with his own misjudgments and forced to take measures to retrieve himself, he lost the very quality which his training was meant to insure—a carefully calculating eye and a cool head. His strategic moves consequently proved to be ridiculous errors that led to his own confusion.

In a brief sojourn in America he moved in the shadows of mystery, employing the vast network of German spies, hiring Americans, using thugs and setting in motion manifold plans for gigantic enterprises that involved the entire governmental, industrial and financial organizations of the country. When he went away, his work unfinished, his aims unaccomplished and a large amount of money wasted, there remained a multitude of trails, isolated facts and incidents suggesting his activities. Seizing these clues, Federal agents under A. Bruce Bielaski and William M. Offley, began to dig up von Rintelen's associates, to get their stories and to obtain proof of his doings—his letters and telegrams, his agents' speeches and the instructions which they tried to carry out. Taking these facts, Raymond H. Sarfaty, then Assistant United States Attorney in New York, working with patience and skill, fitted the details together into a series of great mosaics—depicting conspiracy, fraud, purchases of strikes, bribery, perjury, forgery, sedition, almost treason. Those pictures show how hidden forces—Americans land Germans working in secret—during von Rintelen's presence in this country, plotted to cause commotions in political, industrial and financial spheres, and all to aid Germany in derogation of our rights.

PICTURES OF VON RINTELEN

In every one of them, von Rintelen looms as the audacious plotter, man of mystery, user of a hundred aliases, supreme egotist, a vaunted aid to the Kaiser and a Teutonic Dr. Jekyll and Mr. Hyde. In one picture, you see him in exclusive homes on Fifth Avenue, a "mold of form"—scarcely thirty-eight years old, slim and upstanding, with stalwart shoulders, the bearing of an aristocrat, short stubborn hair, a mustache with a like independent twist, and greenish-gray eyes that sparkled defiance. He garbed himself in the cut of London's most artistic tailors and selected the colors of his ties, his shirts and his socks with a view to perfect harmony. He was the "glass of fashion" on the tip-toe of courtesy, beguiling with his gallant quips and charming his hearers by his fascinating stories and comments.

Other pictures show him under an assumed name, in conference with conspirators. He might meet them secretly in offices, or in hotels, or he might pick them up in an automobile, whizzing along at full speed and handing gold to hirelings who for a price were ready to undertake some criminal job. He might be seen dining in one of Broadway's most alluring cabarets, ordering the rarest of wines and boasting of his schemes to accomplish in America what would be equivalent to Germany's capture of Paris.

VON RINTELEN'S VALUE

And who is this man? He is so important that when made a prisoner in England, the Kaiser offered to exchange for the nobleman any ten British prisoners that King George might select. He is so esteemed in Germany that large amounts of gold were placed at the disposal of Americans to go to England and by hook or crook effect his escape. Rumor has sought to make him a relative of the Hohenzollerns. Another report has put him down actually as the Duke of Mecklenburg-Schwerin. But persons, who knew him well in Berlin, saw him in the United States and at the prison camp in England, say he is von Rintelen. He is said to be the son of a former member of the Kaiser's Cabinet; but the German "Wer Ist's" does not credit that man with a son. Still, von Rintelen married into one of the wealthiest families in Berlin, his wife being a member of the von Kaufmann family, and he had a commanding social position in Germany.

He is wealthy in his own name, his fortune being estimated at $15,000,000. He is a director of the Deutsche Bank and the National Bank für Deutschland. He is, or was, a member of the big financial group of Germany, and as such was one of the Emperor's financial advisers. His knowledge and advisory sphere included England, the United States and Mexico; and of the financial and industrial resources of these countries he was supposed to have a broad and comprehensive knowledge. He had influence also because he was a friend of the Kaiser and a close associate of the Crown Prince.

A SECRET AGENT'S TRAINING

Von Rintelen's work was cut out for him in his early youth. His qualifications were considered and he was assigned to studies in preparation for the tasks he gave promise of performing most efficiently. At the gymnasium and the university, he divided his time between economics and finance. In addition, he spent considerable time in the navy, finally became a Captain-Lieutenant, and as such qualified for the General Navy Staff. He, too, was one of von Tirpitz's young men chosen for definite lines of naval secret service and financial campaigns that would be of value to the further development of the navy.

Finance may have been a mere cloak for the real nature of von Rintelen's naval assignments abroad, or his secret service training may have been a necessary part of his training for a high place in the Teutonic financial world. Graduating from the university and finishing the prescribed part of his tutelage under von Tirpitz, he went to London where he obtained employment in a banking house. While there, he was learning not only finance, but he was a part of that branch of Germany's spy system that radiated through banking institutions to the various concerns allied therewith. Under the guidance of wise heads in Berlin, he grasped far more facts about banking conditions than ever were suspected by his English associates.

Next he came to America. He entered the banking house of Ladenburg, Thalmann & Co., spending a short time there and then moving to other banking institutions, some of which were branches of English and Canadian banks. He obtained letters of introduction from big bankers to bankers scattered throughout the United States. He grew in knowledge, learned American banking methods, the connections of banks with big industries, and sought to make affiliations of benefit to German institutions. He served, meantime, as Germany's naval representative at the exercises in commemoration of John Paul Jones. His entrance into New York's society was paved for him through the German Embassy's friends. He was a guest at social functions where only the most favored were invited. He was accepted as a member of the New York Yacht Club. He was entertained at Newport. He made friends among the biggest men in New York; for he was attractive, a remarkable cosmopolite, extremely learned, versed in international questions, speaking English, French and Spanish fluently, and, above all, he was an inimitable raconteur. He showed himself at all times an ardent pro-German, arguing for a union of Germany and the United States in the event of war.

Through his wide acquaintanceship and innumerable avenues open to him, he gained information about America such as only the most favored business men in America possess. He left this country finally saying he would go to Mexico to investigate conditions there, hoping that eventually he might be able to open Mexican and South American branches of a German bank. But before going, he had acquired insight not only into American banking connections with Canada, but also with Mexico. He knew the big financial groups interested in the development of the natural resources of those countries and he knew thoroughly America's actual and industrial preparedness for war.

BACK TO GERMANY

So, returning to Berlin in 1909, he again took up his banking business and continued his close affiliation with von Tirpitz and the Big Navy crowd, setting forth the facts he obtained and making recommendations for the development of Germany's secret service in America. He became more prominent socially than ever, making it a point to entertain Americans. When his American acquaintances turned up in Berlin, they invariably found von Rintelen a most cordial and extravagant host. He obtained introductions at court for some; and he introduced others to the Crown Prince. When the war started, Americans who besought von Rintelen for help in the exciting days, found him most obliging.

But before circumstances that brought von Rintelen to this country arose, he received several Americans. One was a wealthy American manufacturer who owns a large factory in France. Being on intimate terms with von Rintelen, he called upon him and explained how the plant had been closed down with the invasion of the Germans, causing a big financial loss. He appealed for von Rintelen's intercession to have the concern continue business. He got von Rintelen's promise of aid but returned to the United States before any definite action was taken as von Rintelen was too crafty to make any move before he was ready to ask his compensation.

Von Rintelen was ordered, in January, 1915, by the General War Staff to come to America. It had become necessary to send a man here to buy supplies of copper, rubber and cotton and to take extensive precautionary measures against the Allies getting war munitions from America. He was scornful of American facilities for filling Allies' orders and backed by the authority of the War Staff and a group of Berlin's ablest bankers, he made arrangements for his trip. Knowing he must elude the English, he obtained the Swiss passport of his sister Emily V. Gasche, who was with her husband in Switzerland. He erased the "y" of Emily and had the passport altered in other ways to suit his needs, traveling as Emil V. Gasche, a Swiss citizen. As he bade goodbye to his wife and two little daughters, he talked arrogantly of a quick trip to America past English spies, promised big accomplishments for the Emperor and an early return home.

Von Rintelen, confident and daring, is said to have gone first to England. After gathering facts about the manufacture and importation of munitions of war and England's method of increasing the supply, he disappeared suddenly and is believed to have gone to Norway. When he was on the high seas due to arrive in New York on April 3 he sent a wireless message to the American owner of the factory in France, asking an interview at the pier. Von Rintelen, acting at what was the time best suitable to himself, had succeeded in having the American's factory opened. He wished, on landing, to give him this information and in return get help in the plans that he wished to put into effect. As the American did not go to the pier, the nobleman, always alert and suspicious, hired a detective who spent a week investigating. He finally met this man, told him in part the purpose of his trip to America, and used him as a means of getting introductions to men who would prove valuable to him.

JEKYLL AND HYDE

Herr von Rintelen, having dropped the guise of E. V. Gasche, immediately began to play Dr. Jekyll and Mr. Hyde. Dr. Jekyll, visiting the Yacht Club, and calling upon wealthy friends, proved a more charming, more delightful von Rintelen than ever, meeting influential business men who were selling supplies to the Allies. He was presented to society matrons and débutantes, whom, by flattery and subtlety, he sought to use to further his purposes. To these, he was Herr von Rintelen in America on an important financial mission. But occasionally, he made wild boasts of plans. As a typical Mr. Hyde he sought information from I von Bernstorff, von Papen, Boy-Ed, about the production of war supplies. Astounded by what he learned from them and corroborated from other sources, he began to realize how utterly he had misjudged America's potential resources and what a blunder he had made in his statement to the General War Staff.

Within a brief time von Rintelen realized, with a vividness that chilled him, the capacity of America to hand war materials to the Allies and her rapidly increasing facilities to turn out still more ammunition and bullets. The facts which he obtained struck him with triple force because of the knowledge he had about the war moves. *It is upon a basis of the supplies of munitions in the Allied countries, particularly Russia, as von Rintelen knew them, that his acts are best judged and upon this basis only can sane motives be assigned to the rash projects which he launched.*

He understood these three striking facts thoroughly: (1) that the German drive on Paris had failed because in two months the Germans had used up ammunition they confidently expected to last a half a year; (2) that the English and French in the west could not take up the offensive because ammunition was not being turned out fast enough; and (3) that the Russian drive on Germany and Austria would soon fail for lack of arms and bullets.

In the winter and spring of 1915 the Russians had made a drive into Galicia and Austria, hurling the Austrians and Germans back. In May they had advanced victoriously through the first range of the Carpathian mountains. Meantime the German General Staff, as von Rintelen knew, was preparing for a big offensive against the Russians. The War Staff knew of Russia's limited capacity to produce arms and ammunition, knew that during the winter with the port of Archangel closed by ice, her only source for new supplies lay in the single-track Siberian railway, bringing material from Japan. He realized that by spring the Russian resources would well nigh be exhausted, and that with the beginning of the projected Austro-German offensive the crucial necessity lay in shutting off supplies from Russia. He knew that England and France could not help her, and, therefore, the American source must be cut off absolutely. But spring had already come, ships were sailing for Archangel laden with American explosives, shells and cartridges.

A PLOTTER AT WORK

Von Rintelen, startled by his mistaken estimate of American industrial preparedness, and frantically determined that Russia's supplies must be crippled, that the cargoes going to France and England must be held back, began mapping out his gigantic enterprises. These conditions were the big compelling motive; for von Rintelen's reputation was at stake. *The work for which he had been so carefully trained was bound to fail unless he acted quickly.* Desperate measures were necessary. With that situation in view he exchanged many wireless communications with his superiors in Berlin—messages that looked like harmless expressions between his wife and himself in which the names of Americans who had been in Berlin were used both as code words and as means to impress upon the American censor their genuineness. He obtained as a result still greater authority than he had received on the eve of his departure from Germany.

In his quick fashion, he often boasted, and there is foundation for part of what he said, that he had been sent to America by the General Staff, backed by $50,000,000 to $100,000,000; that he was an agent plenipotentiary and extraordinary, ready to take any measure on land and sea to stop the making of munitions, and to halt their transportation at the factory or at the seaboard.

He mapped out a campaign, remarkable for detail, scope, recklessness and utter disregard of American laws. These plots proved von Rintelen, or the German General Staff, a master of thoroughness and ingenuity, for he took into consideration the psychology, the customs, habits, and reported weaknesses of Americans.

His schemes in brief were (1) *the purchase of war materials for Germany as a means of inflating prices;* (2) *the fomenting of war between the United States and Mexico as a means of compelling the American Government to seize all available war munitions;* (3) *a campaign of publicity and the arousing of public sentiment to bring about an embargo on arms shipments;* (4) *strikes in American industries; and* (5) *a series of acts of violence against factories and munition-carrying vessels.*

Von Rintelen rapidly mobilized his forces of money and men. He went first to the Trans-Atlantic Trust Company, where he was known by his right name and where he arranged his finances. Money was transferred from Berlin through the usual German channels—large corporations with German affiliations—and placed to his credit in various banking institutions. He deposited large amounts in the Trans-Atlantic Trust Company and large amounts, totaling millions, in other banks. He next rented an office on the eighth floor of the same building that housed the trust company and had a telephone running to it through the switchboard of the banking institution. He registered with the county clerk as the E. V. Gibbon Company, a purchaser of supplies, signing his name to the document as "Francis von Rintelen."

Using the name of Fred Hansen, he received persons in that office. There he summoned to his help a part of the German espionage system. He did not hesitate to call upon any German for assistance, and thousands of willing workers were at his disposal. If he wished a naval reservist, he knew where to get him; if a member of the landsturm was needed for any detail, he was called. From Boy-Ed, he received data about the sailings of ships; from von Papen, facts about munition factories. He met Koenig and assigned numerous tasks to him, particularly the location of munition factories, their products and exports.

His first task, merely incidental in importance compared with his other aim, was the succoring of the Fatherland and the blocking of the Allies through purchases. He participated with influential Germans in the scheme of buying the leading munition factories. He attempted the running of the British blockade. Dr. Albert also was buying goods, but von Rintelen, working on a much larger scale, commensurate with his fertile imagination, and employing a staff of agents, took charge of the shipments of raw products and food. Carrying on these purchases through E. V. Gibbon Company, using the name of Gibbon and Hansen, he had as aid Captain Steinberg, a German naval officer. *Through him, von Rintelen chartered ships, purchased materials, caused false manifests to be made for the cargoes, and arranged for shipment to Italy and the Scandinavian countries, whence they were trans-shipped.*

IN THE MAZE

This officer, it is charged, had dealings with Dr. Walter T. Scheele, the alleged manufacturer of fire bombs, and arranged with him to mix lubricating oil, so urgently needed in Germany, with fertilizer, and ship the oil as "commercial fertilizer." The oil was to be extracted by a chemical process in Germany. Von Rintelen, through Steinberg, importuned Dr. Scheele to ship munitions as farming implements, giving him $20,000 for that purpose. Dr. Scheele did bill the shipment as requested, but he did not lie because he shipped farming machinery, taking a fat commission. Again von Rintelen was hoodwinked. The officer, von Igel and Dr. Scheele have been indicted on a charge of conspiring to defraud the United States by false manifests.

"*The British blockade,*" von Rintelen used to boast with purring pride, "*is a myth. I can send to Germany all the goods that I wish.*"

So skilfully did he plan—he was a master of detail and a consummate artist in concealing his movements—and so many different aliases did he employ, that at first he attracted no attention, and after a time his doings were credited to a German Red Cross lecturer. Because of the German method of switching agents to cause confusion to the enemy's spies, it is probable that some Red Cross agents did figure in the purchases. The investigations of the Federal authorities, however, have laid to von Rintelen the schemes carried on from April to June, 1915.

Von Rintelen boasted that he bought provisions, amounting to $2,000,000 a week, for shipment to Germany through Denmark. More than $25,000,000 was consumed by von Rintelen in his blockade-running, many of the boats being seized by British warships.

Von Rintelen also took a flier at the most elusive and puzzling diversions of war-brokers, namely the purchase of the 350,000 *Krag-Jorgensen rifles which the United States Government had condemned just prior to the outbreak of the war.* Around those rifles was centered more intrigue and deceitful scheming than was incited by almost any other single article connected with the war. Even after the Government had announced emphatically that they were not for sale, and *President Wilson had told one banker: "You will get those rifles only over my dead body,"* every belligerent tried to get them.

Von Rintelen heard that by bribing Government officials he could obtain the guns. He was stirred; for if an official would accept money for one thing, he could be influenced to do other things to help Germany. Sending out agents, he offered to purchase the rifles. He encountered a man who put a price of $17,826,000 on them, part of the amount being intended, von Rintelen was told, as bribes of several millions of dollars for Government officials.

Things looked bright to von Rintelen. *"So close am I to the President,"* said the agent who promised to deliver them, *"that two days after you deposit the money in the bank you can dangle his grandchild on your knee."* But von Rintelen apparently came to realize that he was dealing with the secret agent of another government, who was laying a trap for him, and he quickly withdrew.

THE "LUSITANIA" GOES DOWN

Then the Lusitania was torpedoed. Americans who were connected with von Rintelen's schemes to ship supplies to Denmark and to buy the Krags, became alarmed over the prospect of war with Germany. They cut off negotiations with him and fearing possible government investigations, they began to talk. Part of the activities of a mysterious German of the name of Meyer and Hansen reached both the Government officials and newspapers. A reporter on the New York *Tribune* who got a "tip" of the real facts and who hunted for von Rintelen, frightened the German agents from the office of the E. V. Gibbon Company. Steinberg skipped back to Germany disguised as a woman carrying a trunk full of reports showing the necessity of concerted action to prevent the Allies from getting American war materials.

Von Rintelen slipped away to an office in the Woolworth Building. On disclosing something of his schemes to men there, he was quickly ordered out. He moved to the offices, in the Liberty Tower, of Andrew M. Meloy, who had gone to Germany hoping to interest the German authorities in a scheme having the same purpose as von Rintelen's. In Meloy's office he posed as E. V. Gates—still retaining the initials of E. V. G. So effective was von Rintelen's "getaway," that he was reported to have gone abroad as a secretary. Those newspaper stories again gave von Rintelen cause to chuckle over his cleverness and his elusiveness, and encouraged him to still more reckless projects.

He was reporting meantime to Berlin by means of apparently innocuous commercial messages sent by wireless, and also by cablegrams *via* England and Holland.

Von Rintelen, always scheming to prevent arms and ammunition from going to the Allies, reached into Mexico to use that country as another angle from which to harass the United States. *He planned*—and this project was a part of his vast campaign—*to embroil Mexico and this country in war, or to cause such a jumble of revolutions within the Mexican borders that the United States would be compelled to intervene. He pictured this country in war with Mexico, a mobilization of the regular army and the militia, an assembling of the American fleet. That would require a large part of the output of the munition factories. The horses that were being shipped to the Allies, the arms, the clothing for soldiers, the shoes and the hundreds of other things which American factories were busily turning out, would be required for a large American army moving south of the Rio Grande.*

STIRRING UP MEXICO

He seized, therefore, upon President Wilson's opposition to General Huerta, and he planned to start a revolution in Mexico with the aim of returning Huerta to power and thus placing the United States in a position where it would be compelled to go into Mexico and restore order. The United States would not be in a position then to dictate terms for the settlement of the *Lusitania* controversy, would seize the war supplies going to the Allies, and, incidentally, would be hampered for the remainder of the European war.

Ensconced in Meloy's office, von Rintelen had as his daily associate a man of his own age and of much the same appearance, tall, slender, splendidly dressed, namely, a Mexican of German ancestry and a banker of Parral. These two, who had known each other for years, met in New York. The banker was versed in Mexican affairs, and the young German-Mexican knew some of von Rintelen's plans which had been set in operation before the latter's arrival in America.

German agents had been sent to Barcelona, Spain, to confer with General Victoriano Huerta, former dictator of Mexico, and dazzle him with the prospect of returning to power. Von Rintelen appreciated keenly the fact that Huerta in Mexico virtually meant a declaration of war by the United States, and, therefore, he wanted to put him there.

Having coaxed the old warrior to the United States, von Rintelen got Boy-Ed and von Papen to map out Huerta's plans. The two attachés, with von Rintelen standing, invisible, far in the background and pulling the strings, had many secret conferences in New York hotels, overheard by Federal agents. They developed the plans for Huerta's dash into Mexico, and the uprising of Mexicans to support him. Von Rintelen, Boy-Ed and von Papen made trips along the Mexican border, arranged for the mobilization of Mexicans, for the storing of supplies and ammunition and for furnishing funds. Von Rintelen deposited in Cuban banks and in banks in Mexico City more than $800,000 for Huerta's use. When the aged general, stealing away from New York, reached Texas, he was nipped, while attempting to jump the international border.

While the Huertista faction was amply financed, it was only one of seven groups, five of which were in Mexico, to which von Rintelen passed out money. Striving to stir up trouble and still more trouble for the United States, he poured gold upon gold into Mexico, hoping that President Wilson, nervous and harassed, would raise a big army for a march.

Next, as an English banker making a special study of Mexican railway securities, he called one day upon Villa's representative in New York, and discussed the Mexican situation with him, and afterwards he sent money to Villa. He gave support to Carranza. He financed Zapata, and he started two other small revolutions in Mexico. He gave $350,000 to one agent who hurriedly left the country carrying the cash with him. He sent $400,000 traveling through devious channels to help one of the revolutionary parties; but that money was recovered by von Rintelen's superiors after a most exciting scramble. The reckless agent is reported to have expended $10,000,000 in his Mexican enterprises, and airily he said he would spend $50,000,000 if necessary

VII

CAPTAIN FRANZ von RINTELEN, GERMAN ARCH-PLOTTER

BUT VON RINTELEN HAD STILL BIGGER projects afoot. While his precise, swiftly moving mind supervised the Mexican conspiracy, and carefully watched over shipments of supplies to the Fatherland, *he was launching a series of concerted conspiracies designed to cut off this country almost entirely from Europe.* His vivid imagination had led him to picture a Utopian fantasy wherein Americans who believed so absolutely in universal peace—despite the war raging abroad—that the laborers would refuse to make munitions of war, the farmers would decline to sell food to warring nations, and the Government would take over all the war factories. *Von Rintelen, accordingly, determined to bring such a dream into real life, not for altruistic purposes, but to help Germany conquer the Allies.*

He had made his plans before he left Germany, and he had sent ahead for information concerning Americans as his aids, who were skilled in finesse and underground work. *He wanted men who, while men of brains, might be led by lust for gold or hatred of England to espouse the criminal schemes which he had originated. He sought leaders whose logic and oratory could sway the rank and file.* The man of whom he had heard while in Berlin as a likely assistant was David Lamar, now serving a term of imprisonment for having impersonated a Congressman, whose craftiness and ingenious methods in using politicians in his stock operations had won him the title of "The Wolf of Wall Street." The two men were brought together.

One can see von Rintelen, enthusiastically speaking in millions of dollars, as he outlined his schemes to Lamar, his equal in grace of manner and deceit, and Lamar cloaking his avarice with smiles and sophistry.

BEFUDDLING THE PACIFISTS

Von Rintelen's first step, as he outlined it to Lamar, *was to use the horrors of the European War as an appeal for universal peace, and to enlist the laboring men and the farmers of America in raising their united voice against the exports of arms and ammunition. And thus a great labor peace propaganda* was orig-inated by a German whose patriotism had driven away his scruples, and an American who had gone money-mad. The details of the organization were set forth, and soon von Rintelen had a staff of workers at his command, though they all may not have known he was paying their salaries. His agents, in secret interviews with labor leaders, were soliciting their aid, flashing rolls of gold-tinted certificates. The men who guiltily handled the money which von Rintelen drew from the bank had only one complaint, namely, that the denominations of the bills were entirely too large.

Two of von Rintelen's agents following Samuel Gompers, president of the National Federation of Labor, to Atlantic City one day, offered him $500,000 for his services in endorsing the peace propaganda and participating in the work. Mr. Gompers scorned the offer. Other big labor leaders, whose aid was solicited, began immediately to warn their associates against the anti-American activi-ties of German agents.

By June, 1915, von Rintelen's schemes were moving apace. A big advertis-ing campaign had been started in the early spring with von Rintelen's cash. Newspaper propaganda picturing the glories of universal peace began to appear.

By the aid of Lamar, who kept von Rintelen in the background, the Ger-man soon had many persons working and talking in the interest of universal peace. It has been stated that the services of Frank Buchanan, Represen-tative in Congress and former labor leader, and of H. Robert Fowler, ex-Congressman, were obtained. Whether they were aware of von Rintelen and his motives is a question for a jury to answer, for they have been indicted in connection with the alleged activities of the Labor's National Peace Council.

Within a short time, thousands of invitations were scattering through-out the country to labor leaders, small and large, and to heads of farmers' granges, to attend the national convention of the peace propaganda at the expense of the organization. All railroad fares, hotel expenses and a liberal allowance for spending money were promised.

Under the fostering financial auspices of von Rintelen, who hovered conveniently near the New Willard Hotel, the members of a peace movement gathered in Washington, expenses paid. They adopted resolutions saying they desired "to promote peace." *The resolutions demanded the enactment of laws that would enable the Government to take over as exclusive government business the manufacture of all arms, instruments and munitions of war; demanded an immediate embargo upon shipments of war supplies to the belligerents; denounced the maintenance of military and naval forces, and called for a special session of Congress to promote "peace universal."* The executive board went immediately into executive session.

PAYING THE HIRELINGS

"How is this movement to be financed?" one of the newly-elected executive board asked another. He and one of the vice-presidents waited for an answer. They got none, he says, and the question was repeated by another. Then one of the officers answered:

"This thing is big enough, so that I do not care where the money comes from to finance it."

Another member asked:

"What, after all, does this council want to do?"

"We want," was the answer, "to stop the exportation of munitions to the Allies. Germany can manufacture all the munitions she wants."

Von Rintelen's deposit in the Trans-Atlantic Trust Company meantime was growing smaller by jumps of $100,000. It was drawn by cheques payable to cash, placed in another bank, quickly withdrawn, and on one occasion the money in bills was taken to the headquarters of a peace organization in a suit-case. *Bank accounts of von Rintelen's peace propagandists began to jump.*

The executive board was busy. One of the first moves was a statement filed with Secretary of State Lansing alleging that nine ships in various American ports were taking on cargoes of ammunition in violation of the neutrality laws. That charge, undoubtedly prepared with von Rintelen's aid upon information gathered by German spies, showed an accurate knowledge of the merchantmen loading with supplies for the Allies. *There was, however, no violation of law,* because the vessels were officered and manned by ordinary seamen who had no connection with the Allied governments.

The second step was the preparation of a complaint charging as a violation of law the issuance of Federal Reserve notes by national banks on the ground that the New York banks had lent money to the Allies which was being used in payment for war supplies, and that some of those banks had rediscounted notes with the Federal Reserve Bank. Here again was displayed a remarkably detailed knowledge of the business of the Federal Reserve Banks. *This charge also fell flat.*

A third move was against Dudley Field Malone, Collector of the Port of New York. Resolutions were adopted accusing him of exceeding his authority in having granted clearance papers to the steamship *Lusitania* when that vessel was ladened with munitions, and authorizing an action to be started against him. No suit, however, was begun. In this connection, it may be mentioned that one member of the peace committee was attorney for a woman of Chicago, who, months afterwards, started suit for $40,000 against Collector Malone and Captain Turner, of the *Lusitania,* on the ground that the ship illegally carried explosives.

CONSPIRACY GROWS BOLDER

These public acts mentioned above, however, are stated by the Federal Government to have been merely a cloak, covering a more extensive conspiracy financed by von Rintelen. By a series of strikes in munition factories, humming with the Allies' war orders; on railroads carrying the articles to the seaboard, and on steamships, von Rintelen, it is alleged, sought to cut off commerce among the United States and the Allied countries. Von Rintelen and several others are accused in the Federal indictment of doing six different acts in a conspiracy in restraint of foreign commerce. They are charged with conspiring to use "solicitation, persuasion and exhortation" to influence the workers to go on strike or to quit work, to bribe officers of labor unions to get the men to strike, and "by divers other means and methods not specifically determined upon by the defendants, but to be decided as the occasion arose."

Von Rintelen was busy now jumping from town to town, sending orders under one name, then another, and paying out money. *There took place in June and July,* 1915, *many strikes which, the national labor leaders of the respective trades said, were absolutely unauthorized by the national bodies.* The German agent was delighted to read in the newspapers of strikes at the Standard

Oil plant in Bayonne, N. J.; of strikes at the Remington Arms Company in Bridgeport, Conn., and in the General Electric Plant in Schenectady, N. Y. His agents would approach him gleefully with the newspapers containing these accounts, and immediately would receive another bundle of bills with the exhortation, "That is fine. Go out and start some more."

Another projected strike in connection with which Germans were mentioned in correspondence, but in which von Rintelen is not named, is presented here because it fits in the general scheme of the German plotting. That is the conspiracy on part of moneyed representatives of Germany in May and June, 1915, to start a strike simultaneously among the 23,000 'longshoremen on the Pacific and Atlantic coasts. *Such a walkout would absolutely have paralyzed American shipping, completely stopped the movement of explosives to the Allies at a most critical moment.* A leader of the big 'Longshoremen's Union told Chief William J. Flynn, of the United States Secret Service, that $1,035,000, or $45 for every man, was offered to keep the men out on strike for four weeks. After the sinking of the *Lusitania,* the man who approached the 'longshoremen wrote under the name of "Mike Foley," asking if an "S." (strike) was to be called, that because of the "L. (*Lusitania*) affair," his people were not going to do anything at present, and because the "Big Man" (who preceded von Rintelen) was going away. It will be recalled that after the sinking of the *Lusitania,* Dernburg was dismissed from the country because of his comments concerning the attitude of Germany towards submarine warfare.

CRIMINALS SET TO WORK

While von Rintelen was reaching out in so many directions in his frantic endeavor to build a barrier between the United States and the Entente Powers, he did not hesitate to resort to criminals. Keeping his quick eyes on the progress of the peace propaganda, he had schemes which, while distinctly separated from that organization, were designed to work in harmony with the developments in the strike propaganda. Von Rintelen planned by aid of reservists and crooks to take other measures in munition factories to stop, delay, injure the production of materials destined for the Allies' battle fronts.

He sent trained German reservists to get employment in factories with orders to collect information and do what they could to cause trouble. Resorting again to the well-developed system of German secret agents in New York, under new aliases, he got in touch with organized bands of criminals in New York, and, the authorities say, hired them *to start depredations on the ships being loaded with supplies* for the Allies in New York harbor. To von Rintelen or some other person associated with him is attributed the origin of a plot for widespread attacks by thieves on cargoes being lightered from railroad piers to merchantmen. These thefts of sugar, automobile tires and magnetos have amounted to millions of dollars. For instance, one of the sugar thieves stealing bags of sugar from a lighter said to a comrade:

> "Take some more bags. The ship won't ever reach the other side, anyway, and nobody will know."

To the persons who doubt these varied, reckless and extensive activities of von Rintelen, it may be suggested that von Rintelen asserted frequently to his associates that he had come to America to take every step, including peaceful or violent measures, to stop the shipment of munitions.

The doubter must not overlook the supervision which von Rintelen exercised over the manufacturer of fire bombs which German reservists are accused of hiding on the Allies' merchantmen, and the fact that von Rintelen's aid visited a bomb man in his Hoboken laboratory frequently; that on one occasion he scored him roughly because the fire bombs were not proving effective. Furthermore, Fay, after his arrest, and long before the indictment of the bomb plotters, told Captain Tunney of a wealthy German, then a prisoner of war in England, who had paid $10,000 to a Hoboken chemist to make fire bombs.

Though von Rintelen, during the months of June and July, was exuberant over the reports—most of them false—which were carried to him concerning the progress of peace, the strikes and other schemes, and though he was kept drawing money from the bank until the $800,000 in the Trans-Atlantic Trust Company was reduced to $40,000, he began to have doubts about Lamar and about the effectiveness of the latter's management of some of the projects. He knew that Lamar and his associates were planning for a second rousing meeting in Washington, but, becoming suspicious, he suddenly cut off the money. He had received estimates of activities that required more money. After deliberation he finally decided to slip away to Berlin, get away from Lamar entirely and after making a report to the War Office return to America to broaden his scope of work.

All told, von Rintelen had failed to perceive any falling off in the exports to the Allies. They were, in fact, rapidly increasing, and von Rintelen's schemes thus far had proved ineffective, though he still was optimistic that eventually he would have all his forces working in unison and thus accomplish his aims.

He did not go to Washington when a second peace convention was in session, and the word had slipped out to some of the workers that von Rintelen was about to sail. Still, the meeting with the members claiming a representation of 8,000,000 voters, was more denunciatory and enthusiastic over its aims, than ever. There were attacks on President Wilson and demands for an embargo on war munitions. There was an intense pro-German feeling.

Differences, meantime, began to arise among the members of the executive board. One of the vice-presidents resigned just before the second session convened, saying emphatically that the financing of the organization was under suspicion. Another quietly quit, not making the fact public until weeks afterwards. Lamar flitted away to a magnificent country home which he had bought in Pittsfield, Mass. There was no money left. The propaganda died.

EXIT VON RINTELEN

Von Rintelen was on the high seas. He had left $40,000 in the bank in charge of his friends, and some of the plotters tried to get that on the strength of a promise to stop the Anglo-French bond sale of $500,000,000. Before sailing he had applied for a passport as an American citizen named Edward V. Gates, of Millersville, Pennsylvania. But whisperings concerning von Rintelen's activities had reached the White House from society folk who had heard von Rintelen's rash talk and who knew of some of the unscrupulous things he had attempted. The State Department ordered an investigation and finally sent his passport on to New York the day before the sailing of the *Noordam,* in care of Federal agents; but von Rintelen did not claim it. Though he had bought a ticket on the boat under the name of Gates, and had obtained drafts payable on that name, he did not occupy the Gates cabin but at the last minute engaged passage under the name of Emil V. Gasche, a Swiss citizen.

On board ship, he set to work preparing for the close scrutiny of British naval officers when the ship neared Falmouth. He handed over many of his documents to Andrew D. Meloy, his traveling companion, and Meloy's secretary. He dictated a long document about financial conditions of Mexican railways purporting to be the report of himself as commissioner for a group of English bondholders. He sought to make it appear that he had been sent to the United States as a representative of the bondholders' committee of Mexican railways. When the British officers came on board and searched him, von Rintelen put up a skillful bluff, but finally surrendered as a prisoner of war. Meloy, who had aided von Rintelen in his application for the American passport, was sent back to this country by the British authorities.

A VALUABLE PRISONER

While von Rintelen, after his strenuous days in America, was resting comfortably in a luxurious prison camp at Donington Hall, England, the American authorities were busily delving into his record. Mr. Sarfaty presented witness after witness and thousands of documents to the Federal Grand Jury. Von Rintelen and Meloy were indicted, first, for the fraudulent passport conspiracy; and Meloy finally made a confession to the Government authorities. Von Rintelen's agent, called before the Grand Jury and refusing to answer, was adjudged in contempt of court and spent a night in the Tombs prison. Another agent, summoned before the Grand Jury and asked about his dealings with von Rintelen, refused to answer on the ground that it might tend to degrade and incriminate him, but he afterwards was arrested on a firebomb charge.

Von Rintelen was indicted on the charge of forgery on the passport application, and upon that as a basis, application was made to the English authorities for his extradition. After months of investigation, indictments finally were filed against von Rintelen, Lamar, and his associates on a charge of conspiring to restrain foreign trade.

The moment a United States District-Attorney, equipped with a mass of documentary evidence, telegrams, letters, minutes of secret meetings, and the statements of hundreds of witnesses, laid facts before the Grand Jury who brought an indictment against a Congressman, the House of Representatives, without waiting for the trial of the defendant, immediately ordered an inquiry which in substance amounted to a fishing expedition by the subcommittee to ascertain just what evidence Mr. Marshall and Mr. Sarfaty had dug up against one of their members. Congress did not take any action, and finally, after a spectacular play, decided to let the matter drop.

A COSTLY FAILURE

From the viewpoint of picturesqueness, fantastic conceptions, reckless-ness, extravagance, and a remarkable mastery of detail, von Rintelen stands forth as the most extraordinary German agent sent to America. Boy-Ed and von Papen are now telling their friends in Berlin that their recall was due not to what they did but to what von Rintelen did and said.

The energetic nobleman had hoped to cause an absolute cessation of exports from this country to the Allies and to create a political situation where the United States would be powerless to make any protest on Germa-ny's submarine warfare. To bring these conditions about *he had not hesitated to try to foment war between the United States and Mexico, to violate various American neutrality laws, to attack American institutions and American ideals with the aim of causing an industrial stagnation.* Yet how little he actually accomplished!

His Mexican plans were a failure. His schemes to influence legislation came to naught. While a few strikes were started and quickly settled, the activity of the Germans proved hurtful to the working men. Von Rintelen did get a few supplies over to Germany; but many of his ships were seized by the English. His enterprises are said to have cost many millions of dollars, and the supplies which he shipped are about the only thing that Germany got out of his gigantic schemes. U. S. Attorney Marshall has a passport issued to Edward V. Gates which von Rintelen can have any time he wishes to come and get it. Should he ever step upon American shores, he will face charges which upon conviction furnish a total sentence of anywhere from fifty to sixty years. *Never did Germany aim through one man to accomplish so much yet effect so little as through Franz von Rintelen, the Crown Prince's friend.*

VIII

The STORY of the *LUSITANIA*

THE *LUSITANIA* WAS, IN THE eyes of the German Admiralty, the symbol of Great Britain's supremacy on the seas. The big, graceful vessel, unsurpassed in speed, had defied the German raiders that lurked in the Atlantic hoping to capture her and had eluded the submarines that tried to find her course. Time and time again, the Germans had planned and plotted to "get" the *Lusitania,* and every time the ocean greyhound had slipped away from them—every time save when the plot was developed on American territory.

To sink the *Lusitania,* the German Admiralty had argued, was to lower England's prestige and to hoist the black eagle of the Hohenzollerns above the Union Jack. Her destruction, they fondly hoped, would strike terror to the hearts of the British, for it would prove the inability of the English navy to protect her merchantmen. It would prove to the world that von Tirpitz was on a fair way of carrying out his threat to isolate the British Isles and starve the British people into submission to Germany. It would be a last warning to neutrals to keep off the Allies' merchantmen and would help stop the shipment of arms and ammunition to the Allies from America. It would—as a certain royal personage boasted—shake the world's foundations.

Gloating over their project and forgetting the rights of neutrals, the mad war lords did not think of the innocent persons on board, the men, the women and babies. The lives of these neutrals were as nothing compared with the shouts of triumph that would resound through Germany at the announcement of the torpedoing of the big British ship, symbol of sea power. The attitude was truly expressed by Captain von Papen, who on receiving news of the sinking of the *Lusitania* remarked: "Well, your General Sherman said it: 'War is Hell.'"

So the war lords schemed and the plots which resulted in the sinking of the *Lusitania* on May 7, 1915, bringing death to 113 American citizens, were developed and executed in America, through orders from Berlin.

The agents in America put their heads together in a room in the German Club, New York, or in a high-powered limousine tearing through the dark. These men, who had worked out the plot, on the night of the successful execution had assembled in a club and in high glee touched their glasses and shouted their devotion to the Kaiser. One boasted afterwards that he received an Iron Cross for his share in the work.

On the night of the tragedy, one of the conspirators remarked to a family where he was dining—a family whose son was on the *Lusitania*—when word came of the many deaths on the ship: "I did not think she would sink so quickly. I had two good men on board."

WARRIORS AT WORK IN AMERICA

In their secret conferences the conspirators worked their way round obstacles and set their scheme in operation. Hired spies had made numerous trips on the *Lusitania,* and had carefully studied her course to and from England, and her convoy through the dangerous zone where submarines might be lurking. These spies had observed the precautions taken against a submarine attack. They knew the fearful speed by which the big ship had eluded pursuers in February. They also had considered the feasibility of sending a wireless message to a friend in England—a message apparently of greeting that might be picked up by the wireless on a German submarine and give its commander a hint as to the ship's course. *In fact, they did attempt this plan.* Spies were on board early in the year when the *Lusitania* ran dangerously near a submarine, dodged a torpedo and then quickly eclipsed her German pursuer.

Spies also had brought reports concerning persons connected with the *Lusitania,* and had given suggestions as to how to place men on board in spite of the scrutiny of British agents. All these reports were considered carefully and the conclusion was that no submarine was fast enough to chase and get the *Lusitania;* that it was practically impossible to have the U-boats stationed along every half mile of the British coast, but that the simplest problem was to send the *Lusitania* on a course where the U-boats would be in waiting and could torpedo her. The scheme was, in substance, as follows:

Captain Turner, approaching the English coast, sends a wireless to the British Admiralty asking for instructions as to his course and convoy.

He gets a reply in code telling him in what direction to steer and where his convoy will meet him. First, we must get a copy of the Admiralty Code and we must prepare a message in cipher, giving directions as to his course. This message will go to him by wireless as though from the Admiralty. We must make arrangements to see that the genuine message from the British Admiralty never reaches Captain Turner.

That was the plan which the conspirators, aided and directed by Berlin, chose. Upon it the shrewdest minds in the German secret service were set to work. *As for the British Admiralty Code, the Germans had that at the outbreak of the war and were using it at advantageous moments. How they got it has not been made known; but they got it and they used it, just as the Germans have obtained copies of the codes used by the American State Department and have had copies of the codes used in our Army and Navy. While the codes used by the British officials change almost daily, such is not the case with merchant vessels on long voyages.*

The next step of the conspirators was to arrange for the substitution of the fake message for the genuine one. Germany's spy machine has a wonderful faculty for seeking out the weak characters holding responsible positions among the enemy or for sending agents to get and hold positions among their foes. It is now believed that a man on the *Lusitania* was deceived or duped. Whether he was a German sympathizer sent out by the Fatherland to get the position and be ready for the task, or whether he was induced for pay to play the part he did—has not been told. Neither is his fate known.

Communication between New York and the German capital, ingenious, intricate and superbly arranged, was almost as easy as telephoning from the Battery to Harlem. Berlin was kept informed of every move in New York and, in fact, selected the ill-fated course for the *Lusitania's* last voyage in English waters. Berlin picked out the place where the *Lusitania* was to sink.

Berlin chose the deep-sea graves for more than one hundred Americans. Berlin assigned two submarines to a point ten miles south by west off Old Head of Kinsale, near the entrance of St. George's Channel. Berlin chose the commander of the U-boats for the most damnable sea-crime in history.

Just here there is a rumor among U-boat men in Europe that the man for the crime was sent from Kiel with sealed instructions not to be opened till at the spot chosen. With him went "a shadow" armed with a death warrant if the U-boat commander "baulked" at the last moment.

BERLIN GIVES WARNING

The German officials in Berlin looking ahead, sought to prearrange a palliative for their crime. Their plan, which in itself shows clearly how carefully the Germans plotted the destruction of the *Lusitania,* was to warn Americans not to sail on the vessel.

While the German Embassy in Washington was kept clear of the plot and Ambassador von Bernstorff had argued and fought with all his strength against the designs of the Berlin authorities, he, nevertheless, received orders to publish an advertisement warning neutrals not to sail on the Allies' merchantmen. Acting under instructions, this advertisement was inserted in newspapers in a column adjoining the Cunard's advertisement of the sailing of the *Lusitania:*

NOTICE!

Travellers intending to embark on the Atlantic voyage are reminded that a state of war exists between Germany and her Allies and Great Britain and her Allies; that the zone of war includes the waters adjacent to the British Isles; that, in accordance with formal notice given by the Imperial German Government, vessels flying the flag of Great Britain or any of her Allies are liable to destruction in these waters and that travellers sailing in the war zone on ships of Great Britain or her Allies do so at their own risk.

Imperial German Embassy
Washington, D.C., April 22nd, 1915

Germans in New York, who had knowledge that German submarines were lying in wait off the Irish coast to "get" the *Lusitania,* sent intimations to friends before the sailing of the ship.

The *New York Sun* was told of the plot and warned Captain Turner by wireless after the ship sailed. The German secret service in New York also sent warnings to Americans booked on the *Lusitania.* One of the persons to receive such a message signed "morte" was Alfred Gwynne Vanderbilt. Many other passengers got the same warning that the ship was to be torpedoed; but they all laughed at it. They knew she had outrun submarines on a previous voyage and tricked them on another voyage. Besides, before the horrors of this war, optimistic Americans firmly believed the world was a civilized place. It was only after the destruction of the *Lusitania* that many neutral Americans could credit the atrocity stories of Belgium.

FATEFUL MAY 1, 1915

So when the *Lusitania* backed from her pier in the North River on the morning of May 1, 1915, there was more than the average levity that makes the sailing of an ocean liner so absorbing. On the pier were anxious friends somewhat perturbed by the mysterious whisperings of impending danger. Mingling among them also were men who knew what that danger was, and who had just delivered final instructions to German hirelings on board. On the deck of the great vessel, as she swung her nose down-stream toward Sandy Hook, was not only the man who had promised to see that the false message in code reached Captain Turner, but there also were those two friends, good and true, of von Rintelen's—men who, in the event that the *Lusitania* should run into the appointed place at night, would flash lights from port holes to give a clear aim to the commanders of the stealthy submarines.

On board the vessel swinging out past Sandy Hook into the ocean lane were a notable group of passengers, many of them representative Americans of inestimable value to this country. Besides Mr. Vanderbilt, there was Charles Frohman, a talented theatrical producer, who had furnished by his artistic shows genuine amusement to millions; Elbert Hubbard, talented and inspiring writer; Charles Klein, writer of absorbing plays; Justus Miles Forman, novelist, and Lindon W. Bates, Jr., whose family had befriended von Rintelen. Merchants, clergymen, lawyers, society women, a large list of useful men and women in the 1,254 passengers.

These, added to the crew of 800, made more than 2,000 lives under the care of the staunch, blue-eyed captain. *Of that number,* 1,214 were *being rushed over the waves to doom.* And as the ship sped eastward, submarines leaving their bases at Cuxhaven and Heligoland clipped their prows under the waves, and made for Old Head of Kinsale on the south coast of Ireland, where they were instructed to pause, upon sealed instructions, and obey them to the letter.

Meantime, Berlin, counting almost to the hour when the *Lusitania* would near the British Isles, prepared the exact wording for the false instructions to Captain Turner. This was sent to New York by wireless, where it was put into British code. The next step was to have this message substituted for the British Admiralty's instructions to the *Lusitania*. The inside details of how this substitution was effected—can only be surmised. This secret is buried with the British Admiralty and with the Bureau in Berlin.

BERLIN'S DELIBERATIONS

For such intricate action Germany had been preparing with infinite patience both before and after the war began. Prior to the outbreak, representatives of Germany had started the building of the wireless plant at Sayville, Long Island, by which aerial communication was established with Berlin. After the war began, the equipment of the station was increased, and instead of 35 kilowatt transmitters, 100 kilowatt transmitters were installed, the machinery for tripling the efficiency of the plant having been shipped from Germany *via* Holland to this country. Wireless experts, members of the German navy, also slipped away from Germany to direct the work of handling messages between the two countries.

Everything was in readiness at Sayville, consequently, to catch the directions that were flashed through the air. There was an operator specially trained to take the message coded for the deception of Captain Turner, and send it crackling fatefully through the air. Everything was ready and only the request of the operator on the *Lusitania* for directions south of Ireland was needed. *All this was in violation not only of our neutrality laws, but also in disregard of American statutes governing wireless stations.*

Meantime, the vessel had reached the edge of the war zone decreed by Germany in violation of international law, and Captain Turner sent out his call for instructions. Presently the order came. It was hurried to Captain Turner's state-room.

Captain Turner, carefully decoding the message by means of a cipher book which he had guarded so jealously, read orders to proceed to a point ten miles south of Old Head of Kinsale, and run into St. George's Channel, making the bar at Liverpool at midnight. He carefully calculated the distance and his running time, and adjusted his speed accordingly. He felt assured, because he relied on the assumption that the waters over which he was sailing were being thoroughly scoured by English cruisers and swift torpedo boats in search of German submarines.

THE EXPLOSION THAT ROCKED THE WORLD

The British Admiralty also received his wireless message—just as the Sayville operator had snatched it from the air, and dispatched an answer. The order from the head of the Admiralty directed the English captain to proceed to a point some seventy or eighty miles south of Old Head of Kinsale and there meet his convoy, which would guard him on the way to port. *But Captain Turner never got that message, and the British convoy waited in vain for the Lusitania to appear on the horizon.*

The *Lusitania* headed north-east, going far away from the vessels that would have protected her. Swiftly she slipped through the waves on the afternoon of May 7. Unsuspecting, the ship moved directly toward certain death. The proud, swift liner steered straight between two submarines, lying in wait.

The details of what happened after the torpedo blew out the side of the great ship have been told—told so fully, vividly, so terribly that they need not be repeated here. As Captain Turner heard the explosion of the torpedo he instantly knew that there had been treachery. He knew he had been decoyed away from the warships that were to escort him to his pier.

The manner in which the captain had been lured to the waiting submarines was made clear at the secret session of the Board of Inquiry that investigated the sinking of the ship. Captain Turner told at the Coroner's inquest how he had been warned, supposedly by the British Admiralty, of submarines off the Irish coast, and that he had received special instructions as to course. Asked if he made application for a convoy, he said:

"No, I left that to them. It is their business, not mine. I simply had to carry out my orders to go, and I would do it again."

At the official inquiry, the captain produced the orders which he had received, directing him to proceed south-west of Old Head of Kinsale. The British Admiralty produced its message which had directed Captain Turner to go by an utterly different course. It produced also orders which had been issued to the convoy to meet the *Lusitania*. The orders did not jibe. *They showed treachery, and further investigation pointed to Sayville.*

AMERICA REVOLTED AND APPALLED

The indignation and the revulsion of Americans against Germany because of the destruction of the *Lusitania* with the appalling loss of life was a surprise to the Kaiser and his war staff. They apparently had believed that the warning contained in the official announcement of Germany, declaring the waters about the British Islands a war zone, and the advertisement published would be sufficient excuse, and that their act would be accepted calmly by

America. They were not prepared for Colonel Roosevelt's invective stigmatizing the act as piracy, or the editorial denunciation throughout the country. Their effrontery was displayed by one of their agents, who announced that American ships also would be sunk. But this agent's removal from the country and mob violence threatened other agents was emphatic proof of America's state of mind.

Immediately Germany turned as a defense to the argument that the *Lusitania* carried munitions of war and other contraband in violation of the United States Federal statute. But the American laws were quoted to Ambassador von Bernstorff to prove to him that cartridges could be transported in a passenger ship. That argument proved of no avail.

Secretary Bryan's note, written by President Wilson, and forwarded to Berlin, demanded a disavowal of the sinking of the *Lusitania,* an apology and reparation for the lives lost. But Germany sought to parley with a reply that would lay the blame on Great Britain, and asserting that the *Lusitania* had been an armed auxiliary cruiser, requested an investigation of these alleged facts, and refused to stop her submarine warfare until England changed her trade policy. But this note again aroused the wrath of Americans.

LIES AND DECEIT

German secret agents began to manufacture evidence to support the Kaiser's contentions. Here a hireling of Boy-Ed looms as an obedient servant of the naval attaché, whether he knew all the facts or not. It was Koenig, who, using the alias of Stemler, obtained from Gustave Stahl an affidavit to the effect that he had seen four fifteen-centimeter guns on the decks of the *Lusitania* before she left port on her ill-fated voyage. There were three other supporting affidavits. All these documents were handed to Boy-Ed on June 1, 1915, and the following day were in the hands of von Bernstorff, who turned them over to the State Department in Washington.

It required but little work on the part of Federal agents to establish the untruth of Stahl's affidavit. Stahl, a German reservist, appeared before the Federal Grand Jury, where he again repeated his lies. He was indicted for perjury and upon a plea of guilty was sent to the Federal prison at Atlanta.

It was Koenig who had hidden Stahl away after the latter had made his affidavit, and it was Koenig who, at the command of the Federal authorities, produced him.

So here again Germany's efforts to deceive and to justify her piratical act came to naught, and left her even more damned before the world. Time came within a few days for President Wilson to reject forcibly the flimsy defense made by Germany, but before that note was drafted, the United States authorities by a thorough investigation of Sayville, and a scrutiny of the German naval officers employed there, discovered that the fake code message that drove the *Lusitania* to her grave in the sea had been flashed out from neutral territory; that the conspiracy had been developed in America, though the details were not obtainable at that time as they are presented here.

President Wilson was determined to demand absolute safety for Americans at sea. Though Bryan resigned, Mr. Wilson sent a note, asserting that the *Lusitania* was not armed, and had not carried cargo in violation either of American or international law. The action of Bryan weakened the position of America in demanding a cessation of Germany's submarine warfare. It gave encouragement to Austria, after Germany had promised to obey international law, to try a series of similar evasions. It gave impetus to Germany's plans to make a settlement of the submarine controversy and to try to divide Congress on the issue.

The loss to America was 113 lives and a great amount of prestige; to Germany, a tremendous amount of sympathy. But through it all stand out the pictures of secret agents, boasters, schemers and reckless adventurers, one of whom, having aided in the sinking of the *Lusitania* and the drowning of hundreds of her passengers and crew, had still the audacity to dine on the evening of this ghastly triumph at the home of an American victim. One agent high in international affairs, overcome by the force of the tragedy done in answer to the Kaiser's bidding, had still enough decency left to remark:

"Oh, what foul work!"

IX

Dr. HEINRICH F. ALBERT, GERMANY'S BAGMAN and BLOCKADE RUNNER

"AND TELL HIM THAT THE struggle on the American front is sometimes very hard."—Dr. Albert.

To outwit John Bull on the high seas by running his blockade is a big task. To compete against the combined commercial generals of England, Russia, France and Italy in seeking trade in the Americas is a still larger undertaking. But for one man to attempt both, while incidentally keeping watch on the industrial growth of the United States and being a big factor in Germany's spy system, seems like a pigmy grappling with a Hercules. The qualities requisite for the man who would accept such a battle are diplomatic finesse of the highest degree, strength compared to one of America's kings of industry, a vast economic knowledge, the shrewdness of a Yankee and the cleverness of the Kaiser's ablest strategist. Yet the responsibilities of such a manifold enterprise, romantic in its infinite details and its vastness, were assumed by one German.

You could find him almost any day until the break with Germany in a small office in the Hamburg-American Building, the Kaiser's beehive of secret agents, at No. 45, Broadway, New York. He was a tall, slender man, wonderfully supple-looking in spite of the conventional frock coat and the dignified dress of a European business man. His clear, blue eyes, his smooth face, thoughtful and refined, his blonde hair, and his regular features suggested a man of thirty-eight, or even younger, though you would look for a middle-aged or older man as selected for a position requiring so many nice decisions. When you entered his room—and few persons gained admission—he would rise and bow low and most courteously. He spoke in a soft, melodious voice, was deliberate in the choice of his words and encouraged conversation rather than made it. He was the quintessence of politeness, a marked contrast to the clear-cut, energetic, brusque, American business man—a smooth polished cog in the steel machinery of Prussian militarism.

Yet this man was the center of Germany's business activities in America. Upon him has rested the task of spending between $2,000,000 and $3,000,000 a week for the German Government in the purchase of supplies and in propaganda. His expenditure in furthering the cause has cost him thirty millions of dollars outside the vast amounts spent in the purchase of supplies, and he admits he wasted a half million or more dollars.

He was Dr. Heinrich F. Albert, privy councilor to the German Embassy and fiscal agent in America for the German Government. He was the source of the funds used by the representatives of Germany, her secret diplomatic and consular agents. He was the channel through whom money flowed from the Imperial exchequer—unwittingly it may have been on his part—to men who, in the interest of Germany, have violated American laws.

His job was a big one because this war has demanded the help of industry, as no other previous war. Just as it has resolved itself into an enormous race between the industries of the combating nations in turning out shells and arms, so Geheimrath Albert's duties became all the more multitudinous, really a part of the great conflict itself.

Dr. Albert had just as important work as his colleagues, the military and naval attachés, but in a different field. With industrial preparedness of greater importance in this than in any other war it is natural that the commercial attaché and his staff of agents should prove a most important asset to Germany's secret service in America. Geheimrath Albert's duties in the economic field have been bound inextricably with the aims of the Fatherland's secret service. While directing and financing the collection of data for use in the preparation of reports to the home government, he has also worked side by side with the other representatives of his Government.

THE EQUIPMENT OF A COLOSSUS

Albert was equipped for the gigantic task, as few men in the world have been equipped. He knew finance, the economy of industry, the finesse of diplomacy and the odd, yet scientific twists of the inventor's mind. He had been trained in the things that interested kings and the problems that appealed to the laboring man. His field of knowledge was broad, for in preparation for his tasks he had to seek the best commercial, banking, industrial methods and inventions of the world to help Germany. So successful was he that his friends have termed him "The German Yankee."

Around no German official in America has there hovered so much mystery. A great bulwark of Germany's propaganda—though no participation in any illegal or criminal acts has been charged against him—he might have remained the greater part of the war under cover had it not been for the activity of secret service agents and for a little nap which Geheimrath Albert, the courteous and overworked, took upon an elevated train one day. When he awoke, his dossier was gone. That portfolio contained a mass of wonderfully illuminating documents, so many and so varied that if the privy councilor is accustomed to take up in one day so many diverse matters it almost staggers the imagination to try to conceive of the tasks which this war brought him. Through them public and official attention was fastened upon him, serving to deepen the folds of mystery about him. Through them the public in America first learned of the vastness of German propaganda. Dr. Albert lost his portfolio in August, 1915.

In the quietness of his little office above humming Broadway and within calling distance of the gold-lined Wall Street into which he so constantly pried, Geheimrath Albert discussed momentous economic problems with Germany's other big men. In the German Club in the evenings he continued those consultations. In trips to Washington and Chicago and New Orleans and San Francisco, he and his agents conferred with big German business men.

His close confidant was Count von Bernstorff, with whom he had a joint account of several millions of dollars in the Chase National Bank, New York. His two active colleagues were Captain von Papen and Captain Boy-Ed. The association with these men must have been very close and keen; for on von Papen's recall Dr. Albert wrote him: "I shall feel your departure most keenly; our work together was excellent and was always a great pleasure to me. I hope that in the Fatherland you will have an opportunity for making use of your extraordinary talent in dealing with economic questions. When I think of your and Boy-Ed's departure and that I alone remain behind in New York, I could—well, better not!"

Dr. Albert learned the output of the steel industries and the financial connections of the big corporations. He had accurate information about the electrical manufacturing concerns in this country, their output, their inventions, the ability and the accomplishments of the engineers at the head of those plants, their training and personal history. He knew all about America's transportation systems, their financial strength and the real mechanical and constructive ability of the scientific men connected with those systems. His information was as broad as his American activities. Suffice it to say that it was Dr. Albert's business to get these facts—and he did so.

HIS VIEW OF THE FUTURE

How Dr. Albert looked to the future is set forth in a report which was prepared for him on June 3, 1915, by a trade representative in the German General Consulate, New York, on the effect of the British embargo. This document, compiled by a scientist, was undoubtedly only one of hundreds of such instruments worked out by Germans in this country for the help of the Fatherland. In this paper the writer, named Waetzoldt, says:

> There can be no doubt that the British Government will bring into play all power and pressure possible in order to complete the total blockade of Germany from her foreign markets, and that the Government of the United States will not make a strenuous effort to maintain its trade with Germany. . . .
>
> It has been positively demonstrated during this time that the falling off of imports caused by the war in Europe will in the future be principally covered by American industry. . . .
>
> The complete stopping of importation of German products will, in truth, to a limited extent, especially in the first part of the blockade, help the sale of English or French products, but the damage which will be done to us in this way will not be great. . . .
>
> The *Lusitania* case did, in fact, give the English efforts in this direction a new and powerful impetus, and at first the vehemence with which the anti-German movement began anew awakened serious misgivings, but this case also will have a lasting effect, which, unless fresh complications arise, we may be able to turn to the advantage of the sale of German goods. . . .
>
> The war will certainly have this effect, that the American business world will devote all its energy toward making itself independent of the importation of foreign products as far as possible. . . .
>
> If the decision is again brought home to German industry it should not be forgotten what position the United States took with reference to

Germany in this war. Above all, it should not be forgotten that the 'ultimate ratio' of the United States is not the war with arms, but a complete prohibition of trade with Germany, and, in fact, through legislation. That was brought out very clearly and sharply in connection with the still pending negotiations regarding the *Lusitania* case.

Dr. Albert received among many reports one giving an analysis of the trade here in war materials:

> The large war orders, as the professional journals also print, have become the great means of saving American business institutions from idleness and financial ruin.
>
> The fact that institutions of the size and international influence of those mentioned could not find sufficient regular business to keep them to some extent occupied, throws a harsh light upon the sad condition in which American business would have found itself had it not been for the war orders. The ground which induced these large interests to accept war orders rests entirely upon an economical basis and can be explained by the above-mentioned conditions which were produced by the lack of regular business. . . . These difficulties resulting from the dividing up of the contracts are held to have been augmented, as stated in business circles, by the fact that certain agents working in German interest succeeded in further delaying and making worse American deliveries. . . .
>
> So many contracts for the production of picric acid have been placed that they can only be filled to a very small part.

A MAN OF MYSTERY

Naturally one of the most vital problems that stirred Dr. Albert was the British Order in Council in regard to the blockade of Germany from which resulted the seizure of meat and food supplies and cotton by British war vessels. He was always on the alert for information as to what was the attitude of the Administration and the people of the United States toward the blockade. That he used secret and perhaps devious means to get it is revealed by a confidential report which he received under most mysterious circumstances concerning an interview by a man referred to as "M. P." with President Wilson and Secretary Lansing. "M. P.," according to the conversation, claimed to have received from the President "a candid, confidential statement in order to make clear not only his own opposition, but also necessarily the political opportunity." A striking part of this conversation follows:

L. advises regarding a conference with M. P. Thereafter M. P. saw Lansing as well as Wilson. He informed both of them that an American syndicate had approached him which had strong German relations. This syndicate wishes to buy up cotton for Germany in great style, thereby to relieve the cotton situation, and at the same time to provide Germany with cotton. The relations of the American syndicate with Germany are very strong, so that they might even possibly be able to influence the position of Germany in the general political question. M. P. therefore asked for a candid, confidential statement in order to make clear not only his own position, but also necessarily the political opportunity. The result of the conversation was as follows:

1. *The note of protest to England will go in any event whether Germany answers satisfactorily or not.*

2. *Should it be possible to settle satisfactorily the Lusitania case, the President will bind himself to carry the protest against England through to the uttermost.*

3. *The continuance of the difference with Germany over the Lusitania case is 'embarrassing' for the President in carrying out the protest against England. . . .*

4. A contemplated English proposal to buy cotton in great style and invest the proceeds in America would not satisfy the President as an answer to the protest. . . .

5. The President, in order to ascertain from Mr. M. P. how strong the German influence of this syndicate is, would like to have the trend of the German note before the note is officially sent, and declares himself ready, before the answer is drafted, to discuss it with M. P., and eventually to so influence it that there will be an agreement for its reception, and also to be ready to influence the press through a wink.

6. As far as the note itself is concerned, which he awaits, so he awaits another expression of regret, which was not followed in the last note— regret together with the statement that nobody had expected that human lives would be lost and that the ship would sink so quickly.

The President is said to have openly declared that he could hardly hope for a positive statement that the submarine warfare would be discontinued.

WHAT HIS SECRET
CORRESPONDENCE REVEALED

Dr. Albert also was in close communication with the American branches of German industries. This fact is apparent from secret correspondence found in his dossier, showing how after much deliberation and consultation a group of German representatives in America forbade the American branch of a German firm to fill a Russian war order. This correspondence shows that the American branch first sought information as to whether or not it should fill the order either as a means of making money or, secondly, as a means of delaying the Russian Government in getting the material. One of the Embassy staff wrote suggesting that the Ambassador approve of the acceptance of the order as a means of hindering the Allies. After a conference it was reported:

> In my opinion it would be hazardous for your firm to ship locomotives, cars, or wheels to Russia. All these transportation means would lighten the transport of troops, ammunition and provisions for the Russian Government, and your firm would, within the meaning of Paragraph 89 of the (German) Penal Code, be rendering aid to the enemy thereby. . . . That you are in a position to delay the delivery of the order to the prejudice of the hostile country ordering them will in no measure relieve you from liability.

GERMANY IN THE STOCK MARKET

When it appeared that the Kaiser would not yield to demands made by the President, the prices of stocks went down and Germans bought stocks cheaply. After they loaded up a liberal supply, word would come that Germany was yielding and the stock market would become buoyant, thus allowing the German group to sell hundreds of thousands of shares on a substantial profit. *There is absolutely no doubt that as a result of every crisis the German Government realized millions of dollars in the market.*

An instance of how Dr. Albert had opportunity to get into the market is revealed in a secret letter written to Dr. Albert on July 8, 1915, by a well-known Board of Trade German in Chicago, and associated with a group of German traders. In this letter he refers to Dr. Albert's "principal," presumed to be no other than the German Government or the Kaiser himself. His letter says:

> Provisions have been horribly depressed by severe liquidation. We firmly believe that purchase of September lard will make your principal a great deal of money. September lard closes tonight at $8.65. This, with high freight added, will cost under 10 cents delivered Hamburg, where actual prices are around 35 cents per pound.
>
> I do not want to appear over persistent, but there never was a better proposition than buying this cheap lard for September delivery.

One of Dr. Albert's functions was to sift this commercial information and make recommendations to Berlin. He would confer with his coworkers on all military and naval matters having a commercial phase. That he did so is proved by the reports which they made and which went to Dr. Albert for his consideration and further recommendation. Captain von Papen, on July 7, 1915, submitted to Dr. Albert a memorandum headed, "Steps taken to Prevent the Exportation of Liquid Chlorine," in which he tells of the efforts made by England and France to buy that chemical in America, tells of the output here, and the firms turning it out.

THE SHIP PLOTS

Another matter of importance to which he gave thought was the problem which had been in every German mind and mouth since the beginning of the war, namely, the prevention of the shipment of war supplies to the Allies. A letter mailed to Dr. Albert from Chicago under date of July 22, 1915, sets forth how zealously his agent was working on an embargo conference with the aim of arousing sentiment in this country against the export of arms and ammunition. The letter says that he had obtained the co-operation of a United States Senator, a Congressman and other Americans in this project.

One letter from Albert's agent runs thus:

I must refrain from communicating the above facts in my report to the Ambassador, as the matter could be too easily compromised thereby. Perhaps you will find an opportunity to inform Count von Bernstorff verbally. As soon as the matter has first gained more headway, I believe Mr. von Alvensleben, who has taken part in the whole development here, will come to New York in order to inform the Ambassador fully regarding prevailing frame of mind here as well as regarding the movement, provided, however, that is desired.

Letters from Detroit suggested a plan for a general strike of the automobile workers in that city as a mighty protest against shipment of arms. The strike would cost about $50,000.

NEWSPAPER PROPAGANDA

To Dr. Albert also was assigned the task of studying sentiment in this country regarding the war and taking steps to influence it in favor of Germany—in other words, highly paid press work. Through Dr. Albert arrangements also were made for many German professors, either in Germany or connected with American institutions, to give up their occupations as teachers and devote themselves in America exclusively to lectures before high-class audiences. In these talks the speakers devoted themselves to showing the friendly relations between Germany and the United States, the similar aims of both countries in industry and international affairs, and to arguing for the cordial support of Germany's cause.

A complete organization was tabulated of journalists throughout the country who were sympathetic with the German cause. These men received news for publication in various papers, also instructions. By the aid of these men a vast amount of information was gathered and shunted along to Dr. Albert. In addition Dr. Albert gave consideration to still more elaborate plans for the purchase of newspapers, the starting of news syndicates and information bureaus which, apparently neutral, should be secretly allied with the German cause and supported by German money. These facts were shown by a number of papers bearing on publicity and methods of acquiring it which were found in his dossier. The papers show that in one instance he was subsidizing a weekly paper and that in return he demanded a certain policy.

The following letter throws some light on the subject:

I request the proposal of a suitable person who can ascertain accurately and prove the financial condition of your paper. From the moment when we guarantee you a regular advance, I must—

1. Have a new statement of the condition of your paper.
2. Practice a control over the financial management.

In addition to this, we must have an understanding regarding the course in politics which you will pursue, which we have not asked heretofore. Perhaps you will be so kind as to talk the matter over, on the basis of this letter, with ——.

Plans for the purchase of an English daily in New York which would support the German cause were worked over at length by Dr. Albert and his assistants. Proof also that Dr. Albert and his associates contemplated the creation of news bureaus in New York and Berlin which would furnish and disseminate throughout the United States news favorable to the German Government is given in the memorandum prepared apparently by an expert newspaper man, outlining the plan and cost of organization and giving certain suggestions.

Dr. Albert gave consideration to the suggestion of paying the expenses of American newspaper men who would go to Germany and send back articles favorable to the German cause. He did so under orders from von Bethmann-Hollweg, the German Imperial Chancellor, who caused one of his aids to write to the German Ambassador a letter suggesting that certain journalists be invited to visit Germany.

EFFORTS TO OUTWIT
THE BRITISH BLOCKADE

Varied and important as were these various duties, already mentioned, still the paramount task to which Dr. Albert devoted himself was a scheme to outwit England's blockade of Germany. This tall, silent man, working in his little office, was concerned with the purchase of millions and millions of dollars' worth of supplies—cargo after cargo—for shipment to Germany, direct or through neutral countries. In this campaign he used every means of deceiving the enemy that were in his power.

Let it be said that this is meant as no reflection on Dr. Albert. In war one nation may establish a blockade and the other nation will attempt to run it. International lawyers agree that one nation has a right to establish such a blockade. If the shipowner obtains ingress to the port he makes big profits by the sale of his goods, but if he is caught by the other belligerent he loses his ship and cargo. It is a gamble.

It has already been established as a part of international law, through decisions of Lord Stowell in England more than a century ago and of the United States Supreme Court during the Civil War, that if it can be shown that shipments of supplies to a neutral country are really designed for transhipment to a belligerent, then the enemy has a right to seize and confiscate those goods.

After the Orders in Council were issued by England, Dr. Albert sought first to make the embargo unpopular in America. Letters and other documents in his dossier show that plans were submitted to him for stirring up sentiment in this country against what was denounced by pro-Germans as arbitrary seizures on the part of Great Britain. For instance, Edward D. Adams of 71, Broadway, New York, who for many years was a representative in that city of the Deutsche Bank, sent a letter to Dr. Albert in which he makes the following suggestion:

> The South politically is of very great importance to the Democratic Party and to the re-election of its representatives at our next Presidential election. The Cabinet and Congress have represented in them Southern men to a considerable number who are keenly alive to the importance of keeping the Democratic Administration in close touch with the Southern voters, and it takes such action from time to time as will secure their sympathy and support.

Likewise plans were worked out for the arousing of the meat packers in Chicago to protest to Washington over the seizure of meat ships bound for Germany by way of neutral ports.

German representatives studying public sentiment in this country also suggested to Dr. Albert that indignation against Great Britain could be aroused by making it appear as if the British blockade was hurting America in preventing the receipt here of various non-contraband articles from Germany. One associate wrote to Dr. Albert:

> From a German standpoint, the pressure on the American Government can be strengthened by the interruption of deliveries from Germany

even if the British Government should permit exception. Those shipments especially should be interrupted which the American industries so badly require; withholding of goods is the surest means of occasioning the placing before the Administration in Washington of American interests. Those protests have the most weight which come from American industries which employ many workmen.

In the early months of the war Dr. Albert was a buyer of enormous supplies of cotton, wheat, copper, lubricating oil and other articles needed by Germany for the prosecution of the war. He signed contracts for meat and other supplies amounting to millions of dollars and he made payment the moment the ships were loaded here so that the American seller got his money regardless of what happened to the cargo while on the high seas. Of course, after the German Government seized all food supplies, the British Government took the attitude that all food supplies bound for Germany were intended for the Government and were therefore contraband. In the next place all purchases of food or other material by Dr. Albert as the official representative of the German Government made them Government supplies and therefore contraband of war. The moment the British Government discovered that these articles were purchased by Albert, no matter whether they were bound for neutral countries, or not, England argued she was justified in seizing the ships and confiscating them. But as a fact, England paid the American shippers in most instances.

All the facts in the vast scheme mapped out by Dr. Albert for outwitting John Bull's blockade, have been developed by the Attorney-General of England and set forth in the prize courts there. It has been shown that Albert backed the purchase of cotton by the shipload, that he acquired vessels under neutral flags for carrying these cargoes to neutral countries. He spent millions of dollars in the purchase of meat. For instance, Dr. C. T. Dumba, Austro-Hungarian Ambassador, writing to Baron Burian from New York, tells of an interview in Chicago with a beef packer.

No fewer than thirty-one ships, with meat and bacon shipments from his firm to Sweden, with a value of $19,000,000, have been detained," he says, "in British ports for months under suspicion of being ultimately intended for Germany. The negotiations have been long drawn out,

because Mr. Meagher and his companion will not accept a lame compro-
mise, but insist on full compensation or release of the consignments in
which the bacon may still remain sound.

A TWO-FACED PROPAGANDIST

Dr. Albert issued a statement which purports to be a complete reply to the
charges in regard to a secret German propaganda in the United States. He
said that the purchase of ammunition plants in this country was justifiable,
argued for an embargo on arms and ammunition, charged Great Britain
with piracy on the high seas, denied that the German Government financed
press agents, and asserted that the German Government had not started any
under-cover newspaper campaign in this country. He said it was inevitable that all sorts of wild and irresponsible offers, proposals and suggestions
should be addressed from every conceivable quarter to one holding the official position in which he was placed as an accredited agent of one of the
great nations engaged in this unfortunate world-wide war. He referred to
the strike letters as junk, and said that he should not be held responsible for
every crank that wrote him a letter.

That statement was for the American public. Dr. Albert's real sentiments
are shown vividly in a letter which he wrote to Captain von Papen from San
Francisco after the announcement of the President's decision to send the
military attaché out of the country. Here is part of it:

> Well, then! How I wish I were in New York and could discuss the sit-
> uation with you and B. E.! Many thanks for the telegram. The 'Patron'
> also telegraphed that I was to continue the journey. So we shall not see
> each other for the present. Shall we at all before you leave? It would be my
> most anxious wish; but my hope is small. For this time, I suppose, mat-
> ters will move more quickly than in Dumba's case. I wonder whether our
> Government will respond in a suitable manner! In my opinion, it need
> no longer take public opinion so much into consideration, in spite of its
> being artificially and intentionally agitated by the Press and the legal
> proceedings, so that a somewhat 'stiffer' attitude would be desirable,
> naturally quiet and dignified!

If you should leave New York before my return, we must try to come to some agreement about pending questions by writing. Please instruct Mr. Amanuensis Igel as precisely as possible. You will receive then in Germany the long-intended report of the expenses paid through my account on your behalf. I would be very thankful to you if you would then support the question of a monetary advance which you know of, although I know that I was mistaken in my opinion, that I acted as your representative and according to your wishes

When all the work of Dr. Albert is summed up and taken into consideration with his propaganda in association with Captain von Papen and Captain Boy-Ed, the impression remains that he, a guest of the United States, was immersed in plans that were aimed at the honor and integrity of this republic.

X

AMBASSADOR DUMBA, GERMANY'S CO-CONSPIRATOR

"IF I WANTED TO FLATTER the American people, I would make a statement before my departure, but I say nothing."

This was the sentiment of Dr. Constantin Theodor Dumba, veteran diplomat and Austro-Hungarian Ambassador at Washington, just after he had received his passports from Secretary of State Lansing. He was dismissed from this country in September, 1915, because of his pro-Teutonic activities, which were adjudged by the State Department to amount to interference with the internal affairs of the nation.

The diplomat, regarded at the time as the ablest in Washington, did not relish the notoriety of being the ninth diplomat to be expelled from America; and, when questioned by reporters on the eve of his departure, he revealed the acrid feeling regarding Americans which his wonted suavity and self-control hitherto had enabled him to conceal. The next day, however, he did unbend to the extent of saying something about "wonderful United States"—and then sailed away.

Dumba, master of intrigue and remorseless in the attempted execution of any scheme that he regarded as beneficial to the welfare of his country, had been the supervising authority of the Austro-Hungarian espionage system in America, which was linked almost chain for chain with the German machinery. The joint activity of the German and the Austrian organizations was aimed at the same end as those described in connection with the duties of the German agents and their executives. He had as his active assistants, Baron Erich Zwiedinek von Sudenhorst, counsellor to the Austrian Embassy, and after the dismissal of Dumba, Chargé d'Affaires; Dr. Alexander Nuber von Pereked, Consul-General in New York, and several other Austrian consuls throughout the country. He is said to have been the originating genius of many of the ideas which the German agents tried to put into effect.

The charges against him are based on a series of exposures concerning the secret propaganda in which Dr. Dumba participated and concerning which evidence was gathered by the Secret Service and the Department of Justice. They rest on secret diplomatic messages which Dr. Dumba wrote and entrusted to Captain James F. J. Archibald, an American, traveling in August, 1915, on the steamship *Rotterdam* for Holland, whence he expected to confer with the Foreign Offices of both Germany and Austro-Hungary. Those documents were captured by the British and turned over to the American authorities. They expose much the same sort of illicit activity as set forth in German documents.

MORE PASSPORT FRAUDS

Attorney-General Gregory caused a thorough investigation of these documents and also of von Nuber's office in New York. Many consular employees were taken before the Grand Jury and practically every member of the Consulate, excepting von Nuber and his immediate associates, was rounded up one night in the office of Superintendent Offley in New York. They were questioned, and they gave much information.

Baron Zwiedinek was a busy person at the summer Embassy at Manchester-by-the-Sea after the outbreak of the war. Hundreds of Austro-Hungarian reservists were bobbing up at various consulates and registering, eager for directions and for means of getting back to their country. Evidently, these matters came under his jurisdiction, for he wrote the following letter to von Nuber:

Manchester, A. M., 24 August, 1914.
To the Imperial and Royal Consulate-General in New York:

On the 21st inst. the Imperial and Royal Embassy received the following telegram from the Imperial and Royal Consulate in San Francisco:

Nine employees arrived here on the steamer *Yokohama* seek transportation New York at expense of State. Beg for telegraphic instruction whether Consulate should pay traveling expenses. Stay here would cause embarrassment.

The Embassy has instructed the Consular office mentioned to send these employees to New York. Thereupon the following telegram of the 22nd arrived:

Attaché Hanenschild, Interpreter Nanternatz, Embassy, Tokio, as well as six employees, journeyed onward.

Since the Imperial and Royal Embassy is of the opinion that it is a patriotic duty of the reservists to do their utmost to reach the monarchy, will the Imperial and Royal Consulate please make all efforts in this connection to discover the proper transportation facilities for these employees who are shortly to arrive. Perhaps it would be possible also to produce suitable passports of neutral countries at comparatively slight expense.

Concerning that which is done in this connection please report in due time.

For the Imperial and Royal Embassy,
ZWIEDINEK

When that letter was shown to Baron Zwiedinek by Secretary of State Lansing, he admitted the authenticity of the signature, but denied he remembered anything of its contents. He explained that it was probably dictated by a clerk, and that in his haste he signed it without reading it. He also disclaimed any responsibility for it on the ground that Dr. Dumba was at the date of the letter the Austro-Hungarian Ambassador.

MUNITION PLOTS

Part of the schemes considered and recommended by Ambassador Dumba to prevent the exportation of war munitions from the United States is set forth in the secret communications which he gave to Captain Archibald to carry to Baron Burian, Austrian Foreign Minister. The first document discusses the diplomatic efforts that have been made toward that end, deprecates the arguments put forth by the State Department in declining to take any action to forbid the export of war munitions.

"The true ground for the discouraging attitude of the President," wrote Dumba, "lies, as his confidant, Colonel House, already informed me in January, and has now repeated, in the fact that authoritative circles are convinced that the United States in any serious crisis would have to rely on foreign neutral countries for all their war material. At no price, and in no case, will President Wilson allow this source to dry up.

"For this reason I am of the opinion that to return to the question whether by a reply from your Excellency or by a semi-official conversation between myself and the Secretary of State would not only be useless, but even, having regard for the somewhat self-willed temperament of the President, would be harmful."

Dr. Dumba's plans for causing strikes in munition factories in the United States are related by himself in the following official document which he sent to Baron Burian:

New York, August 20.

Your Excellency: Yesterday evening Consul General von Nuber received the enclosed *aide mémoire* from the chief editor of the local influential paper *Szabadsag,* after a previous conversation with me in pursuance of his verbal proposals to arrange for strikes at Bethlehem in Schwab's steel and munitions factory and also in the Middle West.

Archibald, who is well known to your Excellency, leaves to-day at twelve o'clock on board the *Rotterdam* for Berlin and Vienna. I take this rare and safe opportunity of warmly recommending these proposals to your Excellency's favorable consideration. It is my impression that we can disorganize and hold up for months, if not entirely prevent, the manufacture of munitions in Bethlehem and the Middle West, which, in the opinion of the German military attaché, is of great importance and amply outweighs the comparatively small expenditure of money involved.

But even if strikes do not come off, it is probable that we should extort under pressure more favorable conditions of labor for our poorly downtrodden fellow-countrymen in Bethlehem. These white slaves arc now working twelve hours a day, seven days a week. All weak persons succumb and become consumptive. So far as German workmen are found among the skilled hands means of leaving will be provided immediately for them. Besides this, a private German registry office has been established which provides employment for persons who voluntarily have given up their places. It already is working well. We shall also join in and the widest support is assured us.

I beg your Excellency to be so good as to inform me with reference to this letter by wireless. Reply whether you agree. I remain, with great haste and respect,

Dumba

PLANS FOR STRIKERS

The enclosure, or *"aide mémoire,"* written in Hungarian, outlines the scheme which the diplomat recommended.

I must divide the matter into two parts, Bethlehem and the Middle West business [says this paper] but the point of the departure is common in both, viz., press agitation, which is of the greatest importance as regards our Hungarian-American workmen. It means a press through which we can reach both in Bethlehem and in the West. In my opinion we must start a very strong agitation on this question in *Freedom* (Szabadsag), the leading organ, in respect to the Bethlehem works and the conditions there. This can be done in two ways and both must be utilized.

In the first place, the regular daily section must be devoted to the conditions obtaining there, and a campaign must be regularly conducted against these indescribably degrading conditions. *Freedom* already has done something similar in the recent past, when the strike movement began at Bridgeport. It must necessarily take the form of strong, deliberate, decided and courageous action.

Secondly, the writer of these lines would begin a labor novel in that newspaper much on the lines of Sinclair's celebrated story. This might be published in other local Hungarian, Slovak and German newspapers. The *Nepszava* ('Word of the People') will undoubtedly be compelled willingly or unwillingly to follow the movement initiated by *Freedom,* for it is pleasing the entire Hungarian element in America, and is an absolutely patriotic act to which that open journal, the *Nepszava,* could not adopt a hostile attitude. Of course, it would be another question to what extent and with what energy and devotion that newspaper would adhere to this course of action without regard to other influences, just as it is questionable to what extent other local patriotic papers would go. There is a great reason why, in spite of their patriotism, American-Hungarian papers hitherto have shrunk from initiating such action.

In these circumstances the first necessity is money.

Bethlehem must be sent as many reliable Hungarian and German workmen as we can lay our hands on, who will join the factories and begin their work in secret among their fellow workmen. For this purpose I have my men, roll-turners and steel workers. We must send an organizer who in the interests of the union will begin the business in his own way. We must also send so-called 'soap-box' orators who will know how to start a useful agitation. We shall want money for popular meetings, possibly for organizing picnics. In general, the same applies to the Middle West. I am thinking of Pittsburg and Cleveland in the first instance, as to which I could give details only if I were to return and spend at least a few days there. I already have shown that much can be done with the newspapers. We must stir up the men's feelings in Bethlehem. A sensation was caused by the articles which appeared at the time of the strike at Bridgeport. They brought Bethlehem into the affair.

It is evident that the start of a movement from which serious results are to be expected requires a sufficiency of money at the very start. The extent of subsequent expenditure for the most part depends on the work effected. For example, the newspapers must not receive the whole sum intended for them all at once, but only half. To union agitators only a certain amount should be given at first, and a larger sum in case of success or of a serious strike on the formation of the union. It is my opinion that for the special object of starting the Bethlehem business and the Bethlehem and Western newspapers campaign $15,000 to $20,000 must be at our disposal, but it is not possible to reckon how much ultimately will be required.

When a beginning has been made, it will be possible to see how things develop and where and how much it will be worth while to spend. The above-mentioned preliminary sum would suffice partially to satisfy the demands of the necessary newspapers and to a considerable extent those of the Bethlehem campaign. If circumstances are lucky and leadership is good, we can arrive at positive results in the West comparatively cheaply, whereas Bethlehem is one of the most difficult jobs.

I will telephone at 8 a.m., and request you then to let me know where and when I can learn your opinion of my proposal, which requires a considerable amount of verbal exposition. Finally, I make bold to point out the fact that hitherto I have said nothing on the subject to any one connected with the newspapers, and am in the fortunate position that in the case of giving effect to the plan I can make use of names in case of necessity, for I have already in other matters made payments through other individuals. In any event, in the case of the newspapers the greatest circumspection is necessary. No one but the proprietor must know that money is coming to the undertaking from any source.

THE GERMAN SPY IN AMERICA » 273

EXIT DUMBA

Following the receipt of those documents by the State Department, Dr. Dumba and Secretary Lansing were in conference. The Ambassador admitted he had written the letter, and had consigned it to the care of Captain Archibald. He defended his course on the ground that he was under orders from his home government, and that he wished to prevent Austro-Hungarian workmen from committing high treason by helping turn out munitions for the Allies. President Wilson, however, insisted on the Ambassador's recall, and Secretary Lansing, in his note to Austro-Hungary, made these charges against Dr. Dumba:

> By reason of the admitted purpose and intent of Mr. Dumba to con-
> spire to cripple legitimate industries of the United States and to inter-
> rupt their legitimate trade, and by reason of the flagrant violation of
> diplomatic propriety in employing an American citizen, protected by an
> American passport, as a secret bearer of official dispatches through the
> lines of the enemy of Austria-Hungary, the President directs us to inform
> your Excellency that Mr. Dumba is no longer acceptable to the Govern-
> ment of the United States as the Ambassador of his Imperial Majesty at
> Washington.

After the departure of Dr. Dumba, Baron Zwiedinek and von Nuber began a series of advertisements in racial newspapers, calling the subjects of Austria-Hungary out of the munition factories. If any workman wrote him regarding the matter, he sent a reply, in which he said: "It is demanded that patriotism, no less than the fear of punishment, should cause every one to quit his work immediately."

XI

GERMANY'S LOBBY in CONGRESS

PRESIDENT WILSON SAID IN PART of his Flag Day address in June, 1916:

> There is disloyalty in the United States, and it must be absolutely crushed. It proceeds from a minority, a very small minority, but a very active and subtle minority. . . . If you could have gone with me through the space of the last two years and could have felt the subtle impact of intrigue and sedition, and have realized with me that those to whom you have entrusted authority are trustees not only of the power, but also of the very spirit and purpose of the United States, you would realize with me the solemnity with which I look upon the sublime symbol of our unity and power.

The President in those few words summed up the conspiracies of the Teutonic Powers aimed at the integrity of the United States. When he made his charge, he had behind him a vast amount of evidence which never has been and never will be made public. *He had as proof the details of Germany's scheme to control the Congress of this nation and to manipulate it in a manner that would have rendered not only the legislative bodies an absolute check to the administrative functions of the Government, but would have dictated the course of the Republic in international affairs just as if the United States were a dependency of the Fatherland.*

DISLOYAL CITIZENS

"The subtle and active minority" to which the President made such a sensational reference is a group of Americans—German-Americans swayed by sentiment for Germany and Americans influenced by gold—who have been following the dictation of Teutonic agents in America. They have received orders and sought to carry them out. They have been puppets that worked and argued in the interest of the Central Powers when certain men pulled the strings. They have been active workers in carrying out clever political policies and agitations that were part of schemes devised in Berlin to benefit Germany against her enemy. True, there have been faithful American citizens who have sided with Germany's arguments—and their loyalty cannot be questioned—*but there have been citizens who knowingly worked with German agents against the best interests of the nation.* When a man strives and schemes with foreign agents against the honest endeavors of an American official, who is seeking to execute the law, he is guilty not only of disloyalty but of sedition.

From the outset of the war Teutonic agents intrigued to get their clutches upon the Federal legislative body. They schemed to use it as an obstacle to any move by the President. They sought legislation that would prevent the shipment of munitions from this country, that would have prevented the Allies from floating any war bonds in America, and that would have stopped Americans from sailing on passenger vessels of Allied merchantmen. Their aim was to make Congress vote and the President act just as the Emperor of Germany deemed most suitable to the interests of the Fatherland.

To that end they tried to manipulate sentiment among the voters by means of insidious propaganda. They hired lobbyists to work among Representatives and Senators at the National Capitol, and so thoroughly and accurately did these men do their work that the line-up of the House of Representatives and of the Senate was reported almost daily to Berlin on any important legislation bearing on Germany's interests in the war. They reported the change from day to day of any Congressman's attitude and the reason therefore. They strove to create a sentiment among the voters so that appeals would pour in upon Congressmen, filling them with fear of defeat at the polls if they did not obey what amounted to the Kaiser's dictation.

At the start of the European War there began in Congress a vehement debate over the question of imposing a legislative embargo on the shipments of arms and ammunition to the Allies. In these debates men participated who undoubtedly were sincere in the convictions they expressed. Nevertheless, they were button-holed by Americans working for German agents, but all the flowery oratory in favor of "universal peace" proved unavailing.

In the late winter and early spring of 1915, a hireling of the Germans began to seek secret conferences with Congressmen in a Washington hotel and to outline to them plans for compelling an embargo on munitions. *Money was mentioned and offers were made to seven or eight different Congressmen.* It is charged by Government officials that a large amount of money was spent—but the project was in vain.

UNDERGROUND DIPLOMACY

Meantime, Count von Bernstorff and Dr. Dumba were seeking by diplomatic means to effect a stoppage of the flow of war equipment to the Allies. Each addressed appeals to the Secretary of State and each presented notes from his respective Government protesting against the shipment of munitions as unneutral. Their protests were unavailing and the answers of the Secretary of State were so clear and determined that it became clear to the Teutonic agents that their efforts along such a channel would be without success. Dr. Dumba ascribes the failure of Congress to shut off the export of munitions and the decision of the Administration against the Teutonic Powers, to the President, for in one of his letters to Burian he said in August, 1915:

"As last autumn, he (President Wilson) can always, through his personal influence, either force the House of Representatives to take his point of view against their better judgment, or, on the other hand, in the Senate can overthrow the resolution already voted in favor of prohibiting the export of guns and munitions. In these circumstances any attempt to persuade individual States to vote parallel resolutions through their legislative bodies would offer no advantages apart from the internal difficulties which the execution of this plan presents."

With that letter Dr. Dumba enclosed a memorandum adroitly suggesting the use of England's seizure of ships as a means of inciting Americans to support embargo legislation.

President Wilson [he wrote] will not hear of Congress laying an embargo, for the reason, as he clearly explains, that to do so would be un-neutral. The result of this is to stultify all attempts at agitation based on embargo. This is a matter entirely in President Wilson's hands. It is, of course, always possible that, despite the President's declaration, a resolution might be laid before Congress contemplating the prohibition of the export of munitions as a measure of reprisal against England for her illegal seizure of American ships; but we should indulge in no illusions as to the success likely to attend such an enterprise.

HOLDING THE CLUB TO CONGRESS

The German agents, as has been told, did not cease their efforts to arouse the sentiment of the country, hoping to force Congress and the President to take steps in the direction that the Germans wished.

The fear which a Representative in Congress has of displeasing his constituents was a factor carefully taken into account by the German agents. Every means of impressing upon a Representative the belief that the men who voted for him wanted an embargo were used. These were the motives behind a plan for holding an embargo conference in the Middle West in the summer of 1915. The details were carefully developed and the conference would have been held had not the secret workings been divulged through the publication of the Albert papers. One letter addressed to Dr. Albert by Herr P. Reiswitz, in Chicago, reveals the scheme in detail and shows that Count von Bernstorff was aware of the inner organization. The letter, dated July 22, 1915, says in part:

> Everything else concerning the proposed embargo conference you will find in the enclosed copy of the report to the Ambassador. A change has, however, come up, as the mass meeting will have to be postponed on account of there being insufficient time for the necessary preparations. It will probably be held here in about two weeks.
>
> H— seemed to be very strong for the plan. He told our representative at a conference in Omaha: "If this matter is organized in the right way you will sweep the United States."
>
> For your confidential information, I would further inform you that the leadership of the movement thus far lies in the hands of two gentlemen (one in Detroit and one in Chicago), who are firmly resolved to work toward the end that the German community, which, of course, will be with us without further urging, shall above all things remain in the background, and that the movement, to all outward appearances, shall

have a purely American character. I have known both the gentlemen very well for a long time, and know that personal interest does not count with them; the results will bring their own reward.

PULLING WIRES BEHIND SCENES

Germans made it a point to get behind resolutions presented to Congress in the early part of 1916 bearing on the submarine controversy. These measures, regardless of the aims of the legislators, had features that would be helpful to Germany in her desire to sink merchantmen on the high seas.

Senator Gore introduced a resolution "to prohibit the issuing of passports for use on vessels of a belligerent country," and another bill "to prohibit a belligerent vessel from transporting American citizens as passengers to or from ports in the United States and to prohibit American and neutral vessels from transporting American citizens as passengers and contraband of war at one and the same time." Representative Stephens of Nebraska and Representative McLemore also introduced bills and resolutions of similar character.

This lobbying and other secret propaganda in Congress was designed to render the President powerless in his demands upon Germany to cease torpedoing passenger ships. The Germans almost succeeded in getting Congress to enact resolutions, forbidding Americans to travel on such passenger vessels. While this legislation was under discussion, Berlin was kept accurately informed concerning the attitude of both the House and the Senate on those measures. The schemes of the Germans, however, fell through and President Wilson was upheld in his policy.

After President Wilson had sent his ultimatum to Germany, insisting that the attacks on passenger ships and merchantmen, in violation of the rules of international law, must cease, the entire horde of German propagandists, German spies and German sympathizers were lined up in a countrywide appeal to Congress to maintain diplomatic relations with Germany, no matter what her answer to America's note might be. By a systematic scheme put into operation throughout the country, thousands of telegrams were sent to members of Congress and of the Senate beseeching harmonious relations with Germany. In the majority of instances these telegrams were according to formula and all the sender had to do was to sign his name to it. The telegraph charges were paid by an organization financed by German agents.

But their pleas were not needed, for Germany, facing at last—after many months of exchange of notes—the anger of the American people, finally yielded on the submarine question and the *Lusitania* controversy. All of Germany's legislative propaganda and secret work had been futile. The exposure of the activities of her agents resulted only in causing many neutral Americans to revolt against her.

XII

CHANGING the SYSTEM

AFTER ALL THE RAMIFICATIONS OF the Teutonic system in America had been unearthed through the work of the Federal authorities, an order went forth to the spies to cease activities that were in violation of the laws. *Meantime, the Chief Spy in Berlin began immediately to construct an entirely new system of espionage, for use in an emergency.* The remnant of the old system, however, was kept at hand for the furthering of propaganda and such activities as could not arouse the objection of the Government, even though detected.

Count von Bernstorff, German Ambassador, took steps following the seizure of the von Igel papers, rather the papers showing the directorship of the system in America, to issue a warning to all Germans of the necessity of leading a purely and righteously neutral life. He sent forth a statement, which had been prepared by an attorney in New York, to all German consuls in the country, and took care to see that the State Department obtained a copy of this notice. The notice, dated some time in the early spring of 1916, said:

> In consequence of cases which have occurred of late, German Ambassador Bernstorff sent instructions to all German Consuls in the United States to strongly impress on German citizens living in their districts that it is their duty scrupulously to obey the laws of the states in which they reside.

That notice, however, was simply a subterfuge employed by the Chief Spy in Berlin to throw Americans off his trail. In December, 1915, following the arrest of Paul Koenig and other German agents, a formal notice was sent forth from Berlin asserting that no citizen of Germany ever had been asked to disobey any laws. But that statement had proved merely a blind to cover other activities in the United States. With the seizure of the von Igel-von Papen papers, however, it had become necessary to make a strategic retreat, so to speak, and to rebuild the spy system.[3]

The necessity of such a move is clear because of the fact that the papers, documents and other evidence developed by the Secret Service and other Federal agents proved that the warriors and statesmen of Germany had, at the outset of the war, decided upon a campaign in America to injure the Allies and to weaken the American Government. The General War Staff had at their disposal in America a vast army of German reservists and secret agents, and straightway set them to work upon plans in violation of American laws.

TWO AND A HALF YEARS
OF HIGH TREASON

Go back over the events since 1914, and study them in the light of the moves made by Germany or by her secret agents here, and you will realize how, in America, Germany has had a hand in practically every domestic or foreign event of any importance. *Her agents sought to control the Congress. They planned trouble between the United States and Mexico with the aim of stopping the shipment of war supplies to the Allies, and of getting this country so absorbed in other matters that we could not call Germany to account for her murderous submarine warfare. They fomented trouble among laboring men. They schemed to bring abou seditious uprisings in Cuba, and in the dependencies of the Allies, using this country as a base of operations.*

By means of this secret organization, Germany carried on the scheme of buying fraudulent passports for the use of her reservists, developed a scheme for the illegal provisioning of the German cruisers, set on foot various military enterprises from the United States against Canada, schemed to destroy munition factories in America, to blow up merchantmen of the Allies sailing from American ports—and planned crimes of bribery, arson and assault.

But the alertness of the American Secret Service and the Bureau of Investigation of the Department of Justice prevented the consummation of these plans. There was need for a shifting of the Germanic spies. Immediately after the publication of Count von Bernstorff's warning, an exodus of known

3 How a new system was devised, and how Americans were employed to gather information about the Allies is now coming to light. Still more startling revelations of plans for attacks upon the United States will shortly be unfolded

spies to South America began, and the development of *an effective system of espionage in every country in South America is now under way.*

AMERICA'S VITAL QUESTION

The great question that confronts the American people is one of preparedness against this or a like system. Any foreign government that knows the moves of the United States before they are made is in a position to do the country much harm in peace, and tremendously greater harm in war. In view of the crimes perpetrated by Germans and Austrians in America in 1914, 1915 and 1916, it behooves the American Government to take steps to destroy the system, root and branch; to see to it that no nation ever builds up a similar system in these United States.

This Government must take such steps as will ensure it against treachery from within. The citizens of the United States must stand in time of danger as one man in defense of our lives, our liberties, our rights on land and sea, our homes and our national honor.

— **THE END** —

www.ingramcontent.com/pod-product-compliance
Lightning Source LLC
Chambersburg PA
CBHW071715120626
46550CB00001B/245